I SURVIVED
Evolved against all the odds

Ruth Mantile

Copyright © 2019 by Ruth Mantile

All rights reserved.

No part of this book may be reproduced in any manner, mechanically or electronically, including tape or other audio recordings and photocopying, without the written permission of the author, except for reasonable excerpts for research and reviewing purposes.

Print: 978-1-77605-620-0
E-book: 978-1-77605-619-4

Layout & typesetting by Janet Von Kleist
jvonkleist@yahoo.com

Published by Kwarts Publishers
www.kwartspublishers.co.za

I SURVIVED
Evolved against all the odds

Contents

Foreword		9
Acknowledgements		13
Introduction		15
1	Possible infantile amnesia	21
2	A long journey to hell	26
3	Love conquered all	43
4	Shattered dreams	50
5	Life without meaning	58
6	Finding my purpose in life	63
7	No turning back	84
8	ANC: My home, my life	100
9	The best decision and a new identity	139
10	Joining the altruistic army	144
11	The family I never had	156
12	Turned into a young Marxist	186
13	A taste of the battlefield	202
14	A presumed curse turned into a blessing	268

FOREWORD

'Happy' Ruth Mantile

I first took notice of Comrade Ruth Mantile when she joined our group at Vienna Camp, Luanda, Angola in 1981 as we were assembled into a platoon that was destined for basic military training in Kamalundi, Malanje Province in eastern Angola.

Apparently, she had been a refugee in Maseru, Lesotho in 1980, the same time I was also a refugee in the same city. Since the first time I met her, she has always been a happy bundle of joy. I simply cannot remember a single moment when Comrade Ruth would miss an opportunity for a hearty, spirited laugh when such presented itself. Throughout the trials, tribulations, and deprivations that went with our hard and intense guerrilla training and survival, Comrade Ruth's playful and jolly spirits never ebbed. Be it the absence of something to eat, or a long, exhausting and energy-sapping training regime, Comrade Ruth would always derive amusement from such.

There was never a dull moment for her, and her pleasant personality and sense of humour eased the bitter sting of the intense conditions we had to endure. By her easy-going character and happy companionship, she helped our platoon sail through whatever hardships we encountered, whatever the magnitude.

She was in a way our platoon cheerleader. Young as she was, she was a pleasure to have in our platoon. Through her pleasantness, playfulness, and joyfulness, she imbued us with high morale, thereby enabling us to perform our assigned tasks with the expected enthusiasm.

I have never seen her down and under. She enjoys a good, hearty laugh, and in doing so, she lifts the spirit, even when everyone around her is feeling down. It is a pleasure to be acquainted with her, and she was indeed the toast of our company.

–Dumisane Mafu (Mazolo Msomi)

Growing up in Mangaung with Mpoetsi Morake

We were just a bunch of kids in 1973, attending St Mary's Primary School in Bochabela Township in Mangaung. Our class consisted of dark, skinny girls except for one Dipuo Moqhetsola, who was very light in complexion and very big in stature, and of course, Mpoetsi Morake, who was light in complexion, tall, slender and beautiful with a lovely smile. Mpoetsi had a beautiful heart and was very popular at school because of her intelligence.

Dipuo was a person who took no nonsense and would put you in your place at the slightest provocation. Other popular girls were the likes of Fana Seema, Mookgo Mofana, and the cousins Tokelo, Pat and Nthabiseng Pebane. We also had Tshepiso Mokhali and Nohayazi Mkhwetha.

Mpoetsi fitted into all the groups because she was friendly, intelligent, and beautiful. Unlike us, she did not have a group she belonged to, and as a result, she was free to move around with whomever she wanted. Almost every Friday, there would be fights between two groups of girls; those who were streetwise would pick fights with my group of naïve girls according to the other group. I do not remember Mpoetsi being part of those fights because she would leave the moment a fight started.

During school breaks, we would buy fat cakes from Tlale store and eat it with snoek, fali (liver spread) or atchaar, but Mpoetsi would just sit there with us without buying anything. She even refused to eat with us when we offered. She always said that she was full, and we did not understand because we were all in the same class and never saw her eat anything. Mpoetsi would always walk barefoot while we were in shoes and socks.w Some of us wished to do the same, but our parents would not allow us to walk barefoot because it was against school regulations. Mpoetsi would be so comfortable, and the way she walked showed that she was happy and contented.

After school, we would usually play the jukebox at a nearby shop, and Mpoetsi would dance to her favourite song, which was the original hit by Clarence Carter, "Don't bother me". If we wanted to see Mpoetsi very happy, we would just go to the jukebox where we would watch her dance because she had remarkable moves, iyo.

The other place we used to meet with Mpoetsi was at church. We attended St Rose Catholic Church near our school, and we never missed a service until one Sunday. We normally attended the 8:00 am service, and we would meet around 7:45 am so that we could have time to talk about girls' stuff, but that particular Sunday in 1980, Mpoetsi did not show up which was unusual for her. The following Monday, Mpoetsi did not come to school. A week passed without hearing anything from her or her family. Mpoetsi disappeared like that, and nobody knew what happened to her, and to us, life was never the same without her. It was only later that we heard that she left the country to fight for our freedom and we realised that Mpoetsi was not only brilliant and clever, but she had a vision. We learned so much from that, and we started to see things differently.

-Shono Njiva

'Little Girl' Ruth Mantile

It was in 1981 when I first met Ruth Mantile in Kamalundi, where I became a platoon commander of Platoon One and Ruth Mantile was in Platoon Two. When I saw Comrade Ruth, I became so worried because she was very young, but besides that, she was a female, which worried me. The thing with me was that I always felt sorry for our female comrades because I regarded them as being physically weaker than their male counterparts, but that does not mean I undermined them; I just thought the situation in the camps was not conducive for females.

It was worse when I met Ruth; I wondered how she was going to cope with training and camp life. To my surprise, Ruth was a happy soul that always smiled, even under extreme physical exhaustion. She even laughed at some of her comrades who showed signs of weakness.

Our soldiers underwent Commanders' Course, which was to assist them when they go inside the country to fight the enemy. We trained them in military engineering, tactics, politics, firearms, topography and physical training. Our soldiers trained on how to use ZGU, 2 mm mortar and Grat Pe.

Later on, I was so impressed when I realised that I was worried for nothing because I saw Mantile growing as a soldier and as a young woman. I would listen to her during political discussions and felt proud that we had produced a political soldier in her. She will always be one of the females I honour.

-William 'Moropa' Moadira

ACKNOWLEDGEMENTS

I would like to thank my daughter, Tshepiso, for giving me the courage to write this book. If it was not for her encouragement, I do not think I would be where I am today. Tshepi, you have been a shining star in my life, and I will always cherish the time we have together. You are unique in your own way. Do not change who you are and continue to love yourself. I love you a lot.

To Tshepo (Maele), Malizo, Tokollo, Thabang and Thoriso – thank you for loving me and supporting me throughout this journey. I am indebted to all of you, and I will always love you.

Throughout this journey, I met people to which I would like to say that I believe our paths crossed because we had to meet for reasons we do not know yet. For now, I want to thank you for your kindness, words of encouragement, love and allowing me to be myself. I love all of you.

To the ANC-family – thank you so much for planting seeds of love, forgiveness, and humility in my life. I will always be indebted to the ideals we shared; that of ensuring that our people are free from fear and want.

I would also like to thank the Kwarts Publishers team for their professionalism, guidance, and patience.

Above all, I thank God for loving me so much, even when I thought I did not deserve His love.

INTRODUCTION

Does the world still believe that one's upbringing determines one's destiny? Does this narrative say that, if you were born from a rich family, you would also be rich, or if your mother abandoned you at childbirth, you would also abandon your children? I agree with the notion, but not in its entirety. Yes, if I was abandoned as a child, I may have trust and commitment issues, low self-esteem, and anxiety, but it does not define who I am and does not determine my destiny. The choices I make in life define who I am and determines my destiny.

I was abandoned by Mama at the age of around two. I only got to know her and stayed with her when I was almost seven years old. Even then she was very cold and indifferent towards me. I could see her physically, but I did not feel her presence as a mother figure in my life. The usual mother and daughter maternal connection was not there, and we remained emotionally detached from each other.

Mario Balotelli, the Italian footballer, said the following about abandonment: *"They say that abandonment is a wound that never heals. I say only that an abandoned child never forgets."*

Besides being abandoned by Mama, I survived being bullied in the township I grew up in. At the young age of twelve, a stranger raped me. At the age of fourteen, I was raped twice by people who were supposed to protect me. At the age of eighteen, one episode resulted in an unplanned pregnancy. These things could have easily led any person to self-destruction, but not me, for I knew that my purpose was larger than what I was going through physically. My spirit was always stronger than my physical being, which made me survive against all the odds.

I knew from a very young age that I was an introvert. Whether it was by choice or not, I do not know, but I enjoyed my own company and the company of very few people. I found that being in a big group drained my energy.

I preferred reading books, playing with Babsy, our dog, or just lazing around. I loved reading books by Jack Schaefer (*Shane*), James Hadley Chase (*No Orchids for Miss Blandish, An Ace Up My Sleeve, You Have Yourself a Deal, Mission To Siena, Tell it to the Birds* and *A Coffin from Hong Kong*). I used to enjoy the suspense that came with the crime stories of James Hadley Chase; it would take me a day or two to finish a novel, and besides doing my daily work, reading kept me going.

My life experience caused me to fight for justice, develop empathy, forgiveness, and developed a love for humankind very early in life because I did not only survive the harshness of the world, but I even evolved to become a better person in the society against all the odds, which surprised many people including Mama. Satchel Paige, a former African American baseball player, taught me this when he said, "Work like you don't need the money. Love like you've never been hurt. Dance like nobody's watching."

By writing this book, my main objective is not for people to feel sorry for me, as one of my rapists insinuated. Let me make it clear: I never felt sorry for myself, and as it is, I do not expect anyone to feel sorry for me because I knew then, as I know now, that my rape episodes, abandonment by Mama and her hatred of me did not, and do not, define who I am. The purpose of this book is to indicate to the world that no matter what your circumstances are, the choices you make can build or destroy you.

The last objective is to give assurance to women, men and children who are experiencing, or have experienced, abuse of any kind, whether sexual, verbal, physical or psychological, that there is life after all those calamities that befell you. We can change those calamities into joy, happiness and peace by giving out unconditional love, forgiveness and prayer to those who have offended us because that is what I did. Love attracts love; absolute love attracts love absolutely.

The fact that I love myself as I am and love my children, and many other people who crossed my path, motivated me to live a happy life and to write this book. Through this book, I want to tell men and women out there who were made to believe that they are ugly, inadequate, useless and do not deserve to be loved, that one's upbringing does not determine one's future or destiny.

Healing from any kind of abuse, especially emotional abuse from childhood, is a very difficult exercise to go through, but as Andrew Vachss, American author and federal investigator, said, "*Adult survivors of emotional child abuse have only two life-choices: learn to self-reference or remain a victim. When your self-concept has been shredded, when you have been deeply injured and made to feel the injury was all your entire fault, when you look for approval to those who cannot or will not provide it, you play the role assigned to you by your abusers.*"

At a very young age, I made a decision that I would never allow myself to be a perpetual victim of abuse of any kind. I also bet with my life that none of my children or any person under my responsibility has ever experienced physical and emotional abuse perpetrated by myself. I remain true to my decision. Steve Maraboli, American author and motivational speaker, said, "*Letting go means to come to the realisation that some people are part of your history but not a part of your destiny.*"

At the age of thirteen, I wrote a poem out of bitterness. It reads like this:

Her womb suffocated me
Lying in her womb, I felt unwanted
There was no space for me to breathe
Everything in my mother's womb was suffocating me
I was never free in my mother's womb
Her womb suffocated me

I tried to breathe, but I could not
I tried to cry, but nobody heard me
I tried to kick, but I could not because I could not feel my legs
Her womb suffocated me

I wanted to leave this ungodly place
I wanted to be free from this bondage
I wanted to be able to sing a love song
Her womb suffocated me

The fact that Mama did not love me made me feel sad, and I felt it was contrary to what we were taught in church, that we should love each other as God loved us. I always gave my poor mother the benefit of the doubt because I never saw Mama go to church; therefore, she would not understand the Tenth Commandment: "Love thy neighbour", or what Jesus said to his disciples before he was crucified, "Love each other like I loved you".

I was astonished later in life when some of my former school mates told me that they used to envy me for walking barefoot and that they actually thought it was part of swagger. I could not understand why they would think that any child in her good mind could enjoy walking barefoot throughout the years and throughout all seasons. I would have understood if they were saying they only saw me barefooted at school, but I even went to church on Sundays without shoes. I should say I did not mind that, but my concern was that I was the only one amongst my siblings who would not get anything, including shoes. The first time

Mama bought me shoes was in 1980, which was a surprise to me. Whatever I had were handouts from Mama's employer, Mr Christos, who owned a photo studio in the city of Bloemfontein. Therefore, I thought that it had nothing to do with affordability from Mama's side and that it was her choice not to buy me necessities. Despite this, I appreciated the fact that she sent me to the best school. For me, that was more important than anything in the world.

For the pain I endured in Mama's house as a child, and as an adult, I used to feel as if my heart was bigger than my body because I could feel its heaviness and the pain would be as if somebody was piercing it with a spear. The worst part was that, because of my smile that concealed my pain and hurt so well, nobody saw, or knew, what I was going through in my life. Everybody who came across me at any stage of my life saw this happy, confident and energetic person. I was a happy child in people's eyes, and some even called me Smiley, which I did not understand. No one knew what I was going through, and if my suicide attempts had succeeded, people who knew me would have never understood why I committed suicide. With my experience of hurt and pain, I realised later on in life that I unconsciously internalised people's pains and hurt because I experienced pain and hurt early in life and it was my wish that nobody should go through the pain and hurt as I did. As an adult, I came across as a crying baby to some people, but I understood them because they did not know where I came from. I had untreated depression from a very early age, which resulted in three failed suicide attempts at the age of ten, twelve and thirteen.

In the late eighties, I so much wished to sing a song for Mama which was composed in 1987 by Labi Siffre, and was, later on, sung by Kenny Rogers, "Something Inside So Strong". I might not have known why Labi composed that song, but I felt it was relevant to my situation. Mama needed to know that whatever she did to me, she would not succeed because I was a woman on a mission, and I had a vision. Nothing would deter me from achieving that, not even her.

I got strength from knowing that family is not only people you are related to by blood but even people you meet in the streets. As long as you share the common purpose and love, they become your family. I survived and evolved because of the love and care from that family I did not have any blood relations with.

Let me assure you that one's upbringing does not determine who you are or who you will become. One's destiny is in God's hands, and you can choose to lead a positive life and surround yourself with people who add value to your life. Or, you can choose to believe the voice of your toxic parents and family, which would ultimately lead you to self-destruction. It took me almost eight years to complete this book because I had to endure flashbacks of sexual assaults which had a negative impact on my life, but over and above that, the experience of not being loved by a mother was the worst nightmare. Mama was a typical toxic parent who never accepted any wrongdoing and would never take responsibility for anything. She blamed me for her divorce. She blamed me when Iris got pregnant with her first child at a very young age, and she also blamed me for almost losing her eyesight and her limbs due to diabetes, which she claimed I caused because I left for exile. That was funny because her own father was diabetic.

My life experience made me develop empathy, forgiveness, and love for humankind very early in life because I survived the misfortunes of my life. In that process, I also evolved against all the odds to become a better person in society. In the process of healing, I have learned to love unconditionally and to forgive without any reservations. Most importantly, I have forgiven myself, which gave me inner peace. I must say it was not easy, but I made it and so can you!

ONE

Possible infantile amnesia

I KNOW THIS MIGHT sound funny or unreal, but it is the truth. I do not have any recollection of things that happened to me when I was younger, and I can only remember things from when I was around six years old. For some reason, I have a feeling that something traumatic happened to me when I was an infant, which resulted in infantile amnesia. What made matters worse was that even my family would not talk about my childhood, and I only saw photos that were taken when I was about eight months old and another one when I was about two.

The other thing is that in 1980, when I arrived in Lesotho seeking political asylum, I was required to give my date of birth. I was fourteen then and seen as a minor and thus could not give them the correct date because I did not know it. I just thought of April 28, 1965, which I still use as my official date of birth. The irony is that no one at home, even Mama, had ever wished me a happy birthday on that day or any other day for that matter, but she would wish my siblings happy birthday without fail. As a result, birthdays do not matter to me.

I can only remember staying in Aliwal North in the Eastern Cape in 1972 with two women I referred to as o-Makhulu (grannies). My name was Vuyiswa Gibisela, and I had two cousins. The one was older than me, and Xoliswa was a bit younger. In our yard, we had many fruit trees, which included grapes, apricots, peaches, and prunes. Summer was my favourite season because I had a lot to eat, unlike in winter when our fruit trees would be 'dead' with no sign of life. What I liked most during the summer was that I could climb the trees and eat whatever I liked. To me, it was as if I was in the Garden of Eden before the serpent appeared. Ironically, I still enjoy fruits that I pick up directly from trees, unlike those I buy from the fruit markets. My favourite fruits were apricots, grapes and plums that I still enjoy, but now, unlike then, apricots, pears and apples cause my tummy to bloat, something that did not happen as a child. I guess the changing environment is the cause of that. I still cherish those days.

For long periods the five of us would not get any visitors, and the only time our house was full of people was when the garden was full of fruits. I only realised later in life that the reason why we had visitors during that time was that it was Christmas and those people were family. They were Xoliswa's mother, uncle Shone-Shone and our grandfather, the husband to Mam-Gcina, as her neighbours called her. They would bring things like big bags of maize meal, samp, and many other things that I did not know existed. Xoliswa's mother, whom I later came to know as 'Dadada Chocho', brought us beautiful clothes and shoes. Dadada Chocho would cook delicious food, and she would buy sweets. It was nice at home for those few days, until they had to leave, which was not nice. Xoliswa would cry for her mother until she would fall asleep. It did not bother me at all when they left because I had Mam-Gcina.

My grannies were traditional healers, and their knowledge of herbs was so good that even the people in the neighbourhood used to come for consultations. They treated everything from flu to diarrhoea. They were just amazing, especially the eldest, because she was the one who would talk to the people while Mam-Gcina would be the one who dispensed medication. Sometimes she and I would go to the veldt to dig herbs for the people who suffered from different illnesses. The walk would be long, but the journey would be very interesting because Mam-Gcina would give me pap and soft, sour porridge mixed together. I used to enjoy that mixture with all my heart. We would come back from the veldt with herbs and sometimes when we were lucky, Mam-Gcina would catch a rabbit, and we would have a feast at home.

One day, as we were in the middle of the veldt, something very strange happened – you would think that I was delusional, but this is the truth. Mam-Gcina said to me, "Vuyiswa if you see anything strange, pass it and do not look back, do you hear me?" She said this with a straight face, and I answered, "Yes, Mom, I hear you."

She did not say anything further, and we just continued walking, passing many trees. As we walked, I saw a tree lying in the middle of the path. Of course, there was nothing strange about it, but as we came closer, a dead man was lying on the trunk. There was blood all over his body to such an extent that one could see it on the ground beneath the trunk. Seeing this made my knees numb; I was so scared that I was actually terrified, but because I trusted Mam-Gcina, I just passed without looking back as instructed.

About two kilometres from the tree, Mam-Gcina said to me, "Vuyiswa, let's turn back." I looked at her, thinking that she would use another route, but she just turned around and faced the way we came. I looked at her and thought, *"What is she thinking? Is she mad? How could she expect me to look at the dead man's body again?"* but I obliged, and we turned back. We walked in silence until we reached the trunk of the tree where we saw the body, but to my surprise, the body was not there! The only thing that remained of the mystery was the trunk and the blood on it; there was no dead body! The other thing that convinced me that I was not dreaming was the bloodstains that were visible on the trunk and in the soil. Otherwise, I would have thought that my brain was playing games with me. After this discovery, I just looked at Mam-Gcina and continued walking without a word, and we never spoke about it ever again.

At the age of seven, I still wet the bed and Mam-Gcina was not impressed because she used to say I was too old to wet my bed, and she considered it as an abnormality. I remember she would always say, "We are going to kill a rat and give it to you to eat so that you can stop wetting your bed." I would laugh it off because, to me, it was almost impossible for a human being to eat a rat. A rat was considered to be a very filthy thing; it was the same as a white cockroach. There was a general belief that if one had white cockroaches in one's house, it meant that the individual was extremely dirty. Therefore, it was inconceivable that she, with such a good heart, could make me eat a rat.

One morning I was woken up by the voices of men in the house. As I was still contemplating waking up, Mam-Gcina came into the room and pulled me towards the 'sitting room' where I found two men whom she referred to as uncles. Both were short at almost 1.53 m, chubby with unkempt beards. I must say that those men were far from being tidy; they looked very clumsy, and they had a terrible smell, which I thought was from the long tobacco pipes they held. I wondered if they brushed their teeth before putting those pipes in their mouths because the smell was disgusting. I greeted them, and they ordered me to sit down. As I was sitting down, I realised that the men had things in their hands; one of them had reeds, and the other one had razor blades. They both instructed me to kneel of which I did. One then held my left hand and tightened a reed around my little finger and wrist, while another one was tightened between my arm and my shoulder.

I was still puzzled by the turn of events because no one explained anything to me. I was like a sheep taken to a slaughterhouse. As I was trying to find answers, the man with a razor cut off my little finger without any indication of his intentions. With one cut, it was on the floor without any pain. The funny part was that there was no blood coming out of the wound.

As if looking at a slaughtered chicken's head, I saw my little finger jumping up and down on the floor. After the 'operation', the two men placed cow dung on the wound, bandaged it and gave me Makhulu's scarf to use as a sling. After this, they left without saying anything to me.

"Mama, why did they cut my finger?" I asked Mam-Gcina almost in tears.

"Vuyiswa, my child, there are things that cannot be explained because 'nga masiko' (It is our custom). We just do them." With that response, I guessed there was nothing more I could get from her, and I let it go. I wore the sling for a long time because, according to Mam-Gcina, the wound was not healing fast enough. This really frustrated me because I did not understand the purpose of the whole thing, and anyway, being a child, what could I have done? I was supposed to give my consent before being mutilated.

TWO

A long journey to hell

ONE DAY IN DECEMBER 1972, after all the visitors had left, Mam-Gcina came outside where I was playing to tell me that we were going to travel to Bloemfontein to see some relatives.

"What about uMakhulu, are we taking her with us?" I asked.

"No, uMakhulu will be looked after by your cousin and the neighbours. Anyway, I'm not going to stay long."

"What is she saying now?" I wondered.

"Why are you saying 'you' are not going to stay for long? What about me?" I asked with tears in my eyes. She mumbled something about school, which I did not understand, but I decided to ignore everything and concentrate on the trip, which was exciting because finally, I was going to meet other people besides the two Gogos, cousins, and those two old men who had cut my finger.

Although we used to go with Mam-Gcina to places like Hershel, Sterkspruit and Burgersdorp, Xoliswa and I were so excited because it would have been our first trip by train. Two days after we were told about the trip, the three of us left for town to board a train, which I saw for the first time.

During the trip to the station, Mam-Gcina explained to us how the train worked. She explained that the train is driven by people who are trained and that they were taught to be careful so we should not worry. On our arrival at the station, she gave money to a man who looked weird; his skin was not like ours, and he had a lot of hair on his arms. I must say he really scared the hell out of me. In return, he gave Mam-Gcina something like a piece of cardboard, which I later learned that it was a train ticket.

"Mama, yintoni la mntu angafani nathi?" (Mama, why is that man different from us?) I asked.

"Ngumlungu Vuyiswa," (That is a white man) she said, and I got the sense that she did not want to continue with that discussion.

We boarded the morning train and arrived in Bloemfontein in the afternoon. I must say I enjoyed the journey, especially seeing long, green trees. Actually, everything was green, which reminded me of the veldt back in Aliwal North. As I was admiring nature, I actually thought of the Garden of Eden – God made the world to be so beautiful and peaceful. The other thing that made the journey enjoyable was the food that Mam-Gcina had prepared for our journey. She had slaughtered a chicken and made steam bread, and that is what we had throughout our journey.

At the station, I saw many people going up and down and looking at them made me anxious. Remember, it was the first time I saw such a crowd. Their presence overwhelmed me, which made me grasp Mam-Gcina's dress as if my life depended on it. Besides the people, there were buildings everywhere of which some of them were very long, which made me wonder what they were and if people lived in them. I did not bother to ask Mam-Gcina about anything because she walked as if we did not even exist. She did not pay any attention to me as we crossed through the streets, to what I later came to know as a taxi rank. At the rank, we boarded a taxi, and Mam-Gcina told the driver that we were going to Nyokong Street. As he negotiated his way through the streets of the city, I was surprised to see so many people and cars. The taxi finally stopped near some houses which looked far different from the ones we saw on our arrival. They also looked different from the ones back home. Here the houses were big with big yards, but in Aliwal North, the houses were small, and they did not have such big yards.

As the car stopped, I saw Mam-Gcina giving the driver some money after which she told us to get out of the car. We disembarked and got our luggage, which consisted of a large, old suitcase. The driver then drove off, leaving us in the middle of the street. Mam-Gcina called out to me, "Vuyiswa yeka ukujongeka ingathi ukhwele e-traini erongo masambe." (Stop looking as if you have boarded the wrong train, Vuyiswa. Let's go.)

I came to my senses and walked towards Mam-Gcina, who was walking towards a house that looked better than our house in Aliwal North. As we entered the yard, I saw a beautiful, white puppy which I later named Babsy. When I saw Babsy, I really fell in love with her. She came running towards us, and I thought she was going to attack me, but she just smelled me and ran away towards the door, which was slightly ajar. Mam-Gcina knocked for a while without any response from inside. After what seemed like a lifetime to me, a girl finally opened the door. She just stood there looking at us without a greeting. She looked at us as if she was looking at aliens from another planet, and without a word, she went back from where she came from. We stood by the door with our suitcase without saying anything to each other. After a while, the same girl came back, accompanied by a boy whom I presumed to be her brother. He greeted us with a smile and asked us to come in and sit down.

"Who are you? And who are you looking for? Actually, where do you come from?" asked the boy.

Mam-Gcina answered with uneasiness, "My name is Mam-Gcina Gibisela, and this is my daughter, Vuyiswa, and granddaughter Xoliswa. We are from Aliwal North, and we have come to see Merriam."

The boy then explained that Merriam was his mother, but she was at work, and she would be back at 18:00 pm. He also told us that the girl who opened the door was his sister Iris and that his name was Joel. The boy, who looked thirteen years old, was friendly, and he did not display any of the animosity that was shown by his sister. He told us to relax and wait for his mother. We just sat there waiting for Merriam.

I was feeling sleepy, maybe due to the long trip, when I heard very strong footsteps and the sweet voice of a woman greeting people who were outside. For some reason, I felt anxious because I did not know what to expect from this Merriam-woman. Maybe it was because Mam-Gcina did not tell me about this woman and her relationship with her. Or maybe I was just afraid that she would react the same way her daughter reacted when she saw us.

I was also very hungry because our last meal was the steam bread and chicken on the train. While I was thinking about my hunger and the possibility of being mistreated by this woman, the door opened, and a tall, petite and very beautiful woman appeared in the door. She entered and politely greeted us, and one could see the surprise in her eyes, but she at least managed to smile at Mam-Gcina who in turn smiled back and extended her hand to greet the beautiful woman.

"You are welcomed. When did you arrive, and what brought you to this part of the world?" the woman asked Mam-Gcina.

"Merriam, the reason I'm here is that, as you can see for yourself, Vuyiswa is growing up, and I am getting old; I am not as strong as before, and I feel that you should take care of her yourself. You have to send her to school like you are doing with your other children."

"What? Is this woman my mother? There was no way in hell that this woman could be my mother!" I thought.

I looked at Mam-Gcina, and she gave me a look that said: "Everything would be fine."

Merriam, without even looking at me, said it was okay; she would look for a school for me. After saying that, she immediately rushed deeper into the house. When we were alone, I asked Mam-Gcina what that was all about because I did not understand why Merriam agreed so quickly to find me a school, while she gave me the impression that I was not welcome in her home.

She told me that Merriam was actually my mother. She said that I was a sick baby and that she offered to take care of me, and that cutting off my finger was part of making me well. She further said that she felt that the time was right for me to know my biological mother. I could not believe my ears, but I said nothing because I probably did not have the strength to say something due to the hunger, which nobody seemed to be worried about.

We sat on soft chairs, which were nothing compared to what we had at home. Remember, back at home, we sat on long chairs that were homemade; they were just planks bound together by nails, without any cloth on top. I think the fact that you had to sit on a plain plank, which did not have any cover, resulted in your bum getting sore, and sometimes it felt numb.

I must say that the house itself was different from ours, especially inside. There were photos on the walls and flowers everywhere. The house was neat with wallpaper, and the floor was covered. The only similarity between the two houses was the neatness. Otherwise, they were incomparable.

As I was comparing the houses, my hunger intensified, and I was relieved to hear what I thought was plates, only to realise that it was them preparing the meal. I wondered when the food would be ready because I remembered that back at home, we ate before sunset, and we went to bed before it got dark outside. I thought to myself, *"Oh! Mam-Gcina, why did you bring me here?"* As I was thinking and nursing my hunger, there appeared a very beautiful little girl who looked younger than me, and as if hallucinating, she had this genuine and warm smile when she entered the sitting room.

She was around Xoliswa's age. I really fell in love with the girl who introduced herself as Pinkie. Her free spirit made me feel easy, and surprisingly, I was not feeling hungry anymore. She sat on my lap as if she knew me from a long time ago. The only problem was the language; she did not speak Xhosa, but for some reason, we understood each other. We ate pap and brown cabbage, which tasted divine, unlike what I knew back at home. We all ate our food in silence, and I guessed that everybody was enjoying the meal. Iris was sitting there eating her food as if saying, "I got little food because of you aliens."

After eating, Mam-Gcina instructed me to wash the dishes, and it was only then I realised that our luggage was still on the floor between Mam-Gcina and me. To my astonishment, nobody bothered to ask us to take the luggage to the room or somewhere. I stood up without the faintest idea as to where and how I was going to wash the dishes. By now, I think Pinkie realised that I was lost because she just grabbed my hand and led me to what she referred to as a kitchen. The kitchen was a lot more organised than the one at home. There, we washed our dishes in one big bowl, which was inconvenient because one had to change the water twice before drying up. I must say that this really took a lot of time. Here there was a sink for washing the dishes and another one for rinsing, and this made things much easier.

I washed the dishes, and Pinkie offered to assist by drying them and packing them away. We were soon done and joined Mam-Gcina, Xoliswa and Merriam, but I just wanted to sleep. I asked Mam-Gcina where we were going to sleep, and I could see that she also wanted to know, but being the person she was, she just played it down. As a result, she did not respond to my question. I think Merriam was also tired because I heard her saying to Mam-Gcina in Xhosa, "Come with me. Pinkie will take the girls with her." I felt so upset about the way Merriam referred to me! I did not mind if she referred to Xoliswa as a girl because she was not her daughter, but I was her child for heaven's sake! She made it a habit to avoid calling me by name, and she also avoided eye contact with me. This really pissed me off, and I wondered what was wrong with her.

I was not aware that Mam-Gcina was also worried until she whispered to me that I should not piss on the bed because that might be embarrassing for both of us. I told her that I would prefer to sleep with her, not Pinkie. She agreed and told Merriam that she would rather sleep with us and that she should sleep with Pinkie. Merriam agreed, and we went to sleep in Pinkie's room. The room was clean, and there was something about it that I could not explain. I felt a lot of peace in this room, something I did not feel in the rest of the house. The room felt like there were angels everywhere or that the Holy Spirit was there with us.

At first, I thought it was my imagination when suddenly Mam-Gcina said, "Bantwana bam, niyaiva lento endiyivayo apha? Ndiva ubukho buka Thixo kweli gumbi. Niya buva?" (My children, can you feel what I am feeling? I feel the presence of God in this room. Can you feel it?) I just gave her a big smile and said nothing. I was so happy to know that God was with us, and even if Mam-Gcina left me here, the Almighty God would always be with me. I knew he would never forsake me.

We decided that I would sleep on the floor in case an 'accident' happened and use our own blankets. We prayed to thank the Lord for saving us throughout our journey and for being with us in that room. We prayed for everything, especially for wisdom, love, and forgiveness. After saying our prayers, we kissed each other goodnight, and I immediately fell into a deep sleep.

I was woken up by the sound of children outside, and I only then realised that I had overslept. I could not ignore the noise and rose from the floor. I quickly made the bed and was delighted to see that I did not wet the blankets during the night. I went out to look for Mam-Gcina, and I found her outside speaking to a woman I did not recognise. I greeted her in Xhosa, and she responded. She was friendly, and she resembled Merriam, so I made the conclusion that she might be her sister. Later during the day, Pinkie actually confirmed that the woman was her aunt, her mother's sister, and that her name was Ngina. She also told me that Ngina was the fourth of five children and that Merriam was the second child. Ngina had two sons who were almost the same age as Joel and Iris.

Kids were playing on the streets, and I was busy trying to see if I could recognise anyone, but there was no one I knew. To my surprise, everybody in the house was still asleep. Maybe the people were used to the noise, and that is why they were still sleeping?

I went back to the house but prayed that I would not bump into Merriam because I felt that it would be better for me not to come into any contact with her without Mam-Gcina. The house was so quiet, and I thought she might have gone to work. I found a basin in Pinkie's room, went outside to get water, and washed my face because I could not dare go outside the yard without washing my face – Mam-Gcina would kill me.

After washing my face, I stood outside, looking at the kids playing. I wanted to play so badly, but my problem was the language. Although they look very friendly, I knew that we would not be able to understand each other. I was still admiring the kids when Pinkie and Xoliswa came out of the house and said, "Dumela." (Sesotho for 'hello'.)

I just figured that she was greeting me and because I did not know how to respond, I just smiled at her, and she smiled back. For a while, she was quiet, her mind focusing on the kids playing and I think they were calling out to her because she kept on shaking her head, which I presumed to be a sign of refusal. Finally, she took my hand, pulled me towards her, and pointed to the playing kids. It looked like she was telling me that we should join them. We went to the kids, and she introduced us as her sister Vuyiswa and cousin Xoliswa from Aliwal North. The other kids introduced themselves as Sono, Ouma, Puleng (who looked as if she had a mental disability), S'tinki (Sono's sister), Nketile, Mamsy, Mado, Kagisho, Mpho, and Maki. (May the souls of those who passed on rest in peace.)

For some reason, Pinkie told the young girls that I only spoke Xhosa. They just smiled, and we started playing with a tennis ball and some empty tins. I remember one of the girls asked Xoliswa something, and she answered, "In the suitcase." All the girls laughed, and we did not understand why they were laughing. One girl, who was Xhosa-speaking, tried to explain to us that they asked her how old she was and when she said it was in the suitcase they started laughing because they thought she was saying her age was in the suitcase. I thought that was funny and started laughing as well.

They played the game as follows: there would be two groups; the arrangement of tins would be like a tower, starting from the biggest to the smallest. The group with the ball had to hit the tins, and as they tumbled down, the other group had to stack them again. In the meantime, the person who had hit the tins had to run around until the other group had stacked the tins in their original position. Watching cricket and softball still reminds me of 'marendas', as the game was called, and I presume that the rules were almost the same. It was the first time we played with other kids. My finger had not healed yet, and it was still painful, so I kept hurting it with the ball until it bled. The girls were so scared and surprised when they saw me bleeding because they did not know why I was bleeding. Xoliswa ran home to call Mam-Gcina who came rushing towards me. She just pulled me into the yard and fetched her medicine bag, which was full of herbs. She then took out a certain herb, which looked like an onion, cut it and put it on my finger. Ironically, the blood stopped, and the pain was gone. I went back to play as if nothing happened.

After the second week in Bloemfontein, I was now free, and I could understand when my 'friends' spoke their language, and for some reason, I would respond from time to time. The sad part was that it was time for Mam-Gcina and Xoliswa to leave for Aliwal North because she left the blind granny with my other cousin and she was still too young to look after her for such a long time.

The morning they left, I did not cry a lot because I thought the situation was okay, especially with God on my side, and the people seemed to have accepted me as part of their own. I never anticipated any problems. Before she left, she promised that she would always pray for me and that I must make sure to always go to church and pray. She also told me that I should always remember that only God loved me unconditionally. I must confess that I ignored this later in my life and that it was my biggest mistake.

Anyway, we waved each other goodbye, and then the taxi disappeared. That night I slept with Pinkie, but I was not free. I was scared that I would wet the bed, even though it had not happened since I came to Bloemfontein. Maybe the reason was that I was careful? Pinkie and I talked about this and that until we fell asleep.

When the schools opened in January, Mama took me to St Mary's Primary School. I was registered there as Anna Mpoetsi Morake. I ceased to be Vuyiswa Gibisela and to be honest, it did not make sense to me, especially when I had to introduce myself to the class. Nevertheless, I accepted my fate, and I was Mpoetsi, the literal translation meaning 'the one who came back to me'. What I hated the most about this name was the fact that everybody in the neighbourhood called me Mpetsi instead of Mpoetsi. Anyway, it did not matter because I never understood why they called me that name in the first place.

I must say that school was fun, and the children were nice. The only problem was that all the children wore new uniforms and looked neat, except for me. My uniform was old and faded, and it was way too big for me. The worst part of it all was that I did not have shoes and had to walk barefoot throughout the year.

I happened to be the favourite of the arithmetic teacher, Mrs May, who was feared by all pupils. I think that the only reason she liked me was that I was good at arithmetic. As time went by, I realised that she was actually empathetic of me. Every Monday she would send me to her house, which she shared with her in-laws, who were my friend Ouma's grandparents, to eat the food she had left for me. I would go to her house, eat, and wash her dishes, and the following day, she would tell me not to wash dishes after eating. It was difficult for me not to do it, and she finally gave up. The most amazing thing about this relationship was the fact that I was one of the most punished pupils in class, especially when it came to discipline and being rowdy. She never compromised, and as a result, I developed self-discipline and did my best in my studies.

It was at St Mary's where I met Father Diaz, who joined St Rose around 1972. He was the second white person I met after the conductor in Aliwal North. The only difference between Father Diaz and the conductor was that the conductor's face looked red and old as if he worked in the sun without putting on a hat Mam-Gcina used to say to us that when we walk in the sun without a hat, the sun will burn us.

Father Diaz was young and healthy. He spoke Sesotho, but his accent was out of this world. Sometimes I could not hear a thing of what he tried to say. Besides the fact that I was not conversant in the Sesotho language at that stage, I could hear when my classmates spoke to me, but not when Father Diaz did.

We would sometimes be required to clean the church and Father Diaz would be there talking to us about God and the development of the Catholic Church, and I would literally understand nothing because he would be speaking in Sesotho. I would then be forced to ask other children to explain to me, and with their help, it did not take long for me to understand the language. I think it took me approximately three months to understand and speak it.

What was amazing about Father Diaz was that he knew every pupil by their surname. Remember, in those days, to be registered at one of the two schools, you had to be a Catholic, and to be a Catholic meant that you had to attend services every Sunday. If not, Father Diaz would visit your home and require an explanation as to why you were not at church on a particular Sunday. The only students who escaped his questions were those who attended church at Fatima in Rocklands, but the ones at St Rose in Bochabela did not have a chance to miss Sunday services unless someone was very sick and bedridden.

In Aliwal North, we were Methodists, but in Bloemfontein, I had to abandon the Methodist Church for the Catholic Church so that I could continue to be a pupil at St Mary's. Anyway, at home, everyone was a Catholic except for my grandfather, who was a Methodist.

I was made to understand that Mama and her siblings became Catholics because of Mama's older brother's influence, who was financially supported by the Catholic Church throughout his academic journey. He even graduated as a teacher in sign language and became one of the first black teachers to teach sign language in Cape Town.

I preferred to be at school more than at home because, although I accepted the fact that Merriam was my mother, and I called her Mama, she never made me feel that I was her child, unlike Mam-Gcina who loved and cared for me. She scolded me without any apparent reason, which made me feel sad and nostalgic. The torment was unbearable, and I felt like running away back to Mam-Gcina, whom I missed very much.

The other thing which was really bothering me was despite everything I did in the house, my siblings, especially Iris, perpetually made me feel unwelcome by making a mockery of me in the presence of her friends. She called me names like 'nine and a half' or 'dummy finger' because of my mutilated little finger. The worst thing was that she would tell everyone who cared to listen that we were not sisters and that I was a monkey found in the veldt.

The fact that Mama laughed at those sick utterances was more hurtful than the utterances themselves. She never said anything about it, and instead, she put salt on the wounds every time she got a chance. She would say my teeth resembled a fork because I had gaps between them. The result was that whenever I laughed, I would put my hand on my mouth to prevent exposing my gaps, which I still do. This made me wonder if she was really my mother because I knew Mam-Gcina would never humiliate me like that. Before I came to Bloemfontein, I was outgoing and happy, but I believe that the utterances of Mama made me a shy and withdrawn child. I lost my confidence and made a decision that I would concentrate on my schoolwork and prove to Mama that I was worth something. I studied very hard, and as a result, I was an A-grade pupil throughout my years at primary school. I always got the first position in class, and on very rare occasions, I got second.

When I thought about it later, I realised that I studied hard to compensate for my 'inadequacies' that were perceived by my 'family'. I was in such a state of confusion because on the other hand, all my teachers were very proud of me, with Mrs May caring for me at school.

Besides the treatment at home, some children in the neighbourhood bullied me, and I did not have anyone to protect me. There was this particular girl who lived a street from us and who made sure to chase or ridicule me in front of her friends whenever she saw me. She would say I am as thin as a pole, or that my eyes are like the devil's eyes. She would even hit me with sticks or throw stones at me. The worst incident was when she sent me to fetch water for her, using a leaking bucket. I walked for almost two hours between her house and the tap, not because of the distance, but because the bucket could not get full due to the leakage. I would get the water from the tap, but before I arrived at her house, all the water would be gone, and I would have to go back to the tap.

While I was doing this, she was sitting with her friends laughing at me. I was getting furious, and I decided that enough was enough. I took the bucket and threw it in her yard, waiting for a reaction from her and her friends. I decided that I had enough of people bullying me; I was prepared to fight to the end, and I told myself that their number was not an issue. At that moment, I puzzled myself because I had so much courage, and I told myself that I had enough of bullies and that it was going to end that day. "Hey, o nagana o ira eng?" (Hey, what do you think you are doing?) she asked while walking towards me. She grabbed me from behind, and I turned towards her and held her throat very tight because I wanted to squeeze the life out of her. She tried to free herself from my grip, but I held her throat very tight. My advantage was that I was taller than she was but thinner, and the other thing was that she did not expect a reaction, so it came as a total surprise to her. Her friends also did not help their 'boss' and just stood where they were.

"Mpetsi, please let me go," she pleaded.

"Apologise for what you have done to me and promise that it will never happen again! Actually, tell your friends that you are sorry for what you have done to me," I instructed.

"Please, set me free first, then I'll apologise," she again pleaded with me.

I loosened my hand and let her free. She coughed for about five minutes, and after a sigh of relief, she said to her friends, which was actually directed to me, "I'll never do it again, sorry."

I just looked at all of them and left without saying a word. Finally, I was a free person on the streets.

As I said, I was doing all the chores at home. When I was in standard three (grade five), I was the one who cleaned the house. After cleaning, I would then wait for Mama to come back from work so that she could give me money to buy whatever we were having for dinner, which would be cabbage with pap or ox intestines. It would rarely be something like tinned fish or 'boerewors'.

We ate pap every day except for Sundays when we ate mealie-rice and chicken pieces which Mama would prepare. Sundays were my 'day off', and I would go to church, although in the afternoon I would be forced to wash dishes. I would start at St Rose at 8:00 am until 10:00 am, and at 11:00 am I would go with my friends Sono and Ouma to St Peter's Methodist Church. After church at 13:30 pm, we would go to either Sono's or Ouma's grandparents to eat.

The food was the same every Sunday and consisted of dumplings, meaty bones and beetroot. I used to enjoy this food because I was free to eat, unlike at home where I would eat while crying because either Iris or Mama said something hurtful to me. I used to feel as if I had a lump in my throat, which made it difficult for me to swallow. Because of that, I never enjoyed the food at home.

After lunch, we would leave, but I would not go home immediately, instead, I would stay at Sono's house to buy time. Around 14:00 pm, I would leave Sono's place to attend the Apostolic Church in one of the houses in our street. I used to enjoy the service the most because we sang a lot while clapping hands, and I would feel the Holy Spirit all around me. The service at the Apostolic Church made me feel complete – as if I was not in control of myself, but controlled by the Holy Spirit, and it really felt good. Normally this would be my last service before I had to go home around 17:30 pm.

Back at home, I would wash the dishes that were used during the day – dishes I had not used. Anyway, I washed it because I was used to it and it didn't bother me anymore. What used to puzzle me was the fact that Iris would be at home doing absolutely nothing sitting like a 'madam' waiting for her maid to do her dirty job. When I look back, I actually think that this has assisted me a great deal, because today I am a better mother and a good cook at that. I take good care of my family because I do not want any of them to go through whatever I went through. Although I take good care of them, I have introduced them to the value system that worked for me as a child and as an adult.

Loving my fellow human being has always been my priority, followed by respect for human beings, especially older people. I believe in justice and equal rights. Another one of my important values has always been to take care of people who are less fortunate than I am. These were values that I inculcated in my children and other children who came into my life at a certain stage. It was their choice to use them in their lives. What was important for me was that I gave them the ABC's of life.

Another thing that bothered me while growing up in Mama's house was the fact that the police raided our house at least twice a week, and although it was not an issue for me, the way they conducted it was frightening and very stressful. They would arrive in the early hours of the morning. They would never knock and would kick the door and shout at Mama from outside demanding to see her passbook. The poor woman would come out with her hands up with some sort of a booklet in her hands, which she would give to the police. They would then look at it and throw it on the floor before taking her away, and she would only be back in the morning, sometimes even after three days.

This really worried me, and I did not understand what was happening. One day I asked Sono's mother, Ausi Khukhwanyana, who explained that every person in a household had to be on a permit that clearly showed who lived in that particular house. So, if one did not appear on the permit, he or she would be arrested for trespassing.

Unfortunately, Mama was not in the permit anymore because she was a married woman, not yet divorced from her husband, who resided in Alexandra in the Transvaal. She only returned to Bloemfontein when she separated from her husband, meaning that she was still using his surname, which was why they harassed and arrested her all the time.

After I heard the explanation, I relaxed because I knew the truth. Before I knew what was really happening, I used to be scared, and as a result, I could not go back to sleep every time they took her away. I would imagine her not coming back home and me being responsible for Pinkie and everybody else. That was scary for an eleven-year-old.

THREE

Love conquered all

BESIDES EVERYTHING THAT WAS happening at home, I was a happy child because outside because of the warmth that I received from our neighbours. When I talk about people who showed me love and had good hearts, I always have one man in mind. That man was Papa Kagisho Maruping, whom I still respect today. He was from a poor background like everybody else in the neighbourhood, but he managed to change his and his family's circumstances. My first contact with the Maruping family happened through Modiegi Maruping whom we knew as a daughter of Papa Kagisho, only to find out later that she was actually his niece.

The family lived in a humble house like the rest of us, but Papa Kagisho started to build and transform it into the most beautiful house in our area. It was like those houses I read about in the James Hadley Chase novels. It had three bedrooms, and the main bedroom had a bathroom with a toilet. There was also another toilet and a separate bathroom in the house. This was the first time I saw a house with a toilet inside, and it was amazing to experience that kind of comfort. Even though I did not want to urinate, I would go to the toilet just to flush it because it was so mesmerising! Remember, this was during the era of the bucket system and imagine my shock when I did not see my waste after flushing!

Papa Kagisho was married to Ausi Kidi, who was originally from Kimberly, and a nurse at Pelonomi Hospital. She was beautiful, humble, soft-spoken and a very accommodating person. I remember we would be at their house in the morning until late, but she would never chase us away. The humbleness of this family blew me away. After some years together, the couple was blessed with a baby boy whom they named Obakeng, a very sweet child who had both parents' personalities. He never treated us badly, and he and Modiegi were always happy to see us at their home.

As a child, one would always admire children who had cars at home because their parents would take them to town and everywhere, which was every child's envy. With Papa Kagisho, we never really realised that we did not have cars at home because he treated us like his own children. He used to drive us in his new Audi and BMW ('China Eyes', or 'Be My Wife'). That inference used to amaze me because BMW was a German car, not a Chinese car, and for a long time, I did not understand why it was called 'China Eyes', but as I grew up, I realised that the shape of the lights were the actual culprits.

When Papa Kagisho was at home, he would always take us to town with other children in the neighbourhood. He would just drive around, showing us places of interests, and sometimes he would take us to the zoo. What I liked about those trips was when he bought us ice cream, especially during rainy days. I still enjoy ice cream when it is raining, and I cannot say exactly what was fascinating about ice cream in the rain, but I guess that was what I enjoyed and still enjoy.

Staying with Mama made me think seriously about my future, and one of the decisions I took very early in life was to become a nun. My decision was based on the fact that I wanted to serve the Lord and His people, especially taking care of the elderly, the poor and the sick. Our house was the second one from the corner; we were in the middle of two houses which were occupied by two grannies. Mme Ma-Wolf was a widow who stayed with one of her sons.

Mme Ma-Lethae was staying with her sweet husband, her son (a policeman), his wife and a son called Kgotso, who was considered by the community as an obnoxious boy. He used to throw other children with stones when they fetched water from a tap opposite their house, and if he wasn't busy doing that, he would chase them away from the tap using sticks from the tree in their yard. He used to annoy many parents in our street. The affected parents would go to Kgotso's house to complain, but his mother, Mamokete, would chase them away. She would be insolent towards the aggrieved families, and because of that, many parents decided that they would not allow their children to play with him. I think the fact that his mother always came to his rescue exacerbated the situation. The poor boy became so isolated, and what made matters worse for him was the fact that people in our street believed that Kgotso's grandmother was a witch and she had 'tokoloshes' under her bed.

She was not the only one who was accused of being a witch. Ma-Wolf was also accused of witchcraft. Her sons were graduates, and the one she stayed with was highly intelligent but an alcoholic. I do not remember seeing that man sober, but despite him being an alcoholic, he would always be clean with a newspaper under his armpit, or he would sit under the veranda reading the newspaper or novels. He was the one who encouraged me to read earlier in my life. He would say, "Mpetsi, you must study very hard and read because knowledge is power. No one will ever take your knowledge away from you. Do you hear me?" After he had read his newspapers, he would give them to me, and he would demand that I narrate to him what I have read.

If I did not pronounce the words right, he would make me repeat them, and it did not bother him how many times I repeated the words; as long as I did not get it right, I would repeat until I did. Ntate Wolf was a funny man, and I enjoyed his company. From time to time, his mother would scold him for delaying me from doing my chores and usually he would just laugh at her.

I took it upon myself to assist those two grannies in cleaning their homes and fetching water for them every day, and it never bothered me that people perceived them as witches. To me, they were just old people who needed my assistance. What used to amaze me was the fact that many people in our street were Christians, but every time they saw me going to assist my neighbours, they would advise me not to enter those houses because the two grannies were witches. Some even asked me to check if there were 'tokoloshes' under their beds! I found those insinuations to be ridiculous, especially coming from people claiming to be Christians. Even today, some elderly people are killed allegedly for being involved in witchcraft, an allegation that is without proof.

Besides the chores I did for the grannies, I also visited patients at Pelonomi Hospital, where I would go to the female wards to talk to and pray for patients. Some would be really sick, and I would give them more attention because I thought that they deserved to be cared for more. This was emotionally draining for me, but I believed that no one deserved to suffer like they were suffering.

During one of my visits, I happened to pass a ward I always tried to avoid – the ward for patients with burn wounds. There were about five patients who were badly burnt, and although I could not see two of these patient's faces, I presumed that they were burnt from their lower bodies up to their faces. There was even one who was placed in something I thought, at the time, was a drum. I stood there for a moment not knowing what to say or what to do to assist because I was afraid that if I tried to touch them or fixed their blankets, I would touch their wounds and hurt them which I did not want to do. The ward smelled awful; I could smell death everywhere, and it felt as if I was in a mortuary. This made me feel uncomfortable, especially because the patients, whether covered or not, were unresponsive to my presence or anyone coming into the ward. To bring back my energy, I decided to kneel and pray:

"God, Father in heaven, here are Your children in this ward. They are between life and death. Father, Your children are going through excruciating pain that no doctor on earth can understand, but with Your intervention as the only healer on earth who could even heal leprosy. Send Your angels to deliver them from these pains and heal them in the name of our Lord, Jesus Christ. Amen."

After I prayed, I stood there for a moment before I waved them goodbye even when I knew they would not be able to respond. I was so emotional after my visit to the burnt patients that I was unable to visit any other wards. I felt that I would not be able to transfer positive energy to those patients. I decided to leave the hospital to mend my broken heart.

One day a classmate's brother, a policeman, was shot dead. The poor girl was devastated because her brother was the breadwinner of the family. When he died, the girl and her other brother had no one to take care of them because their parents were also no more. I felt so sorry for them that I wished that they could give me their burden because I believed that I was stronger than they were. That day I told myself that I was going to do something for them, especially the girl. She was not a nice person but looked so vulnerable that I really felt very sorry for her.

After school, I went home, cleaned the house and went to Ma-Lethae to clean and fetch water. After I did the usual, I asked her if I could do her washing, which she agreed. She promised to give me five rand, but emphasised that she was not paying me; it was just an appreciation of what I have done for her throughout the years. I thanked her and started with her washing, which was only her nightdresses, braziers and underskirts. After doing the washing, she gave me the money, and I went directly to the shops to buy assorted biscuits, sweets and lollipops to give to the girl who lost her brother. I went home and hid the parcel between my books so that no one could see it. The following day during our break, I called her over and gave her the parcel. She looked at me in disbelief, but she took it anyway and with a shy smile on her face, said, "Thank you." She opened the parcel and looked at me with surprise and said, "Morake, you should not have done this, where did you get the money from? You always struggle to get something to eat every break, but you bought this for me? Thank you so much."

I looked at her and replied, "It is true, I do have problems of my own, but the problem you are faced with now is more serious than the ones I have. God knows how I wish I could take your pain away. One thing I would like to leave you with is the fact that God does not make mistakes; everything in our lives has been pre-planned. Therefore, it was not by mistake that your brother died. Maybe his death would bring better things to you and your family. Everything will be given unto you if you seek the Kingdom of God first. Enjoy your biscuits; I shall catch up with you later, bye."

I left her standing there looking puzzled. Like I said, she was not a nice person, and I never expected anything from her, especially friendship, but I felt fulfilled because I did the right thing under the circumstances. I thought I would serve the Lord better if I became a nun. Years went by, and still I thought that I was going to be a nun, until one day, when something terrible happened that changed everything; my life, my dreams, and my faith. All that I believed in throughout my life just diminished, with no hope of survival.

— Ruth Mantile —

My gratitude goes to the following families that taught me humility, respect and love. I owe a lot to these families: Maruping, Sebati, Leepile, Lethae, Sebotsa, Lesia, Wolf, Gaorekwe, Malefane, Njiva, Mkhwetha, May, Kgokgo, Mabote, Molise, Leeuw, Mokgoamme, Moleme, Motloung and many others I did not mention.

FOUR

Shattered dreams

I WAS IN STANDARD five (grade seven) when one of my schoolmates got pregnant. One Sunday after church, I decided to pay her a visit with one of my friends Nyenye. We decided to walk to her place, which was a distance of about five kilometres. Just as we were walking past the shops in Rockland's, we saw a group of boys sitting at the entrance. As we were about to pass them, one of them ran to Nyenye and started talking to her, but I just continued walking towards my friend's house, which was not far away from the shops.

Nyenye stood there, talking to the boy. I must say that Nyenye was a streetwise girl; she already had a boyfriend when I was in standard four (grade six). Even today, I cannot actually remember what standard she was in during that period, maybe because we went to different schools. What used to puzzle me was that she had big breasts, unlike the rest of us. Actually, I did not have breast at all, but hers, God! One would have thought she had a child or two for that matter.

Finally, Nyenye arrived while Montsheng was explaining to me how she became pregnant. She told me that she had a relationship with a certain boy from another school and that he loved her so much that he encouraged her to get pregnant so that her parents would allow him to marry her. According to Montsheng, her boyfriend changed after she got pregnant. He seldom visited her, and if he did, he complained about this and that. The marriage story wasn't an issue anymore because he stopped talking about marriage after she got pregnant. I really felt sorry for her, but I consoled her by saying that things happen for a reason, and she must remember that God will always be there for her and the baby. We had girls' talk, and I realised that Nyenye was not a virgin anymore because she told us that she had two boyfriends and she had sex with both. I was so shocked, and in my heart, I asked God to help me not to lose my virginity the way Nyenye did. As we were talking, I realised that it was getting late and that we had to leave. We said our goodbyes and left Montsheng with her big tummy.

We had to walk back again another five kilometres, and as we were approaching the shops, the boy who was talking to Nyenye came towards us followed by another. The other walked with me and started talking. He asked me my name, and I told him that my friends called me 'Teenage', and he was surprised because that name was for boys. I explained to him that I was a soccer player and I played for the Crocodiles. Surprisingly, he still found that very amusing, and I did not understand the amusement. Yes, I played soccer; I also played basketball and netball at school, and everybody called me 'Teenage' or 'Stylish' because of the way I walked, and I had accepted that. We kept on walking with a boy who said his name was Ace. He was very cool, and he never showed any aggressiveness or anything funny.

As we were walking, he said to me, "Look, you cannot walk back. Let's go and get taxi fare from my mother. We live just behind this house." I thought, "*Oh, God! Where does he come from?"* I agreed because I thought it was noble of him to be so considerate.

It was getting dark, but for some reason, I was not scared. We had just turned at the corner when I realised that there were no more houses and only a veldt. I looked at him, and I think he realised my intention because he just grabbed my hand and took out a knife from his pocket and pulled me towards him. The proximity between us was so close that I could smell his breath, which had never happened to me before. It was the first time I was so close to a person, especially a man, which made me very uncomfortable, and I felt suffocated by his closeness.

I tried to free myself from his grip, but I could not because he really held my hands so tight around my waist. It was now getting darker, and we had left the houses far behind us; I tried screaming, but finally stopped because I realised that we had left the houses and there was no way that somebody could hear my cries. I just left everything in the hands of the Almighty. Also, I thought that if an opportunity could arise, I would run away from this rascal because I knew he would never catch me since my friends did not call me 'Teenage' for nothing.

As we walked, I tried to free myself again, but it was almost impossible. He stopped at a certain spot, and I thought that was the end of me. He released one of my hands and said, "There is no way you can run away from me. If you try, I'm going to slice you into pieces, and you'll never ever see the light again."

He then forced me to the ground with his knife on my back and pulled down his trousers with one hand, after which he used the same hand to pull down my panties. The knife was still on my back. I remember I had red panties on, and I must say I have never again worn red panties.

Still lying on my back with him on top of me, he forcefully opened my thighs and struggled to get inside me. Remember, I was still a virgin. The more he tried to get inside me, the more painful it became, but he did not stop pushing himself into me even though I was sobbing and trying to push him off. Finally, I felt him clinging to me as if his life depended on it, and for some reason, his body seemed to relax on top of me, and that is when I managed to push him away, which I guess it was too late.

I struggled to stand up, and he stood up and held my hand to assist me. When I finally managed to stand up, I felt a sharp pain between my legs. As I was wondering where the pain came from, I heard him saying, "Teenage, I'm so sorry. Please find it in your heart to forgive me. I didn't know what I was doing."

I did not understand what he was talking about. As he was pleading with me – I cannot remember why –something made me touch my skirt. I got the shock of my life when I realised that my skirt was wet. My thighs and private parts were wet as well, but above all, the pain that came from my thighs and private parts was unbearable.

"Did he pee on me?" I asked myself. "What happened?" I did not understand.

"How can an old man like this urinate on me, and why is his urine so painful? The bastard is he not even ashamed of himself," I asked myself. He took off his T-shirt and gave it to me saying, "Skat, please wipe yourself or do you want me to wipe you?" I just looked at him, not knowing what he was talking about because I was so confused. I tried to think of what had actually happened, and nothing made any sense to me. I felt as if I was losing my mind. What had just happened to me was so traumatic; I never thought that somebody could do such a barbaric thing to another person! I also felt delusional because I just could not believe what just happened, and nothing made sense to me. He held his arms around my waist, and I said nothing; I just followed him. He tried to make conversation, but my mind was far away. *"Why did it have to be me? What did I do wrong to deserve this? Where were you, God, when I needed you?"* Tears just rolled from my eyes, and I could not stop them.

Ace's hand was still around my waist when we finally reached the main road. We stood by the roadside for a long time while waiting for a taxi. I could not say what time it was, but I presumed it was late looking at the time I left Montsheng's place, the time we went through the bush and the time …

I said nothing to Ace, who was trying to console me by saying that everything would be okay. "Please stop crying. Everything will be okay! I'm sorry for what I did; it was not my intention, I am sorry. I did not know that you were still a virgin." Whatever he said did not make me feel any better. My thoughts were running wild; all my dreams were shattered. I could not be a nun anymore, and worse of all, I had sinned before God. What was I going to do?

Part of me said it was not my fault. But the other part kept on saying it was and that I should not have listened to him when he told me that he was going to ask his mom for money, that I should not have trusted him …

He stopped the taxi and boarded with me. When the taxi stopped in my street, I disembarked, and surprisingly enough he disembarked too. We walked in silence until I heard him saying, "Teenage, please forgive me, I promise that I will take care of you. I know I cannot bring back your virginity, and I cannot take back the pain, but please forgive me." I just looked at him, and tears rolled from my eyes.

We were almost at my place, and I did not tell him to go back or anything; I just stood in the middle of the street saying nothing. I think he realised that I was nearing home because he looked at me and said, "I think you are going to get it in your heart to forgive me and you must know I'll always be there for you." He kissed me on the cheek and turned away. I just looked at him, and I must say that I was now confused, thinking that a person who has just raped me, took my virginity, my dreams and my dignity, now claims to care for me. The whole thing sounded weird.

When I got into the yard, I realised that it was out of character for me to be outside the yard at that hour of the night. *"What am I going to say to Mama?"* I thought. One thing was certain – I was not going to tell her about my rape because she would never believe me anyway. The possibility was that she was going to say I deserved it. Therefore, I had a good reason for keeping it to myself.

I walked into the yard (remember, this was during the era of the bucket system, and our toilets were outside) and went straight to the toilet where I wiped what I thought was the urine from my rapist, with my panties. After cleaning myself, I threw my red panty in the bucket and went inside, expecting a beating from Mama because I was so late, but as fate had it, there was no one in the house. Thanking my lucky stars, I quickly took the blankets which I used as my mattress and laid them on the floor to sleep. I could not fall asleep that night; I just looked at the black plastic bags we used as a ceiling, wishing that whatever happened to me that evening could turn into a bad dream. I was so confused, and I remember I was shaking and crying, while at the same time blaming myself for the rape. *"If I only did not believe him when he said he was going to ask his mother for money, the rape could not have happened,"* I thought.

A lot of things came to my mind, like the question of screaming. My subconscious mind was saying, *"You should have screamed!"* In essence, my mind was saying, *"It was your fault, you should have prevented it from happening."* You know, I believed what my mind was saying. As I lay there, I felt so helpless and useless. I felt dirty, and the next morning, even though the pain between my legs were really bad, it was far less than my worries.

I was concerned about my community. I thought, *"What if the news reached them? How are they going to react to this? Will they continue to care and love me the way they used to? Are they going to reject and disown me? Oh, God! What shall I do? My community was my only hope; my life depended on them, and if I lose them, I may as well die."* All these questions and concerns ran around in my head. Just the thought of rejection by those mothers and grannies in my community was enough to send me to my early grave.

I got out of bed because I felt that it was useless for me to lie there while I could not sleep. When I picked up my dress from the floor, I was shocked to see a stain of blood on it. I looked at myself to see if there were any wounds I might have missed as it always happens when we play, but there was nothing that indicated a wound or anything like that. As I was wondering, I felt like scratching my vagina, and after scratching, I consciously looked at my fingers and was shocked to see my hand covered in blood. *"Oh! God, what is this?"* I panicked.

I was almost twelve years old, and it was the first time I saw blood coming from that part of my body. Although I knew about menstruation, I had not started yet. Boy! That was scary. I went to the toilet, took a newspaper and poured water on it to make it soft and wiped myself. As I was throwing the newspaper in the bucket, I saw my red panty, which I suspected was also soaked in blood, but because it was red and soaked in urine, there was no way I could recognise blood on it. I quickly fetched another newspaper to cover my red panty and that bloody newspaper so that nobody could see it.

After that, I went to get water, which we had to fetch from outside the yard. I felt so dirty, especially after seeing blood. The water was very cold, but I felt that if I were to heat it, it would take me too long because we did not have electricity. We used a Primus stove to heat water and to cook.

I poured water in the small basin that we used to wash in and started washing my private parts, which was really sore. I kept on washing it because my mind kept telling me that it was dirty and the more my mind told me that it was dirty, the more I kept on washing it until I heard footsteps outside. That was when I realised that there was no blood anymore, much to my delight.

That day after doing my chores, I stayed in the yard, not wanting to go anywhere. I could not eat or do anything because of the pain I was feeling. It was excruciating in both my body and my soul, and it felt as if I had lost a part of myself. Pinkie seemed to be worried about me because she kept on asking if I was okay, and I would say I was fine, but I could see that she was not convinced. The unfortunate thing about the whole ordeal was that I could not visualise my rapist's face anymore. Every time I tried to visualise his face, I ended up with a blank picture of him. His face, or appearance, is still a mystery even today.

What happened that day reminded me of the boys who were from a place called 'di-garteneng' (the curtains), who used to sit around the shop of Norman Mathobisa in our street. Those boys were around nineteen to twenty-one years old, and I believe then that they were not students because they were always around that area. Their area was crime-infested to a point where it was difficult for young girls to walk that route even during the day. Many cases of sexual harassment, attempted rape and rape were reported to the police by parents of victims, but most of the time, nothing happened to the criminals. You know why? Because the houses they occupied were very small and close to each other, so if you did not know the place, it was difficult to apprehend a criminal because he would run into another house and hid behind a curtain. You would not see him because the owner of that house would simply say that she did not see anyone, and you could open the curtain to see if there was anyone.

They were like gangsters who made life very difficult for everyone, including older people who had to pass 'di-garteneng' from work, especially the railway workers who were forced to pass that area. Most of them endured purse-snatching and being assaulted by the same gang. If it could happen to me, a God-fearing child, what happened to other girls out there?

FIVE

Life without meaning

AFTER THE RAPE, I became more withdrawn. I stopped playing with my friends, stopped going to the church choir, but continued going to church. What was amazing was that no one at home realised that there was something wrong with me. I do not know why I bothered because anyway, Mama never cared what happened to me, and I needed to accept it. Although I enjoyed being alone, I continued to go to soccer practices and played in matches. I really enjoyed soccer, and I gave it my all, but there was something else that I was developing, which I did not understand.

I was getting obsessed with being a boy. I started walking and talking like a boy and wore boys' clothes which Mama brought from her employer, Mr Christos. I even stopped wearing two earrings; I only wore one and a 'mosomi' (a black neckband) around my neck. I started hanging out with boys because I thought I would be safer that way. I actually thought that to be a man meant power, and if one had power, one would always be safe. Although I made those changes in my life, I made sure that I was always safe. Safety meant everything to me.

One day during that period of me trying to be a boy, Mama got visitors from Theunissen. It seemed Mama and that woman who brought her son to the hospital in Bloemfontein knew each other from long ago. They laughed at each other's jokes and talked about their experiences with the police who were harassing them because they did not have the correct documents. (Remember, it was during the pass laws.) We went to bed, and Mama and the other woman slept together, and her son slept with Joel.

As I lay on the floor, I heard this other woman saying, "Oh! Merriam, Mamathanzima looks exactly like Phuthuma; it was as if he wanted to deny that she was his daughter. The way she smiles, walks and talks; it is just him. Did you tell her that her father passed away?" I knew she was talking about me because one of my sisters used to call me Mamathanzima. "No! I have not yet," I heard Mama telling the other woman. "Why?" the woman asked. Mama gave a long sigh and said, "You know, after I left Theunissen, she got so sick, and she was admitted to the hospital for a long time. I remember at a certain stage doctors thought they had lost her, and they declared her dead. But a certain woman told me that the baby was still alive. She requested me to persuade the doctors to leave her in the ward for two days, and if she remained in the same condition after two days, they should take her away. At that stage, she was not breathing and had no pulse; we were convinced that she was dead. This woman begged me to talk to them, and two of them agreed under protest.

We had to stay in vigil with that woman at her bedside for two days while she was praying. I was really getting bored, which she noticed, and she decided to let me go home and promised to take care of the baby. I left the hospital without worry because I did not care whether the child died or was stolen, which was a fear of any woman at that time, but I did not care. I left them and came back the following morning only to find Mamathanzima back to life. You know, I did not know what to say to the woman since I had mixed feelings about the whole situation. After thanking her, she introduced herself as Mam-Gcina, a traditional healer from Aliwal North who came to the hospital for no other reason than to heal the child. I was so astonished to hear that, and it made no sense to me. As I was still trying to reminisce about what she said, she asked me to give her the child, but not forever; she just wanted to be with her so that she could heal her. Without thinking, I agreed because I thought if this child was not with me, I still had a chance to save my marriage to the father of Joel and Iris.

Therefore, I am not in the position to tell her now because I do not even know how I feel about her. The other thing is that you know Pinkie, my last-born, is actually Mam-Gcina's granddaughter. What happened was that I visited Aliwal North, to check on Mamathanzima and I met her son Norman and fell in love with him. Before I knew it, I was pregnant with his child. We stayed together for some time, and I thought it was to last, but after some time, I realised that he was a womaniser and we parted ways. It was a very devastating situation because my life revolved around him."

They were quiet for some time and ultimately, Mama asked her exactly what happened to Phuthuma. "We got information that he was shot dead by a farmer, who suspected that Phuthuma sold him a fake diamond, but so far we do not know the truth about what really happened. He was buried in the Transkei somewhere in Kokstad, and most of us went to bury him," she said.

As the two women were talking, I thought whatever I heard meant that I was all by myself; no father, no mother. It was just me against the world. It was then that I understood why Mama was treating me the way she did. She wanted to gratify her children by all means, of which she did not care if she hurt me in the process. Anyway, she told the woman that she did not love me. Although she did not say it in so many words, her statement of not knowing how she felt about me and the way she treated me implied that.

— Ruth Mantile —

My heart was so sore; it was as if somebody had pierced it with a spear. Nothing made sense to me anymore, not even God himself. But I could not blame God for my miseries, and I tried to convince myself that it was actually God who woke me from the dead through Mam-Gcina. Therefore, I couldn't blame Him for things that were done by human beings. The story I heard reminded me of the person who raped me. I started asking myself who was better between him and Mama. Part of me said Mama was worse than that boy was. Actually, I subconsciously blamed her for the rape because if she showed me love and cared for me, I would not have gone to visit a pregnant schoolmate. I would have been at home with her like other families out there.

My life turned into a nightmare. I was now suicidal and wanted to die, but I did not know how to do it. I always convinced myself that there was no reason for me to live anymore; my whole life was a shame. I did not have a purpose in the world at all. At the age of ten, I started to have terrible headaches, and the diagnosis was migraines.

Doctors could not understand why a child of that age could have migraines. I could not explain how I felt, and the only thing I knew was that when those headaches started, I could never bend down, my whole body ached, and I felt nauseous all the time. When I got those headaches, I actually felt that I was going out of my mind, and sometimes I would see something like clouds coming towards me! This was terrifying, and by then, no one was able to explain the cause of the headaches. I could not even go to school for days because of it.

I would be at home trying to nurse the headache, but when Mama came back from work, she would wake me to buy things for dinner even though Iris and Joel were at home. I would wake up and go to the shops, came back and prepare food, then wait for them to eat. After that, I would wash the dishes and Iris would sometimes help me with that.

The unfortunate thing was that the whole thing was starting to affect my studies and as a result, I got a C-grade during my standard five examinations, which according to me was the lowest symbol I ever got since I started school. My teachers were worried about it, but I thought that nobody cared. Look, I am not saying that it was wrong for Mama to make me do all the household tasks, but I was hurt when she made me do those chores even when I was sick.

Because of that, even today, it hurts me so much if my child or anyone expects me to do chores when I am sick. To me, that person lacks compassion for another human being, but as a grown-up woman, I thank Mama for forcing me to do all the chores. She might have thought that she was breaking me, but it turned out the other way; today, I am a good mother and a good cook.

Life is a very interesting thing. You know, during all my miseries I took solace in Babsy. (Remember the dog that welcomed me in Bloemfontein?) She was always there for me; I would get hugs and kisses from her whenever I told her about my problems, and she would listen to me with compassion and empathy. Sometimes I would think that I saw tears rolling from her beautiful brown eyes. She was a wonderful dog, and I used to think she was my guardian angel. I loved Babsy to bits.

SIX

Finding my purpose in life

IN OUR NEIGHBOURHOOD LIVED people from different generations, statuses and beliefs. The first generation, which was elderly people in their sixties, were widows, semi-literate and Christians who were not able to go to church because of their ill-health. These were the elderly who were accused of witchcraft. The second generation was the ones in their late thirties and early forties. These were literate and professionals like nurses, teachers, policemen and social workers. They were also Christians and attended different churches religiously and indulged in alcohol. This generation was politically conscious, but they did not engage in political activities, unlike the younger generation.

The third generation were intellectuals in their early twenties and thirties. This generation included university students and young teachers who were politically conscious and active. They had a direct influence on students who were in high schools in Bloemfontein and surrounding areas and were the ones who persuaded the youth into the Black Consciousness Movement as a vehicle to fight the injustices of apartheid.

I was one of those who were influenced by this generation because, as a soccer player, I had ample opportunity to find myself in their company, especially when they spoke about apartheid and discrimination which I could also relate to because I was discriminated against in Mama's house. I felt the harshness of apartheid as a black child who endured poverty, violence and racism, especially through the education system, which gave a black child limited choice to further his or her studies. Black students were forced to choose trivial subjects which did not assist them to better their situation and kept them subjected to exploitation. That was why I was intrigued by the black consciousness doctrine which Steve Biko, the leader of the Black Consciousness Movement, defined as "Cultural and political revival of an oppressed people".

In June 1979, the young teachers, and some high schools in the Orange Free State (now called Free State Province) joined hundreds of students in Welgespruit (Johannesburg) to form the Congress of South African Students (COSAS). One could say that COSAS replaced the South African Student Movement (SASM) which was banned in 1977. COSAS, like SASM, was inspired by Black Consciousness and I became a member immediately after its formation through Kgabi who was one of the founder members of COSAS and a supporter of the Crocodiles Football Club which I played for.

After joining COSAS, my schedule changed a bit because I had to attend meetings, play soccer, serve Ma-Wolf and Ma-Lethae, visit the hospital, and attend school and church. I was happy with what I was doing, though I was not happy with my school performance, which dropped after the rape, and I told myself that I was going to work harder at St Bernard High the following year. During the December holidays, the only thing on my mind was seeing myself in high school and being active in student politics, which would take my mind off my misery at home, which I never expected to change.

January 1980 came, which was time to go back to school. I was now in high school and felt so enthusiastic and looking forward to being in St Bernard's. I started with a bang! I passed all my tests with excellence, and this really made me happy because, in December, I took a decision that I was going to work hard in school and that I was not going to let anything distract me, even Mama.

I realised that I did not have anyone in the world because my father died before I could meet him. Therefore, I owed it to myself to be a better person. The only thing that would stand between me and my progress would be COSAS and student politics, of which I could minimise my involvement as much as I could to ensure that I achieve my goals.

It was during this time that I had my first period. Fortunately, it did not scare me because at least I knew about it from the biology class, but I did not know what to do. I just used newspapers because I did not know what to use until one day sister Catherine, one of the nuns who taught Biblical study, called me to the staff room.

"Morake, what is that on your dress?" I looked at my dress and saw nothing.

She came around her table and said, "Do you have pads?"

"What's that?" I asked.

She did not answer me; she just gave me money and said I must go and buy pads at any shop, go home and come back the following day. I thanked her and left, and fortunately for me, no one saw my 'accident'. From that day, I knew I had to use pads, but how was I going to buy them?

It was now towards the June examinations, and everybody was preparing. I, on the other hand, attended a meeting where we discussed the pending school boycotts in honour of Solomon Mahlangu, a gallant soldier of Umkhonto weSizwe (MK), who was hanged on April 6, 1979. During the meeting, it was decided that the boycotts would also be in memory of the Soweto uprising of June 16, 1976. I must say I was not impressed because it meant that whatever I had planned would be disturbed by the school boycotts, but I still had hope that an amicable solution would be found. I did not say anything to anyone as I exited the hall and walked home. I continued with my studies while still having hope that the decision to boycott classes would be re-looked at, until one day, as I was walking home from my studies, I met my friend, Sono.

"Hey, Teenage, you are busy studying; don't you know that there are school boycotts? We are not going to write exams. COSAS declared that all the students are supposed to participate in the school boycotts as they did in Soweto in 1976. They are going to chase all the children from different schools and will still decide what they will do with those who are going to resist. So Teenage, don't think that when you are at St Bernard's, you are immune from the boycott," she said.

I did not say anything, and just looked at her, thinking to myself: *"Why can't we write first and then boycott later?"* Although I said that to myself, I was actually not convinced because if we boycotted after the exams, there wouldn't be any impact. Therefore, it was a good time to boycott classes.

At that stage, I did not know when they would come to our school, and I did not want to find out because I was buying time. Maybe by luck, we would be able to write our June exams; hence, I continued with my preparations. The other advantage which I thought we had, was that St Bernard's had a high fence all around the school and the gates were always locked, which would make it difficult for intruders to access.

I continued with my studies until one day, on my way to school, I met many students not wearing their school uniforms. All of them were going in the same direction, which was towards Paradise Hall. I thought about the decision at the meeting, and I realised that it was final and that there was no turning back. Deep down in my heart, I knew the decision was the right one, but I preferred a more peaceful way of doing things. I just continued walking to my school.

When I reached the school, all my classmates were standing by the gate, and everyone looked worried and very serious. I joined them, and I heard that they were actually talking about the planned boycott, but they also shared my sentiments that we were secured and that there was no way that anyone could get into our school.

The school bell rang, and we all ran to the assembly where we were told again about the intended school boycotts. We were advised to stay calm and concentrate on our studies, and that nothing was going to happen to us. We went to our classes after the assembly.

After school, I went home, and on my way, I met Sono, who told me about the meeting they held at Lereko High School. Oh! I forgot to tell you about Sono. She was a comedian; she could definitely compete with the likes of Trevor Noah and other well-known comedians. She was very rowdy and damn, the girl could sing! When Sono told a story, you would feel that you were actually there because she never missed any detail. I must say that she was a good narrator, and I am sure that with good academic guidance, she would have made it into the arts.

"Tomorrow all the students are supposed to gather at Lereko High at 8:00 am, where they will march to the schools where students are still attending classes. After that, they will proceed to Paradise Hall, where there will be speeches. The order is that all students should not wear their uniforms," she told me.

By now, I was getting worried, and I had to decide about the meeting. A part of me wanted to attend, but the other part was saying, *"Do not go to the meeting in case they do a roll call to check who was and who was not at school."* I left Sono by the gate and went inside to clean and prepare a meal of pap and leftover cabbage.

After doing my chores, I made a decision. I told myself that the following day I was going to wear my yellow and white dress to school. The next morning, I woke up as usual and left for school in my dress. On arrival, everybody was in uniform except me. When I was asked by my class teacher why I was wearing a dress to school, I told her about the previous day's meeting. For some reason, she did not say anything, and we just continued with our business.

At 10:00 am, during our break, my class teacher requested me to make tea for her, which was normal for her to ask. As I was waiting for the water to boil, I heard some commotion outside with people screaming and shouting. I went to check, and I was shocked to see the police all over the schoolyard with their batons and dogs. I ran back to the staff room and locked the door. I watched through the window and saw the police beating children with their batons. Some children were lying on the ground bleeding; others laid there without moving, and I thought they were dead. The incident lasted for about twenty minutes, and I think that if it wasn't for Father Diaz's presence, the police would have continued beating the students.

Seeing Father Diaz gave me the courage to leave the staff room to see if I could assist him and the teachers who came out of their classes to assist the injured students. Seeing those innocent, helpless children lying there made me so angry. We thought we were safe at school, but the bastards managed to get into our school and beat up everyone they ran into. I thought I should have attended the meeting instead of being at school.

While they attended to the injured students, I left the schoolyard and told myself that I would never be a spectator again; I was going to fight for the liberation of my people. I was so furious that I even forgot that I was asked to make tea.

On my way out, I saw some students running past me, crying. Puzzled, I stopped to see what the problem was. They were heading to the staff room, and I followed them. There I heard them telling the teachers who were in the staff room that one of the pupils at St Mary's was shot dead. The pupil's name was Papi Makotoko. I knew him because his sister was in my class.

I did not say anything to anyone; I just left the schoolyard. I thought I was going home, but I found myself going in the direction of Lereko High. From a distance, I heard people singing, and I thought that there was now no going back for me; I am going to join the boycotts. Anyway, I had nothing to lose, and it did not matter even if I was going to be the only student from St Bernard's. I could only see dust, and I knew that the students were marching to Paradise Hall. I waited for them, and when they were near, I joined them. We arrived at the hall, and we started singing, "Senzeni na?" (What have we done?) That song opened my own old wound; I used to ask myself, *"What have I done to deserve all these heartaches?"* and it made me realise that my problems were nothing compared to the problems that were faced by millions of black people under the apartheid regime. I, therefore, decided to be part of the bigger picture.

The chairperson of COSAS in the Orange Free State, Mosala Nthatisi, opened the meeting, "Black power!"

"Mayibuye iAfrica," we responded.

"Izwe Lethu, iAfrika," we responded.

"We have gathered here today in preparation for the commemoration of June 16th. The significance of this day, as we all know, is to remember all those heroes who died on June 16, 1976, fighting the system against Bantu Education, including the usage of Afrikaans as a medium of instruction. This is the day where young Hector Peterson was shot and killed by the barbaric apartheid police. We should also remember our martyrs like Steve Biko, Onkgopotse Tiro, and Solomon Mahlangu, who was hanged by the apartheid regime on April 6, 1979, which is very recent, and a lot more. Therefore, we should avenge their deaths by continuing with the struggle to free the black man from the bondage of oppression and exploitation.

Let us remember Tsietsi Mashinini and other student leaders of 1976, not forgetting our own: Leon and others from Bloemfontein who left the country for military training to come back to fight the racist government and free our people. We must assist these combatants in creating political and military cells so that they can be in the position to unleash military attacks on the enemy and their strategic installations without being captured by the enemy. We should also create defence units that will collect information about the planned activities of the enemy so that the combatants can counter the enemy attacks by counterattacks. Black power. One Azania, one nation."

Tiger, together with Sandi Khuzwayo, started singing, "Senzeni na? Senzeni Na? Senzeni Na? Amabono asenza izinja, Amabhunu asenza izinja." (What have we done? What have we done? Boers treat us like dogs.) Another song was "Ityala labo linzima, bazoyi thetha inyani ngesibhamu." (Their charges are heavy, they will confess them through the gun.)

The other song I loved was "Noma kubi siyaya, siyaya, Noma be sidubula siyaya" (Meaning, even if it is bad, we are going; even if they shoot at us, we are going). "Black Power, ilizwe lethu!" Then a chorus, "iAfrika" (Our land Africa).

I was not sure if Tiger was a student at Sehunelo High School or not. To me, he did not look very bright; he looked like those people who would repeat a class twice before he could move to the next class, but boy, he could sing! He sang as if he was far away; he would sound like a person who was on the other side of the world, and he would touch everyone's heart especially me who would cry at every opportunity.

After the speeches, we sang revolutionary songs. There was a comrade who recited poems; his name was Flaxman Qoopane, and he was so good that he made you feel as if you were not doing enough to liberate the country. Those songs and poems encouraged me to join the struggle because it made me realise that there was a bigger picture than my personal problems at home. The bigger picture was to liberate Azania as we all thought South Africa would be named after liberation. One should remember that Tanganyika became Tanzania, and Northern Rhodesia became Zambia after they gained their independence.

Attending all the meetings, reading the pamphlets, and discussing outside meetings, made me conscious of who I was and what my purpose was in the world. I started to ask myself if God really existed and *if* he existed, why He allowed the police to kill Papi Makotoko. With all that was happening in the country, I had a lot of questions about God's intentions for us as a black nation. Were we destined to continue suffering in the hands of white people? Was our faith the reason for our suffering? After asking myself those questions, I decided to visit someone I knew would have answers. That person was Father Diaz. (Remember, I was not attending school anymore because I was too busy attending meetings.) I think when he saw me, he thought I was going to give some lame excuse for not coming to school because he even went to my home to enquire about my absence from school and church.

Father Diaz was one of a kind. As I mentioned earlier, he knew everyone from school and church by their surname. He noticed when you weren't at church on a Sunday and, after church at 14:00 pm, would go to your home to ask where you were. He would do the same with students who were absent from school.

I found him in his office at the Mission reading a newspaper. When I knocked, he looked towards the door a bit puzzled because I was not in my uniform. I entered before he could let me in. I told myself that if he thought I was going to talk about school, he was in for a huge surprise.

"Good morning, Father, how are you this morning? Father, this seems like a beautiful day, and I hope it will continue to be like that even after my meeting with you." The moment I said that he turned his chair to look at me.

"Father, I know you are aware of what is happening around here in terms of police brutality towards students and the Bloemfontein communities. What I do not understand is why is God allowing this situation to continue? Father, God took the children of Israel from Egypt to the Promised Land because he saw their suffering, but he let us suffer from the whites and says nothing about it. Like the children of Israel who were suffering under the Egyptians; what is God waiting for? Why he does not drive the white people in this country to the sea because according to their history, they found us here when they first came to Africa."

Father Diaz was looking at me as if he was dreaming or even confused. I continued to tell him how tired I was of praying and serving the God who did not care about black people and how blacks were capable of liberating themselves from oppression like they did in Mozambique, Angola and lately in Rhodesia (now called Zimbabwe). I even told him about Steve Biko, who said: "Being black is not a matter of pigmentation, being black is a reflection of a mental attitude." I had read about all this from some publications given to me by Kgabi.

Father Diaz's face turned red when I mentioned Steve Biko, but I think what worried him the most was my perception of God at that moment.

"Morake, listen to me. You do not know what you are getting yourself into. Let me tell you something about politics and religion. Discrimination is a problem, and sometimes some people use religion to discriminate against others for both political and economic reasons. South Africa is not the only country that is experiencing repression and discrimination. In 1970 there was a Black Power Revolution in Trinidad and Tobago who were fighting for socio-political change in their country. The movement was greatly influenced by the civil rights movement in the United States of

America. The Black Power movement was supported by trade unions, social organisations, and the black youth."

He even told me about Reverend Martin Luther King, who was a civil rights activist in America who believed in non-violence as a method that could be used to bring social changes. He stood up and opened his cupboard, which was full of books, publications and pamphlets. One book I saw was *Long Walk to Freedom*. As he was going through his collection, I saw his face brighten, and he smiled.

"Morake, do you know Martin Luther King? He asked.

"No, Father, I do not know who he was. Was he like Nelson Mandela?" I asked with keen interest.

He did not answer me and continued with his search.

"Oh, here it is," he said, holding a notebook. "Look, you need to be careful about what you say and what you talk about and most importantly, to whom are you talking to. Never, ever mention Nelson Mandela's name no matter what. I know you have seen some of my collections, but please it should be our secret. Otherwise, we will get in trouble with the police if they find out about this. Do you hear me?"

I nodded my head in agreement and looked at him to continue to say something about Martin Luther King.

"Listen to this speech he made in 1963 during a march for jobs and freedom:

> *'I have a dream that one day, this nation will rise up and live out the true meaning of its creed; We hold these truths to be self-evident, that all men are created equal. I have a dream that one day on the real hills of Georgia, the sons of former slaves and the sons of former slave owners will be able to sit down together at the table of brotherhood.*
>
> *I have a dream that one day, even the state of Mississippi, a state sweltering with the heat of injustice ... will be transformed into an oasis of freedom and justice. I have a dream that my four little children one day will live in a*

nation where they will not be judged by their colour of skin, but by the content of their character.'

"Morake, you have been here for more than three hours, I have some work to do, and I even forgot to ask you about your non-attendance of classes. Look, it is your decision, but you must always know that education is important. However, it is still your decision to make. Martin Luther King once said, '*The function of education is to teach one to think intensively and think critically. Intelligence plus character – that is the goal of true education.*' Think about it and be safe." As he said that, he started to pack away the books. I waved him goodbye and went home.

I started to re-look at myself differently from what Mama made me believe about myself. I became conscious of the fact that I was a young black girl who was prepared to die for the liberation of her country, Azania. As Steve Biko said, God will never come from heaven to solve our problems, we need to solve our own problems, meaning if I became part of the fight for the liberation of our people, I would simultaneously fight for my rights as a child against Mama and Iris.

The preparation for the funeral of Papi Makotoko had progressed, and the COSAS executives assisted the family to organise it by mobilising resources from businesspeople around Bloemfontein. I remember particularly Norman Mathobisa and Steve Bogashu as some of the people who contributed to burying Papi.

I sometimes attended the preparatory meetings, and at one of them, there was a guy called Shakes who lived on a street near ours. Shakes was a very eloquent fellow, and he was always preaching about non-violence. As a chairperson, he said that we needed to discuss how we were going to ensure that there would be a peaceful march from the house to the cemetery. Also at the meeting was Fellow, Kgabi, Kakara, Tunku, Pepe, Hola, Spencer Mbole, and her sister. We all agreed that the march was going to be peaceful and that Comrade Shakes would organise the mass meetings where he would explain the funeral proceedings to the people. A decision was made that the students would start the march at St Mary's and from there walk to the cemetery. All the students had to wear their school uniforms.

After all the announcements, Comrade Shakes said, "We have to select a delegation that would go and talk to the bereaved family so that we would know what they wish for."

The meeting decided that Comrades Agnes, Edith, Fellow, Shakes and Mama Ella would be the ones to go. The meeting adjourned, and I went home and prepared dinner for my family, as usual.

It was the Saturday morning of the funeral. I woke up, cleaned the house and prepared to go to the funeral. A friend of mine, Mohanuwa Molato, had given me a black dungaree, which I was going to wear with a white T-shirt underneath, but my problem was that I did not have school shoes or any shoes for that matter. I decided that I could do without them because I was anyway used to it. I think I looked pretty for the occasion.

I walked to St Mary's and met with my comrades. From there, we joined other students and started marching and singing towards Phahameng. I must say the march was very peaceful. As we passed St Peter's Methodist Church, we saw police armed to the teeth. We passed them still singing, and they did not do anything to us.

After prayers at the bereaved family's house in Phahameng, we all marched to the Phahameng cemetery (known as Mangengenene Cemetery). The police were still visible, and they did nothing to stop us. We got to the cemetery still singing, awaiting the hearse, and after an hour everybody arrived. We stopped singing when it was time for the church proceedings to begin. As Father Diaz was praying, I suddenly smelled something like teargas, which puzzled me. I heard several gunshots, and everybody took cover while others were running all over the cemetery. I took cover, and was trying to think about what could have provoked the situation, but could not think of anything at that moment. I was just thinking of getting out of the cemetery as quick as possible. The smell of teargas was getting very strong, so the only thing I could do was get out of this situation. Still on the ground, I looked around, and I saw that most of the students were also still on the ground taking cover and that the shooting had stopped. I stood up and started walking towards the gate, and I told myself that I was not going to run but walk. I thought that if I ran, the police might justify it by saying that they shot me because they told me to stop. I walked out of the cemetery towards the main road, and that is where I saw Shakes, who was holding a young boy of about eleven who was bleeding. "Teenage, hurry and get water!" he shouted. I ran to a house nearby and got an empty bucket which I filled with water and gave it to Shakes who then washed the boy's face and told me that we needed to take him to the hospital. Shakes was not sure where the blood was coming from, but the boy was seriously bleeding.

"Teenage, just stop a taxi so that we can take him to the hospital!" I obliged, and fortunately, the first taxi stopped, and Shakes took the boy to the hospital.

There were students all over the show. Some were crying, others singing, and there was a lot of confusion. The police had stopped shooting and were just standing there looking at us. Fortunately, we did nothing to provoke them, we just regrouped and continued singing until we reached the Makotoko's home.

I was getting worried about Shakes and the boy. I did not know if he had made it or not, in fact, if that boy died, Shakes would want to take the blame for his death, and I knew that he would never forgive himself for that. Honestly speaking that was Shakes for you. He was a wonderful person; very loving and caring. Although Shakes was from a well to do family (according to my standards), he was humble and a considerate person. With Shakes around, I always felt safe because he would never take advantage of the females and always treated us with respect. As I was busy thinking about Shakes, I heard Edith calling my name, "Teenage, come over this side."

As I looked, I saw a group of people looking at something. I could not establish what it was at that moment and ran towards the group. I then realised that they were singing revolutionary songs standing in a circle. They showed such enthusiasm, and I could see that they were so desperate to attain freedom.

The people who were singing seemed to be ready to take up arms and fight the apartheid regime and its state apparatus. I thought the African National Congress (ANC) should actually seize this moment to arm the people and train them in combat arms and warfare strategies. The time was right for an armed seizure of power, and the people were ready to do just that. I looked at them and thought: *If only we could get arms to fight back the bastards!* Just the thought of us liberating our people gave me goosebumps, and I felt emotional, and tears just rolled down my face. I tried to stop them, but I could not.

"Teenage, there is Shakes, he is back," said Mbole. I looked up and saw Shakes with blood on his hands and on his T-shirt. I ran to him and asked him about the boy.

"He is fine. I was so scared that we were going to lose him, but he's doing well. Thank God for that."

"Did you meet his parents? Are they from around here?" I asked.

Shakes looked at me and said, "Yes, I met his parents. They are wonderful people. They are actually from East London."

Shakes told me that we should go to Papi's home, but before we could leave, he wanted to address the comrades who were gathered around the cemetery and singing.

"Black Power," said Comrade Shakes. "Ilizwe lethu! iAfrika," we responded. "Izwe Lethu, iAfrica." Everybody looked up and paid attention to him.

"Comrades, I know what happened earlier, but I must say I am very proud of all of you. The way you handled the situation showed that you are freedom fighters. What I want us to do now is to go to Comrade Papi's house to wash our hands as a tradition, but comrades, I am warning you now: there will be police and soldiers all around, and I plead with you, do not do anything that will justify their actions. Let us sing peacefully to the house to show these bastards that we respect the dead. Black Power," he concluded. We then very peacefully marched to the Makotoko's house, and no incidents were reported.

After the funeral of Makotoko, I continued to live my life as a child at home doing all the chores, but outside of my home, I continued to attend meetings, distributing ANC material and mobilising the students to join the student's movement. I was now living a double life. Come to think about it, I ceased to go to church because now I was asking myself if God really existed and if he did exist, why he was allowing the killings and suffering of the black nation. Why did he give the system the power to treat the black people this way? Why was he not doing the same with blacks as he did with the Israelites when they were in Egypt? If he loved his children the way the Bible says he does, why did he not stop this? Those were some of the questions I used to ask myself. Remember, I now asked those questions not only for me but for the black people as well.

God's existence was always a debate in our political education, and most of us agreed that God was there, but that He wasn't our God as a black nation. We thought that

He was actually the white man's God because He gave them the power to rule over us.

You should know that in the township, we did not have a good sewerage system, and when it rained, the water flowed everywhere, making it difficult for people or cars to pass. I used to play in those pools of water with my friends Sono and Mpho, and I always thought of the white children who were playing with toys in their warm houses while we were playing outside in the streets in the cold water. One could argue that it was not their fault that they had privileges. Deep down in my heart, I knew that the system in the country was not fair to the black people. I grew up liking Bob Marley and Jimmy Cliff, and for some reason, I started singing "Too Many People are Suffering" by Cliff. These songs and the treatment I got at home made me realise that there was a lot of inequalities and unfairness in the world. As I was singing this song, I did not realise that we had company; I only became aware of him when he said, "What do you know about suffering? You are just a child; leave the rubbish to old people." When I turned, I realised it was a priest from a nearby church. "Do not think about these things. You are a child, and it should remain like that," he said, turning his back to us.

He scolded me and left. I just looked at him, thinking to myself that he does not understand what we go through every day, whether at home or on the streets because he does not have to earn a living. Everything he had, he got for free from his congregation. His children had everything while we had to struggle just to get a plate of food. I actually thought that people like that were informants for the security police. I did not share this with Sono and Mpho because they would not have understood. They were too naïve to understand the political situation in Bloemfontein, or even worse, the country. But they were a good cover because to everyone who knew me, I was just an ordinary child who played soccer and did all the other things children my age did. For some reason, I did not encourage my friends to participate in the school boycotts or anything like that. That is why I was able to do other things covertly. The priest really annoyed me, and after he had left, we decided to stop for the day and left for home without saying anything to each other.

As I mentioned, COSAS, like SASM, was influenced by black consciousness, but in 1980, during the school boycotts, almost throughout the country COSAS declared its support to the Freedom Charter. This was said to be an influence from its president, Ephraim Mogale, whom I later discovered through Kgabi, was one of the underground members of the ANC which were a banned political organisation then.

I was soon recruited into the underground structures of the ANC by the late Comrade Kgabi (May his soul rest in peace) who was very active in the student politics, and he happened to be a member of the underground structures of the ANC. I do not know – actually, it was beyond my comprehension – why I was recruited into that structure in the first place.

The influence that the ANC had on me was amazing. I could not understand the decision, but the truth was that the decision to work for the ANC was the wisest one I had ever made in my life. To be part of the ANC was, and still is, the most unforgettable and significant thing in my life.

I attended both the COSAS and ANC underground meetings, which was fun in the sense that I knew many things that many people knew nothing about. I ended up attending the planning sessions of the underground structures of the ANC together with Comrades, Kgabi, Shakes, Pepe, Papase, Tunku, Lebenya, Oupanyana, Kakara, Spencer, Mbole and her sister. We usually held our meetings at night outside Zenzele Hall in Phahameng location. It was a good place because it gave us a good cover at night. No one suspected that there were people who could use it for anything. The darkness also gave us the perfect cover. The planning sessions involved decisions on who was going to go to Lesotho to fetch banned ANC leaflets, pamphlets, stickers, and to get new instructions from the senior comrades based in Lesotho.

I knew that we were not the only ones who worked for the ANC's underground structures, but because of security reasons we did not know who they were. For me, it was a good thing not to know them in case I got arrested because I would not be able to expose them, but somehow, I knew Kgabi knew them. From time to time I went to Lesotho with Kgabi, though most of the time we would meet the comrades from Lesotho in Ficksburg. They would give us the ANC material, and sometimes they gave Kgabi instructions which I would not be privy to security reasons.

Other decisions involved people who were to distribute those pamphlets and those who were going to mobilise the students to join the underground structures of the ANC. I was part of the group that distributed banned ANC pamphlets in the township and mobilised the youth to join the struggle. In some instances, I was involved in assisting those comrades who were in hiding with food and reading material, and I joined the ANC underground structures at that time.

The good thing about me then was that I was inconspicuous; nobody suspected me of anything. I would go to a place and do what was required of me without anyone bothering me. I remember a particular evening when we had just received copies of the Freedom Charter, and I was supposed to distribute them in the township at night. I took the copies home, and I told myself that I was going to leave some at the Bantu police station.

One evening I walked to the police station with five copies of the Freedom Charter in a paper bag. On arrival at the station, there were many people arrested or who came to open cases. I looked around and realised that I could easily leave the parcel on the counter and nobody would notice it until later. I hung around as if I was part of the crowd, got closer to the counter, and left the parcel on top of it. After that, I just moved back and stood amongst the people who were there. I do not know what happened, but I heard a police officer shouting

"Who has left a parcel on the counter?" There was no answer, and everybody seemed to be puzzled. People looked at that police officer without saying anything. I looked at him, and it was as if he wanted to open the plastic bag and I thought: *Open it, fool!* Because I was just interested in what his reaction would be when he found out what was really in the plastic bag. I could see that he was curious; he actually wanted to open it but was in doubt. He finally opened it, and I heard him say, O, Modimo wa Choaro (Oh, My God).

He looked shocked and frightened as if he had seen a ghost. He just stood there without saying anything. The other police officer who stood nearby took the plastic bag from the shocked police officer and opened it. Shocked, he emptied the bag on the floor, and the other police officers rushed in and picked up the copies from the floor. All their faces turned pale; I was just laughing inside, thinking, *"OH MY GOSH! They are scared!"* The first police officer who saw the copies said, "These copies were left by terrorists, how they managed to leave these things here?"

I left the police station feeling very proud of myself. As I was walking home, I was thinking that it meant it was possible to place a bomb at the police station and leave it there, but my problem was that it was going to kill an innocent person, which was something that we could not afford. Killing all the black police officers crossed my mind as they were part of the system, which killed my people, but those thoughts conflicted with my Christian beliefs, and I ignored it. When I arrived home, I went straight to bed.

The following day there was nothing in the news about the copies of the Freedom Charter that were left at the police station. Even the police did not comment about it, but I understood why. The reason was that it would have exposed their security vulnerabilities. I was still cleaning when I heard a knock on the door, and when I opened it, Kgabi was standing there looking very angry and tired. I greeted him and let him in. Without greeting me, Kgabi said, "Did you leave those copies at the police station? Our comrade inside told me that there were copies of the Freedom Charter found at the police station, and I just knew it was you."

I did not know what to say, and I just looked at him. He was quiet for some time and then said, "That was a very dangerous and stupid thing to do! I do not want you to endanger yourself ever again. Do you hear me?"

"Yes, I understand. I will never do it again," I said.

Kgabi just looked at me and left.

SEVEN

No turning back

THE DAY WAS JUNE 16, 1980, commemoration day for the victims of June 16, 1976. I woke up, cleaned the house and prepared myself to go to St Peter's Church to attend the commemoration. As I was taking my bath, Mama called me Rakgadi, which means Aunt in Sesotho when she was in a good mood, which was very rare. Interestingly enough she and her siblings called me Rakgadi because I was named after their Aunt Mpoetsi. I realised that you do not have school shoes and I want us to go to town and get a pair of shoes."

"*Where is this coming from?*" I wondered in surprise. Of course, I did not have school shoes, but it had been three years without shoes, and the last pair I had was given to me by Mohanuwa, my friend from school. 1980 would have been my fourth winter without shoes, but I was used to it, and it was not an issue anymore. "*What has changed?*" I asked myself.

"Do you hear me?"

"Yes, Mama," I said.

I was still shocked when Mama said to me that we must leave so that I would not be late for the commemoration. We boarded a bus to town and on arrival went to Cuthbert's to look for shoes, but I could not find my size, and Mama suggested that we check at Pep Stores. We went to Pep Stores, and I got shoes. I was very happy about them, and to me, it was the best thing to commemorate on 16 June. I thanked Mama profoundly for the shoes.

Back home, I changed into a dungaree which was also given to me by Mohanuwa, white top and my new shoes. I was so happy inside; it was as if somebody took a heavy load off my shoulders, and I felt content. It was also the first time I looked at myself in a mirror and the beauty I saw amazed me.

I looked amazingly beautiful, and this was contrary to what Mama made me believe throughout the years about myself. For some reason, I avoided looking myself in a mirror because I truly believed that I was the ugliest thing on earth. I must say that this belief affected my self-esteem and self-worth in a big way.

When I arrived at St Peter's, I realised that the police, soldiers and students were already there. I looked around thinking I would see my comrades, but it seemed as if everybody was already inside, and as I got into the church, Comrade Oupanyana ushered me in and showed me my seat.

All the comrades had their seats on the extreme side of the church facing the people. From where we seated, we could see the movement outside the church. Fortunately, on my arrival, the programme had not started yet, so I got a chance to talk to comrades that I have not seen for quite some time. As we were catching up, the programme director, Mosala Nthatisi, who was also the chairperson of COSAS, started to sing 'Senzeni Na' and everybody stood at attention with a clenched fist.

"Black Power! Thank you, comrades, you may sit down. Comrades, I think all of you have seen the police, soldiers and the Special Branch members and I would like to believe that we all understand what that means. We, as the executive, request all of you to be calm and disciplined. We are going to start now with our programme. The first speaker would be Comrade Janie Mohapi, who is a second-year law student from Turfloop University. I don't want to talk much about Comrade Janie; I'll rather let him tell us about himself."

"Black Power! Ilizwe lethu, iAfrica, Mayibuye, iAfrica!" we responded.

"Comrades, as Comrade Mosala said: my name is Janie Mohapi, I am from Bloemfontein originally, and I just went to Turfloop to further my studies. Unfortunately, the situation in South Africa is not conducive for black students who want to further their studies; the education for the blacks is inferior to that of the whites, and that is why I decided to join the struggle. If you are black in the country, you do not have the liberty to study what you want. That is why you would find everybody going for teaching, nursing or join the evil police force. Today, as I stand here, I want us to change that by participating in the struggle to liberate blacks from all forms of oppression and exploitation.

Let us remember this day by picking up the spear of the fallen martyrs like Steve Biko, Hector Peterson, Onkgopotse Tiro and Solomon Mahlangu, recently of Papi Makotoko. Bloemfontein has been quiet for some time. I do not know why, but maybe it is because the active comrades have since left the country to join the ranks of Umkhonto weSizwe, but that has to change.

The ANC was formed in Bloemfontein in 1912; we should ask ourselves what that means. It means we should be active in furthering the aims of the ANC so that South Africa can be free. Amandla!

In 1976, the students in Soweto boycotted classes because they were against the introduction of Afrikaans as a medium of instruction. Therefore, we should do the same. Let us unite and fight the common enemy. There is a saying that 'United we stand and divided we fall'. Comrades, those of you who are afraid must always remember the words of the great leader of the Soviet Union, Comrade Brezhnev, who said, 'Sticks and stones may break my bones, but words will never hurt me.'"

There was a round of applause and comrades started singing revolutionary songs led by Tiger. There was this one song I really liked, and it went like this: "Nantsi indoda emyama Vorster" (which can be translated as 'Here is a black man, Vorster, you must run away'). Comrade Vuyisile Mini was hanged because he was a member of Umkhonto weSizwe and was amongst the first cadres of MK who were sentenced to death by the racist regime.

Speaker after speaker reiterated what Comrade Janie said about continuing with the struggle and taking up arms to fight the apartheid regime. Comrade Mosala was about to conclude the commemoration service when we heard shots outside the church. We were informed that the police started shooting randomly at the comrades who were standing outside because there was no space inside as the church was full. After the shots, I smelled teargas, and before I knew it, there were screams in the church, and everybody was running towards the door.

Comrade Shakes pleaded with the comrades to remain calm, but I do not think that they heard him. I ran towards the door, and for some reason, I found myself outside. I then ran through the fence, which scratched me on my thigh. There was a lot of confusion outside the church, and because of that, I did not know where I was running to.

St Peter's Church was near where Ouma's grandparents lived, so I decided to go there. As I entered, I met Ouma's grandmother, who was hysterical. She said to me, "Mpetsi (that's how she called me too, despite my name being Mpoetsi), you have to leave my house because I don't want any trouble with the police."

I looked at this old woman and thought to myself that there should be another way to get out of this situation.

The disadvantage at this stage was that I was in a school uniform, which was a giveaway.

I went out of the house and looked around to see if there were police in the street, and fortunately, there was no one in the immediate vicinity. I ran as fast as I could, and still, the coast was clear. As I entered the third street from St Peter's, I saw a car coming towards me, and before I knew it, three policemen jumped out of the car and started chasing me. I ran to a nearby house to hide in the toilet. The police got into the yard and started searching for me around the toilet, but fortunately, they did not look in the toilet and left while swearing in Afrikaans. When I thought it was safe, I got out of the toilet and ran home, which was only three streets away but seemed too far.

As I was running, I felt something cold on my thigh, but I kept on going until I reached home without any incident. On my arrival, I realised that I was bleeding. As I entered through the front door, I saw my brother Joel lying on the floor. I found out that he was unconscious because he inhaled teargases, which was thrown at him.

"*Boy! That was scary! Maybe he would never see the sun again,*" I thought. But fortunately, after about twenty minutes, he started to cough, and we were all relieved. As we were sitting around the stove, there was a knock at the door. I thought it was the police and ran to another room to hide. My aunt asked, "Who are you?"

"It is Kgabi; I just want to speak to Teenage."

"Okay, come in, the door is open," my aunt said.

"Mpoetsi, Kgabi wants to see you," my aunt called.

I came out and greeted Comrade Kgabi, who I last saw at St' Peter's earlier that day.

"Teenage, somebody has been shot dead not far away from St Peter's. It seemed as if he was from work or something like that; he was not part of us. His surname is Sejake from somewhere in Rocklands. I thought I must tell you so that we can go and visit the family tomorrow."

"Okay, thank you for informing me," I said.

We said our goodnights and I went into the house and locked the door. My heart was so sore, and I thought we should avenge his death. I stayed awake for a while, thinking about this situation. I was wondering about the events of that day, especially what Comrade Janie said about us continuing with the struggle to liberate the black nation.

My problem was that when I read the Freedom Charter, it stated categorically clear that South Africa belonged to all who lived in it; black and white. How were we going to make sure that the white people lived together with us when they did not show any mercy to the black people? They did not consider us as their fellow compatriots or their equals.

It was on a Wednesday when I decided to attend prayers at the bereaved family's house. The situation was calm, and people were singing gospel songs and praying for the soul of the deceased when suddenly I heard somebody screaming saying that there was a 'mpimpi' meaning there was an informant, who had a two-way radio that was used by police. There was a cry from all corners of the house to catch him. Before I knew it, five people were on top of the alleged informant stripping him of his clothes, and there they found a two-way radio.

They held him very tight and dragged him outside the yard; I followed them with Comrades Oupanyana, Oupa, Kgabi, Shakes, Mbole, Agnes and Edith. Comrade Shakes appealed to the people to remain calm, and as he was talking to them, the bastard managed to escape. He ran to the next street and went into a house, which was later identified as his own. The comrades ran after him and managed to apprehend him before he could lock the door. They dragged him out of the house, and somehow one of the comrades got into the house and dragged a mattress with him. He then put that mattress on top of the 'informant' who turned out to be a police officer. I was still wondering what he was doing there when I heard somebody requesting petrol or paraffin.

This was now getting scary for me; the man was crying and pleading with the people, and the worst thing was that they were not listening to anyone. I heard cries from the house, which I assumed to be from the wife, but this also did not deter the people who were holding the poor police officer down. Somebody brought petrol, and before I knew it, there was a flame on the mattress. The victim was trying to run away, and I should think the more he tried to do that, the more the mattress caught fire because of the blowing wind. I could not stand the agony and the screaming anymore, and I decided to leave. I took a taxi home, but the picture, the cries for help of that police officer was playing in my mind, and I thought to myself, *"Why did he come to the prayers with a two-way radio? What was he thinking? God, what is this?"*

I was almost in tears when I arrived at home. I just got into my bed not wanting to talk about what I had just seen. It was so difficult for me to fall asleep, and I just kept on turning and tossing, thinking about the incident. I have never heard a man crying in my miserable life, especially begging for his freedom. That was a very terrifying situation. I finally fell asleep only to wake up because there was a knock at the door.

"Who is that?" I asked.

"Teenage, open, it's Kgabi." I opened the door to let him in. Kgabi looked as if he just saw a ghost.

"What happened to you?" I asked.

"Teenage, we do not have time. Oupa, Oupanyana and Shakes have been arrested for killing a policeman."

"No! They did not do it; I know they did not!" I cried out, shocked at what Kgabi said.

"Stop this! We do not have time. We have to go to Shakes' place and get all the material that arrived yesterday before the police can get it, otherwise, he will be in big trouble, and so will we."

Without even washing my face, I followed him to Shakes' house, which was in the next street, not far from my home. When his sister opened the door, we just went straight to Shakes' room and took everything that was in the box.

The thing is: Kgabi, Spencer and Shakes went to Lesotho after our meeting the previous week to collect the ANC's pamphlets and the speeches of the ANC president, Comrade OR, as he was popularly known, and everything was still sealed. They had decided to leave the box as it was until after the funeral, but then we had to come up with a plan as to where we were going to hide the box. I knew Kgabi's place was out. I wondered what we were going to do, and we took the box and left.

"Teenage, can't we hide the box in your house because you are still safe so far?" Kgabi asked.

"It is fine. I will hide it in one of my hiding places," I said.

I had a hiding place at home where I would hide sensitive stuff before distributing them to the communities. What amazed me was the fact that it was so easy but almost impossible to find. Keep on guessing!

The following day, Kgabi came to my home and told me that he went to visit the detained comrades and that he was terrified. He said that the police had beaten them up so badly that it might be difficult for some people to recognise them. He also said that he was concerned as to how long they will be able to resist before 'talking'. He also said that the police told him that he would not be able to see them again because they were to be transferred to Modderbee Prison in Benoni, where terrorists were locked up. He just said, "Well, that is part of the struggle," before he left me standing by the door still shocked by the turn of events.

On Saturday, we went to the funeral where Kgabi told the other comrades about the arrested comrades, and people became so sad. I guarantee you, if Tiger was not there, the situation would have remained tense and unbearable. He just started a song, 'Mama-ka –Makotoko siyaya siya Kwa Makotoko' (Makotoko's mother, we are coming to your home), and we joined him singing. The service started on time with prayers from pastors from different denominations.

What really impressed me during the service was the fact that the Pastors expressed their gratitude to the students for the support they have given to the family. They also advised us to remain disciplined and calm, no matter what.

Peacefully, and singing revolutionary songs, we left the church to go to the cemetery. While we were singing and dancing, the police escorted us, and so far, everything was going according to plan, which was to avoid confrontation with the police no matter what they did. Our reason was that we wanted to respect the family of the bereaved by demonstrating discipline and respect. We arrived at the cemetery without any problems. The pastors continued with the service, and we really gave them a chance to do what they knew best. In between prayers and hymns, we sang freedom songs, and some comrades recited poems.

Everybody was so calm. I actually saw satisfaction in the eyes of the family, and I think they did not expect this peacefulness after what happened during the week. As the service was about to come to an end, Father Diaz requested one of the family members to say something on behalf of the family. The family representative was none other than Malome, who said, "We as the family, thank God for giving us strength, but also we thank everybody present for the support they have shown throughout this sad period. We invite all of you for a cup of tea at home. Thank you very much, and may God bless all of you. Thank you once again."

After the prayer, we started singing freedom songs until we reached the family's house where we ate food and drank ginger beer. The atmosphere was very peaceful, and although there were police all around, nothing happened as they were, I think, enjoying the free performance by the comrades.

I remember somebody suggesting that we give the police food because they have 'protected' us throughout the night and now they have been with us throughout the day. Therefore, they should eat as well for the job well done. That made sense; we really felt protected, but somebody said that we had given the police a free performance so we cannot give them food on top of that. After eating, Fellow, Shakes, Tunku, Mbole, Agnes, Edith, Spencer and I went to the family and thanked them for allowing us to be part of the burial. They also thanked us for everything that we did for their son. I was so tired when I arrived home that I went straight to bed and only woke up the following day. As I indicated earlier, after the rape, I started to be what people refer to as a 'tomboy'; in addition to that, I stopped combing my hair in support of the Black Consciousness. One could easily say I was now *'young, black and gifted'* and at that stage, I really felt that I was proud to be black and for some reason, I found my purpose in life again, unlike during the period when I was in the depth of despair not seeing my purpose in life. I was now surrounded by people who appreciated me for who I was, and that alone changed my attitude towards life. I was now very positive about life; I tried to take cognisance of my achievements and contribution to our community.

For the first time in my life, I realised that I was actually a beautiful, loving and caring person, unlike what my Mama wanted me to believe. Throughout my young life, she made me believe that I was an ugly, forsaken creature that did not deserve to be loved by anyone, and you know what? I believed her, especially after the first rape. To me, it made sense because I looked at my friend Sono, who used to play in the street at night while I was in the yard or trying to sleep, but nothing happened to her. Sono never experienced rape nor hurt by anyone. She was always happy, rowdy and free-spirited, I guess like every child.

Two weeks after the burial of Sejake, we had a meeting with the comrades, and information came out that comrades who were in detention for the alleged killing of a police officer were still in detention, but it seemed as if there was no tangible evidence against them. Due to the security situation in Bloemfontein, the advice was that we needed to be extra careful about how we did our operations. Also, we had to be vigilant because there were police informants amongst the students who informed the police about all our plans. Actually, Comrade Kgabi suggested that we should cease all the operations for a while until the situation cooled down.

For some reason, I thought that if we ceased the operations, the possibility would be that the Special Branch would think that the detained comrades were the ones who were inciting the students and that they were responsible for the operations, which would be very dangerous for them. Therefore, I suggested that we should continue making contact with the ANC in Lesotho, distribute the material as usual and have meetings with the students, just to make things easier for the detained comrades. To my surprise, all the comrades supported my suggestion. The question of visiting comrades was an issue, but we felt that we should not go, due to security implications. The meeting concluded that the comrades who were responsible for making contact with the ANC outside should arrange those meetings so that we could continue with our underground work.

We continued with our work, and everything was going perfectly well. As we continued working, Oupa, Oupanyana and Shakes were released from detention because there was no evidence that they were involved in the killing of the policeman. I thought that the decision to release them was maybe because the operations continued during their absence. We were all happy about their release and continued to work, but I made sure that I avoided meeting with Shakes regularly like before in case the police were observing his movements and the people he came into contact with.

The situation continued normally until one day, Kgabi came to me and said that his contact in the Special Branch told him that they got information from their informants that I was the one who was distributing illegal material and mobilising workers to be involved in industrial boycotts. They said I was there when the policeman was burnt to death, and I was a suspect in the case of an AK-47, which was found not far from my home. As Comrade Kgabi was narrating the story, a very cold shiver ran down my spine and for some reason I could not breathe. *"God, what is this now? Who is this informant? What am I going to do?"* I thought.

The truth was that I knew about the AK-47, but it had nothing to do with me. In fact, that AK-47 was not supposed to be in Bloemfontein in the first place. It was part of the merchandise that was going to be used to train comrades who were part of the cells in the Free State. Kgabi told me that the trigger of that weapon was faulty, so it had to be taken back to Lesotho, but the people who were responsible for taking it to back could not go for about two weeks due to security reasons, and that was why the damn weapon was there. The AK was in a pit, covered by soil, and on top of the soil, there was a bin that was always there. It was not that the bin was a new object in that area, it had been there forever. Therefore, it meant that there was a mole amongst us. Yes, I was there when the police officer was killed, but I never participated in it. As if Kgabi was reading my mind, he suddenly said, "Teenage, the situation is bad for you inside the country. We are all aware that the distribution of banned material can lead to a charge of treason. It is even worse if they can link the AK-47 that was found to you. The situation is thus very dangerous; hence, we suggest that you leave the country as soon as possible. Actually, by the end of this week, you should be in Lesotho. So, you have only three days left to prepare yourself."

I looked at Kgabi and said nothing, just thinking about what he had just said. He looked at me and said, "Three days – nothing more. Also, remember to collect money from Janie on Wednesday at 19:00 pm. You will find him at his parent's house in Phahameng."

He then turned away, leaving me still puzzled by what he just said. I just stood there looking at the sky and wondered about my journey to Lesotho in three days. My thoughts were actually with Pinkie, my lovely sister. How was she going to cope without me because I was almost more like a mother to her than a sister? Who was going to read bedtime stories to her, and assist her with homework? That was the only person I thought of and the only one I was going to miss. Pinkie had an inner beauty that you could not miss; she had one dimple on her left cheek, and of course, as a child, she was plump, but with very beautiful legs. She also had light brown eyes, which lit up at night like those of a cat, and lips that were so different. Because of this, her friends used to tease her, saying that her lips resembled that of a fish, and she would just laugh it off. You know, what I loved most about Pinkie was the fact that she was a very loving person, always happy and she really enjoyed the small things in life. I used to call her 'mooi van ver' (beautiful from far away) because from far away you would think that she was more beautiful than Cleopatra, but as you came closer, one realised that her beauty was normal.

At that moment, I was really worried about her because I would have loved to see her growing into a teenager, a university graduate, a young woman, and ultimately getting married having children of her own. Pinkie was my real princess; I loved her to bits, but now it was time for me to leave her, and I knew God would take care of her. Actually, I was leaving the country so that we could all live better.

Wednesday at 18:00 pm, I left home to collect the money from Janie Mohapi, the one who addressed us during the commemoration on June 16. I arrived at his home in Phahameng around 18:45 pm and realised that I was too early for my appointment. I stood by the gate, waiting for 19:00 pm. A few minutes after I started waiting, a man I did not know came out of the house, greeted me and asked me if I was waiting for someone.

"I'm waiting for Janie, but I'm early, my appointment is for 19:00 pm, but it seems as if I did not calculate the distance properly," I said. This person introduced himself as White Mohapi, the younger brother to Janie, who was not at home at that moment. He said I could still wait for him and went back into the house. After a while, White came back and told me that he knew where we could find Janie as he was only at a house not far from there. I followed White, and we indeed got into the third house from theirs. We entered the yard, and the house seemed to be extraordinarily quiet, but I thought nothing of it. We went further and further into the house, and there were no signs or voices of people, but I kept on going until there was nowhere to go. I immediately turned around to face White, who was behind me since we got into the house. I am not sure why it happened that I was in front and I wondered if it was just a coincidence or if he planned it.

As I turned, our eyes met, and I saw that his eyes were looking very serious and vicious. He was actually very serious as if he was about to attack me. I was scared, but I did not want to show him, I just stood there and looked at him straight in his eyes and asked, "Where is your brother? You said we would find him here. Do not play games with me!"

He just looked at me and said, "You know what? I just want to teach you a little game, and then I will take you home because Janie will not be home until Friday. He has gone to Port Elizabeth to meet with the trade unionists, and now, it is only you and me."

"Dear Lord, not again!" I said to myself.

White started to strangle me, I tried very hard to fight him, but he was too strong. He managed to overpower me and then raped me. I was so furious and angry, and I felt betrayed by the comrades, who said I must collect money while they knew that Janie would be in Port Elizabeth. On the other hand, I gave them the benefit of the doubt that Kgabi might not have known that Janie would leave for PE. Maybe I was the problem in the sense that I might have something that says, "Rape me, rape me, rape me and rape me" or maybe it was a bad omen. I arrived at home still wondering why these things were happening to me; was I cursed or what?

It was now Friday, and probably my last Friday in South Africa because I was leaving the country that evening. That morning I woke up earlier than usual and started cleaning the yard first, washed the windows, and lastly, I cleaned the house thoroughly. While cleaning, I was reminding myself that this was my last day in this house and my last day of cleaning it. After doing my chores, I took Pinkie for a very long walk, where we just discussed issues and her fears. You know, for the first time she told me that she sometimes worried that I would one day just leave her because no one at home was going to take care of her as I did. What Pinkie said to me disturbed me a bit, especially because that day was actually my last day with her. I thought I was leaving for a good cause, and there would be greater benefits than staying at home.

"Zaza (as we called her), look, you need not worry about anything. If you ever find yourself without me one day, just know that it will be for a good reason and I want to assure you that you will never be alone. God will always be with you. Everything in this world happens for a reason. As you know, every individual on earth has a purpose in life, so we just have to accept that. Remember, God is the beginning and the end," I concluded. She smiled and kissed me on the cheek; I just held her hand and told her that I loved her.

It was 16:30 pm, and time for me to leave for the station because Stambo would be at the station at 17:30 pm to give me the train ticket. I left the house without saying goodbye to anyone, even Pinkie. I just boarded a taxi to town and arrived at the station at 16:45 pm. I looked around and thought to myself that the situation was quiet as usual, so I just sat there waiting for Stambo to arrive. The agreement was that I was not supposed to say any goodbyes to my comrades because of security reasons. We knew from our contact in Special Branch that they were monitoring comrade's movements all around Bloemfontein. That is why Kgabi felt that I must stop any contact with other comrades. It was a difficult decision, and I had to leave without seeing them, but I knew deep down in my heart that I was going to miss them.

EIGHT

ANC: My home, my life

IT WAS 18:00 PM on September 19, 1980. I was sitting at Bloemfontein station waiting for Comrade Stambo to bring the train ticket to Ficksburg, where I would cross the Caledon River to get to Maputsoe in Lesotho, on my way to Maseru to be a political refugee. I waited and waited for Stambo to bring the ticket, but he never came. I was getting scared because it was now midnight and there was no sign of him. I feared that he had maybe already been arrested and that he might be coming to the station with the police to identify me. I was in a serious predicament; part of me wanted to sleep at the station, but the other part of me wanted to go home.

"Teenage, you cannot go home this time, your Mama will skin you alive!" a voice inside reminded me.

Keeping that in mind, I decided that the only solution was to sleep at the station. I could then decide in the morning what to do next.

I managed to sleep on the floor of the station with the crowd that was there. Awaken by the noise around me, the only thing that came to mind before opening my eyes was that the Special Branch had finally got me. I opened my eyes, and there were police everywhere, kicking and punching people. Men, women and children were screaming and running in all directions, and I could see blood pouring from some of them.

I stood up and ran, not knowing what I was running from, and where was I running to. I just kept on running, leaving many of those people behind me because I was convinced that the police were looking for me. As I was running, I had a feeling that I was alone, and when I looked back, I actually realised that I was indeed alone; there was no one chasing me. I decided to slow down and walked to the taxi rank. As I was walking to the rank, I remembered that I did not have taxi fare, so I decided to walk to the township.

In South Africa, I think Bloemfontein is one of the few cities where the township is not far from the city centre. The distance from the city centre to the first township is not more than five kilometres, so we usually walked from the township to town and therefore, walking was not a problem. I decided that I was going to walk to Park Square to a house that we used as an underground base for our activities. This house belonged to the parents of our two female comrades who were part of the underground structure of the ANC. It was as a hideout for the 'fugitive comrades'. As a group, we had agreed on security measures in our homes, at schools and in our meetings. For security reasons, everyone had to adhere to those measures.

As I was approaching the house, I blew a whistle, which we all understood, and after my whistle, I saw the curtain moving, and I knew that they heard me. As I was approaching the door, Mbole opened the door and behind her was her sister. They both pulled me inside the house, closed the door behind me, and we sat in the kitchen.

"Teenage, do you know what time it is? We were worried sick about you!" said Mbole looking very worried indeed. "Yesterday, police arrested Comrade Stambo, and that is why he did not meet you at the station. He has not been charged yet, but the Special Branch suspects that he knows the people who burnt down the house of Sergeant Morris."

At that moment, Edith interjected, "Comrade Teenage, it is now more important to leave the country than ever before because we are all worried about you and your safety. If the Special Branch can know that you are the one who has been distributing the banned ANC pamphlets and that you were part of the group that burnt down the house of Morris, the situation for you will be even worse. Therefore, we have organised Comrade Spencer to go and gamble to raise a train fare for you. We will get the money at 18:00 pm and we will then take you to the station, but please do not go outside the house because already Comrade Fellow has said that the police were at your house around 23:00 pm looking for you.

They told your mother that they wanted to question you about arson and the murder of a police officer who was burnt to death. There are also charges against you that include distribution of banned material and the two AK's found in a rubbish bin near your home. Therefore, it will be imperative to leave the country as soon as possible to avoid arrest and possible compromise of the underground cells."

She continued, "At this stage, you should not make contact with anyone, the only person who knows where you are beside us is Kgabi and Fellow, and it should remain that way. The other thing is that we have already made contact with the senior comrades in Lesotho; we told them that you will be leaving the country soon and they agreed that the situation would be more dangerous if you remain in the country now than ever before. This is in consideration of the police incident and those two weapons found near your home. We will get you some food, and you will use a bucket instead of a toilet."

I listened to them and said nothing. I was getting very scared, and I thought to myself that this was the right time for me to leave the country and forget about the miserable life I had with my 'family'.

I was at the station at 19:30 pm on Saturday night waiting to board a train, which would leave Bloemfontein at 21:00 pm and arrive in Ficksburg at 5:00 am the next morning. I was strolling around passing the time; I wanted to go to town just to do some window-shopping, but I was scared that maybe something wrong might happen to me, so I decided to just stick around the station. While I was waiting for the train, I saw Oupanyana and another man coming towards me. I suddenly felt numb with fear, and I thought that he was coming to identify me. The worst part was that I stood against the wall, and there was no escape route, meaning there was no chance for me to run away. As I was thinking, Oupanyana and his companion were getting nearer and nearer, and by the time they reached me, I had surrendered already. I was saying to myself that if it was the end of me, let it be.

"Teenage, why do you look so scared? Relax, this is a comrade. He is from Bethlehem. Also, he is joining you on your trip. He has been trying to cross the Caledon but has failed many times. I think he has tried three times already. Therefore, we thought he might get courage if he crosses with a female."

I looked at him and thought to myself that this might be unfortunate days for me, but I had trust in Oupanyana judgment of character. I reluctantly extended my hand to him in greetings, and I said it was my pleasure to meet him, and he said likewise.

I decided that I was going to call him 'Number Seven' because he wore a jersey with 'No 7' printed on it. I actually did not care to know his name and most of all, I did not want to get personal with him. I thought 'Number Seven' would be just fine for me. The train arrived at just the right time for me, so I had little to say to Number Seven and Oupanyana. It was time to say goodbye to Oupanyana, who gave me a very strong handshake and told me to remember to display high morale, discipline, good values and integrity. I thanked him and waved him goodbye. We were booked in second class, and we were five in our cabin; myself, Number Seven, a 'couple' and another old man who looked like a teacher to me because he talked too much. He kept on asking me where I was going to, who my family was, whether they knew where I was. All those questions irritated me, and I felt like telling him to go to hell, but because I learned to be respectful to the elders, I just looked at him without saying a thing. He disembarked in Thaba Nchu, and I thought, *"Good riddance, he was really getting on my nerves!"* I felt that I could not have tolerated him for another hour.

The other thing was that, as he was asking me those questions, I was wondering if he was not a police informant. Maybe I was getting paranoid, but hey, that was part of the game! I think I dozed off because I heard Number Seven saying that we should disembark because we have reached Ficksburg. I looked around and saw people going in different directions. Police and their dogs were all over the station, which made me scared, but I disembarked and told myself that it was the end of my journey; I have nowhere to run, and they have finally found me. As I thought this, I wondered about that idiot who disembarked at Thaba Nchu. My feeling was that he might have tipped the police about my trip and that they were here to arrest me. Although I was scared, I just moved past all the policemen and walked straight to the taxis which were parked not far from the train station.

I was very anxious, and I had even forgotten about Number Seven. Fortunately, he just followed me. We got into a taxi which was going to the border. As I sat in the taxi, I realised that the 'couple' we were with earlier on the train were seated at the back of the taxi we just boarded, but there were other people as well. I only relaxed when the taxi drove away from the station. The four of us remained in the taxi after everyone else disembarked. I wanted to tell the driver to take me to Caledon River, but I was not sure about this 'couple'. To me, this was too much of a coincidence; we boarded the same train, we were in the same taxi, and they also seemed not to know where they were going, just like me. I didn't want the 'couple' to hear and in a hushed voice asked the driver to take me towards the Caledon River, and he obliged. On arrival, I paid him for two, and he wished me good luck. Ironically the 'couple' said, "Good luck, Teenage, we are all proud of you." They smiled at me and made the sign of power. This was so unbelievable! All along, I was protected by comrades without my knowledge! I really felt on top of the world.

I was so proud to be part of the ANC and was now sure I did not make a mistake by joining the organisation. Looking at that 'couple' who might not be a couple, after all, reminded me of that old man on the train. Could it be that he was also a cadre? Experiencing all that made me decide that there was no turning back. I was determined to join Umkhonto weSizwe, the People's Army. Those comrades displayed high discipline throughout our journey, and they were so down to earth. I was smiling alone when I thought about them, they were so convincing that they were a couple in love, and there was no doubt in everybody's mind that they were a real 'couple'. I even forgot that I wanted to commit suicide. Initially, when told to leave the country, I saw that as an opportunity to commit suicide in the Caledon River where nobody would find me. I wanted to die so that I could be free from my miseries. The two comrades made me realise that life is precious, and suicide was not a solution.

We were walking towards the river, not knowing which path to take. We arrived in Ficksburg at 04:30 am, and it was now around 5:00 am. We were just walking around the riverbank when I saw a man sitting on a big rock, not far from where we were. I decided to go to him and ask him to advise me on the best way to cross the river. "Dumela Ntate (Good morning, father), may you please assist me? My grandmother has passed away in Lesotho, and I want to go there, but I do not have a passport. Please help me," I said.

He looked at us and said, "You must get into the river and go straight, don't turn anywhere. The other part of the river is very deep, and if you make any turn, you will drown; therefore, just go straight. Good luck."

I thanked the man and moved towards the river with Number Seven following close behind me. I got into the river and started walking. When I was in the middle of the river, I looked back for Number Seven, but he was just standing there by the riverbank not attempting to get into the river. I just looked at him and continued walking because I did not know why he was not crossing. I finally reached the other side of the Caledon and felt at ease and safe. I stood on the riverbank and looked back to see if I could see Number Seven, who was in the middle of the river, but I was not sure if he was moving or standing.

I then remembered what Oupanyana told me at the station about Number Seven not being able to cross a few times already because he was scared of crocodiles. I decided to wait for him by the riverbank, and that was when I realised that I had lost the address of the contact in Lesotho. Luckily, I still remembered the name. The other thing I knew was that in case I lost the address, on arrival in Lesotho (Maputsoe), I would board a taxi to Maseru, whereby I would look for a police station where I would then declare myself a refugee. That was about all the information I had.

Finally, Number Seven joined me, and we walked towards the taxi rank, which was not far from where we crossed.

As we were walking towards what seemed like a taxi rank, we saw an old woman who was feeding her pigs.

"Dumela Mme (Good morning, mother)," I said.

"Dumela ngwana ka" (Good morning, my child)," she responded. "Where are you from at this time of the morning?" she asked.

"We come from South Africa through the river, and we are going to Maseru to attend the funeral of my grandmother. Where can we get a taxi to Maseru?" I asked.

"Oh yes, just go through my yard, and you will see a fleet of taxis. Just ask there, they will show you a taxi to Maseru. My child, I will advise you to be very careful about which taxi you take. Remember, there are people here in Lesotho who kidnap and kill people for their body parts, which they then sell to the Chinese people."

I thanked her and said goodbye. We were about to board a taxi when she called me. I went back to her, not knowing what she wanted from me.

"Ngoana ka (my child), I called you back because I think I have to tell you this: I see God in you, and it will be important for you to live like a child of God. May the Lord bless you and keep you safe. Go well, child."

I did not know what to say or how to respond to this, and I just thanked her and left.

There were only five of us in the taxi; four men and me. To tell the truth, I was getting scared, especially when I thought about the people who were involved in the kidnapping and killing of people for rituals. For some reason, the three men in blankets resembled the so-called 'makaota', who were alleged to be involved in killing people to sell their body parts for making 'muthi'. The information I got was that they wore their big blankets, and they had woollen hats pulled over their eyes, to avoid being recognised. Though I wanted to commit suicide, I did not plan to die the way the 'makaota' killed their victims. I wanted to drown myself in the Caledon River so that nobody would ever find my remains.

I fell asleep while still thinking about my situation, only to be woken up by Number Seven telling me that the taxi was full, and it was about to leave for Maseru. I did not understand why he had to wake me up, and I just looked at him and said nothing. We arrived in Maseru at around 14:30 pm; I cannot tell you how long it took us on the road before we reached our final destination, but I must say it was a very long and boring trip. We disembarked, and now I had to figure out where to go from there. I told Number Seven that we must just walk to the CBD and we would take it from there. We walked towards the CBD through Kingsway Street, which I later found out was actually the main street in Maseru. As we walked, I felt a bit hungry, and I asked Number Seven if we could find something to eat. He agreed, and we went to a café where we got fish and chips. We ate our food in silence. After eating, I felt all right and energised, ready for action.

As we were standing contemplating what to do next, I saw three men coming towards us, and for some reason, I looked at them very attentively. That was when I realised that I knew one of them; he lived not far from my home back in Bloemfontein. Although I had never spoken to him before (he was one of those students who were in a boarding school outside Bloemfontein, and he was from those families who we considered 'wealthy' in our standards then), I thought he was the only person who could help us. Without thinking about the security implications, I just went to them.

"Sorry," I said. They all looked at us and stopped. I approached them and introduced myself, "My name is Mpoetsi Morake, from Nyokong Street, Bochabela. I am a member of the ANC, and due to the security situation at home, comrades inside the country felt that it was too dangerous for me and they decided that I should come to Lesotho where I would be safe. The contact address had gotten lost in the river, but the name of the contact person was Ngoako Ramatlhodi. I was wondering if you can assist me in getting to him."

They looked at us with suspicion. The one I knew from home asked, "Who is this?"

"This is Number Seven. I was made to understand that he is from Bethlehem. I met him at the station in Bloemfontein. Comrade Oupanyana brought him to me at the station and said I must leave with him," I told them.

"Ok, let us go," Boikie, as I knew him said as if it was an instruction.

Number Seven, who was actually called Tshola (Bizoz Mokoena), joined them and walked in silence for a very long distance. I must say that if I wasn't physically fit, I would have collapsed or something because we walked a very long distance from the CBD. We finally arrived at a certain house.

"Good day, comrades. On our way home, we met these two who told us that they have skipped the country and they have come to join the ANC. Her name is Mpoetsi, and he is Tshola from Bethlehem."

One of the men I did not recognise started introducing himself, and I immediately recognised the other person. He was one of those young teachers who were involved in politics and very powerful at that. He mobilised students to boycott classes, and he was involved in organising stay-aways for the workers. I remember when the police arrested him and fellow teachers for their political involvement, there was chaos in Bloemfontein; students and parents went on a rampage demanding their release. Seeing him was a great relief, and I felt safe. He recognised me as Teenage, smiled at me and said, "Welcome to our world." As Mathata (Menzi) was talking to me, Ike Moroe as he was introduced to us instructed Mathata to take Number 7 with him and the three Comrades for the interviews. He told them that he will be responsible for my interviews. Comrade Mathata and the other comrades left with Number Seven and left me with Ike Moroe. The interview started with me having to explain why I left the country. Hardly twenty minutes into the interview, Ike said that I looked tired and that I could use the bed to rest. I was indeed very tired and climbed onto the bed and fell asleep immediately. I did not worry because I thought I was with a 'senior comrade' and therefore felt safe. How wrong I was! In my deep sleep, I felt someone on top of me, fondling my vagina. I got scared and started kicking and fighting. In my mind, I thought that it was the men I saw outside and never thought that it could be the comrade who said I must rest. I started kicking and scratching him on his back, but he kept on pressing me down. My cries and shouting did not deter him. The pervert finally managed to put his dirty, and probably uncircumcised, penis inside me. The bastard, the son of a bitch, did not even have the decency to say he was sorry afterwards; he just threw me with my panties and opened the door.

After his disgusting act, he acted as if nothing wrong happened, and I believe he felt proud of himself. On the other hand, I felt like strangling the life out of him. The bastard waited for me at the door to put on my panties after which he locked the door and told me that he was taking me to a refugee camp. Every time the son of a bitch opened his mouth, I felt like throwing up. He made me sick to my stomach. I know one might ask why I was feeling this way because he was not the first one to do this to me. Let me ease your mind: the reason I took this so hard was that the bastard was supposed to be my comrade and a 'senior comrade' at that. I trusted him with my life, and I believed that the comrades who brought me to him trusted him as well.

We were about to leave when one of the comrades (Poro, who brought me to the house) came and told him that he was taking me to the refugee camp. As we walked to the camp, I just thought of what that man did to me, especially on my first day in exile. What he did reminded me of the fact that a person who raped me broke my virginity and now, on my first day in exile, someone had raped me again. Was it a coincidence or a curse ...?

You know, the worst thing was that the last time I took a bath was on Friday morning before I left home, meaning I had three days without washing. Can you imagine that? Also, it was exactly four days after my other attack. Oh God, what was it with me? Was I cursed, or what? I kept asking myself those questions in silence.

We walked a long way without a word to each other, and I was comfortable with it because it gave me time to think about what just happened. I thought of the reasons why I did not drown in the Caledon River that morning because that was an opportunity for me to end all my miseries.

We finally reached an area called New Europe, and that was when Poro told me that we had almost reached our destination. When we entered one of the houses in New Europe, I became worried about Poro's intentions, and I think he saw that because he said, "Relax, this is a refugee camp, and the comrades are staying here." Although I did not believe him, I followed him.

He opened the door and entered, then called me to come in. As I entered, there were about fifteen men playing table tennis. Some of them were spectators who were singing revolutionary songs. We walked in, and they continued with their business as if they did not even notice us. We passed through a hall, which led to a passage with about three closed doors. Comrade Poro stopped at one door and knocked. When there was no response, he opened it and called out, "Mamsy, Mamsy."

The room was dark when we entered; I could not see anyone but heard a sweet, feminine voice coming from the direction of one of the corners of the room. You know, except for her white teeth, I could not see the face of this person. I greeted and introduced myself. In return, she introduced herself as Mamsy from Soweto. Still, I couldn't see her. I did not know what was happening, but because of her wonderful voice, I stayed calm. Mamsy showed me where I was going to sleep and asked me if I had any luggage. I said no. She then stood up and switched on the light to give me a nightdress. As I looked towards her, I nearly collapsed because she was so dark in complexion. Please do not get me wrong – it was the first time I saw somebody so dark, especially somebody from South Africa. The people I saw and interacted with were light or coffee-coloured in complexion. I am really not trying to be funny, and what I'm telling you is the truth. Remember, my world revolved around Bloemfontein and Aliwal North, and I never had the opportunity to travel outside the Orange Free State, where I could see dark-skinned people. One should understand where I come from when I say that I was surprised to see Mamsy. And, as if that was not enough, I saw a bundle of what seemed like blankets in the corner where Mamsy was. All of a sudden, a baby started crying. Boy! That really scared the hell out of me.

"Why does she have a baby?" I asked myself.

It was as if Mamsy was reading my mind, and she said, "This is my son, Ofentse (Victor)."

She told me that she joined the ANC with the father of her child, and he had since left Lesotho to go and join MK, and because she was pregnant, she could not go. I was listening to her, but all I could think about was what that bastard did to me. I wished that we could both live so that I can remind him of this day. After Mamsy had shown me the female bathroom, I took a shower and for some reason, I was scrubbing myself, especially my private parts, as if it was infected. I think the effect of water calmed me down because after showering, I went straight to bed.

A lot of noise from the hall, which scared me, woke me up, but I relaxed when I heard Mamsy's voice. I got up and made my bed, then went for a shower. After I had dressed, I just stayed in the room, too afraid to face the people in case they knew about what had happened the previous day. *"Could I use the people who saw me going into that house as witnesses to a rape? No! In their eyes, I was this whore who slept with a man she did not even know – probably a married man for that matter,"* I wondered, and these thoughts kept my mind busy until I heard a knock at the door. "Come in," I said.

A young, petite girl with a killer smile walked into the room.

"My name is Ntombekhaya Matomela from Port Elizabeth," she introduced herself.

"My name is Mpoetsi from Bloemfontein," I said.

"Great, I finally have somebody who is in my age group. I hope we are going to get along just fine," she said while pulling me towards her as if she wanted to give me a hug. She opened the door and pulled me towards the corridor, which led to the hall I saw yesterday.

When we entered the hall, I recognised only Mamsy; the rest of the people were strangers to me. As we entered everybody stopped whatever they were doing and concentrated on us. It was so funny because even those who were playing table tennis stopped playing. I felt so uncomfortable to be looked at in that way. To my surprise, Ntobekhaya was cool about it and introduced me to the comrades. I must say that they all greeted me with respect, and I felt welcomed. As we stood there, watching the table tennis, Ntosh, as I called her, told me that it was time for political discussions, and the presenter was comrade Thabo, who was one of the senior comrades in Lesotho. According to Ntombekhaya, Comrade Thabo was actually one of the founding members of Umkhonto weSizwe. He fought in Wankie in the then Rhodesia, and he belonged to the Luthuli Detachment which comprised of comrades who left the country in the fifties and sixties.

The topic for the day was why the ANC resorted to armed struggle. Comrade Thabo explained in detail the reasons for the armed struggle by saying, "As we all know, the ANC was a very peaceful organisation, and the leadership then believed that the struggle could be won through peaceful means. That was until the apartheid regime banned the liberation movements. The ANC then resorted to armed struggle through the formation of Umkhonto weSizwe popularly known as 'MK' because it was obvious that the only language that the regime would understand was through an armed struggle. The first commander-in-chief of MK was Comrade Nelson Mandela."

Comrade Thabo was relating the events leading to the formation of MK, and that took me back to where the police attacked us inside the schoolyard without any provocation. Therefore, it made sense to me that the apartheid regime actually used violence to defend the status quo and that was why it was important for us to support MK by joining their ranks or giving them the moral support. The discussion was very informative, and it gave me more perspective of the ANC and its military wing, Umkhonto weSizwe.

After the political discussions, Ntosh introduced me to some of the comrades who were staying outside the camp. They congratulated me for joining the ANC, some asked me about the political situation at home, and others asked me if I was going to school or to MK. At that stage, I did not know where I was going, but what I knew at that time was that I wanted to further my studies, although joining MK was also exciting. I just told them that it was too soon for me to know what I was going to do with my life in exile; I could not predict what the future held for me, but furthering my studies was my priority.

Ntombekhaya introduced me to all the people we met. She also explained to me the rules and regulations of the camp and the ANC. She told me that I had to go to the police station to declare myself as a refugee first, and then the police would take me to the Secretary of Internal Affairs, who will, in turn, send me to the High Commissioner for Refugees. After this procedure, I would be sent to the Christian Council to get some clothes. She emphasised the fact that I had to start this process as soon as possible because there was money that I was entitled to as a refugee, which I would get from the United Nations. This would cover the expense of my food and clothing.

She said that the procedure would be that, after having refugee status and getting my money, I would have to contribute some money for food at the camp. I thanked her for all the information, after which she offered to take me to the police station the following day.

The next day, Ntosh and I went to the police station, but she did not enter because, as she had mentioned, if they saw me with her, the police may make an issue out of it by saying I was already a member of the ANC and they might refuse me the refugee status.

I went into the police station and waited for my turn. I was scared because I was thinking about the police back at home. My turn came, and I approached the officer who was supposed to assist me.

"Dumela moroetsana, nka o thusa joang?" (Good day, little girl. How can I be of assistance to you?)

"Dumela, Ntate ke tsoa Afrika Borwa ke tlo ba mophaphathehi naheng ya lona (Good day, sir. I am from South Africa, and I am seeking refugee status in your country), I said.

"Helang! Tlong le tlo nkutlwisa mehlolo ke ena, ebe ke meleko kapa ke eng" (Oh! Please come and hear this, it is a miracle or what?). I just looked at the police officer, not knowing what to say or do. Still puzzled by what he said, I saw a group of police officers coming towards the counter.

"What is it, sir?" another cop asked.

"Just look at this kid, she cannot even wash herself properly, but she claims to be a political activist. Can you imagine?" the first police said.

"You know, we do not know what is happening in South Africa, remember June 16, 1976, a thirteen-year-old boy was shot dead by the police. Therefore, it is possible that even kids like her are political activists," he continued.

"Just give her a form and continue with other processes. Do not worry about things you cannot change. Can you imagine if you send her back and those Boers kill her, how are you going to feel?" the second police said.

They gave me forms to fill in, and fingerprints and photos were taken. After all those things, they took me to Internal Affairs.

On arrival, the receptionist told us that the Secretary of Internal Affairs was out, and he might only be back after 14:00 pm. The police left me with another old man who seemed to me like a puppet of the secretary because of the way he kept on telling me about how good and wonderful the Secretary of Internal Affairs was. Whatever he said to me about the secretary was irrelevant; all I wanted was refugee status in Lesotho. At approximately 14:30 pm, the old man called me and told me that the secretary was ready to see me. I followed him to the secretary's office, and I was amazed at the resemblance of the two old men.

My theory about the old man being a puppet to the secretary was right because as I entered and stood by the door waiting to be given a seat, the secretary said, "You are welcomed." The old man repeated the same sentence. He spoke, smiled and laughed like the secretary. He really made me sick. *"How can a man, an old man for that matter idolise another man like that?"* I thought to myself.

"My name is Mr Sello Mokgele; I am the Secretary of Internal Affairs. How can I help you?"

"My name is Mpoetsi Morake; I am from Galeshewe in Kimberley, South Africa. I have been involved in student politics, and now the police are after me, that is why I have come to Lesotho to seek political asylum. I have reported at the police station, and after they took my fingerprints and photos, they brought me to you," I concluded.

As I said this, I was not conscious of the fact that my thumb was in my mouth until Mr Mokgele said to me, "You must be insane, what politics are you talking about? You are just a child, look at yourself, you are still sucking your thumb, and you want to tell me that you want political asylum? You cannot even wash yourself properly, and you tell me about politics. Get out of my office. I do not want to see you ever again. I said get out before I throw you out! Look at her!"

Before I could say anything, his right-hand man said, "Get out of my boss' office before I throw you out!"

I stood up and left them. I was now confused because it meant that I was an illegal émigré in Lesotho unless if the Secretary changed his mind and declared me a refugee. I could not afford to be an illegal émigré. As I was thinking about this, I was sitting on a chair just outside Mr Mokgele's office. I did not know what to do. Of course, I would go to the refugee camp, but how was I going to survive without clothes and money for food?

I cannot tell what kept me sitting there, but I did, and it paid off. The door to Mr Mokgele's office opened, and the puppet came out, looked at me and called me. As I approached him, he said, "Go inside, the secretary wants to talk to you."

I went inside the office, and the secretary was standing by the window. He just looked at me as if he was looking at his long-lost child who had just returned to him. A few minutes passed without him saying anything, and ultimately he took some money out of his pocket and said, "Take this money and get yourself food and be here tomorrow morning at 8:30 am. Be careful of those boys at the camp; I will be looking after you because I do not want you to end up having children like others. Do you hear me?"

"Yes, Sir," I said.

"Then tomorrow morning," he said, not even looking at me.

I took the money, thanked him and closed the door behind me and left. I went to the same café we bought food on our arrival in Maseru. I got myself some fish and chips and walked back to the camp.

The following day at 7:30 am, I was at the Internal Affair's offices. I arrived very early and just sat on the bench waiting for 8:30 am and wondering what Mr Mokhele was going to say. The other thing was that I was wondering how Number Seven handled the arrogance of the Secretary. To my surprise, he did not struggle to get his refugee status as I was struggling. Was it patriarchy?

At exactly 8:15 am, Mr Mokhele arrived, greeted me and went into his office. After a few minutes, his secretary called me into his office. He was alone, and I felt more comfortable than the previous day when his puppet was there. We went through the questions he asked yesterday and a few more. After the interview of almost three hours, he told me that he intended to deport me because I was too young to be a refugee. Secondly, he had seen many parents coming to fetch their children because they were either too young or they followed their boyfriends, and thus he felt that I was too young to be by myself in a foreign country.

Listening to him made me realise that things were not the way I expected them to be. I came with a very positive feeling, but now I was getting a negative vibe. *"What am I going to do if he deports me now?"* I thought. What I knew for sure was that I was not going to go back home and that I'd rather die.

We just looked at each other without saying a word. Finally, I got the courage to tell him that I was not going to leave Lesotho even if he did not want to give me refugee status and that he could rather kill me.

He looked at me and said, "You know what? You are so stubborn, and that is not going to help you. The fact is that you are very young and immature to be here alone. Tell me who recruited you?"

"Nobody," I said.

"Go out of my office and come back tomorrow," he said.

– Ruth Mantile –

I was now tired of going to the offices of Internal Affairs. I walked that route for almost a month, and still, I was not getting anywhere. My main problem was that I did not have money for food and clothes. Fortunately, I still ate with the comrades at the camp, but sometimes I felt guilty for not contributing money to buy food. At the camp, everybody contributed money to buy groceries for the whole month, but now they had to feed an extra mouth, and this really made me feel very bad. I used to tell Ntosh about it, but she would dismiss me by saying I was crazy to think that. She would remind me that the ANC was a mass movement, and all the people of South Africa and members of the ANC believed in sharing. Therefore, it did not bother them that I did not have money to contribute. To be practical about her theory of sharing, she gave me some of her clothes. Ntobekhaya was a real star!

After two months of travelling to and from the offices of Internal Affairs, I got my refugee status in Lesotho. After all the papers were signed by the Secretary of Internal Affairs, I was sent to the Christian Council to get clothes. I initially thought it would be new clothes, but they were second-hand and were donated by sympathisers of the liberation movements. There was nothing wrong with the clothes because I got better-looking things than the ones I had at home and that I really appreciated. The clothes I chose were very stylish. I mean stylish for the eighties, of course! I really felt like a human being. As a refugee, I was getting a stipend of thirty-five rand every month, and I got a seventy-five rand once-off settlement allowance. I gave the comrades at the camp their twenty rand as a monthly contribution, and I took the rest with me.

I went to buy myself things I wished to have for as long as I lived. I bought a pair of jeans, a dungaree overall, a white T-shirt and a pair of Dunlop 'takkies'. I've mentioned before that after my first rape I just wanted to be one of the boys, so with my overall, T-shirt underneath, one earring and Dunlop's, I really looked fabulous and very cute.

After I bought my clothes, I went to Frasers where I bought myself a piece of cheese, liver polony, guava juice, Russian sausage, viennas, a half-loaf white and Erica butter. I took all my groceries and walked towards the camp. There were two routes to the camp; we used either the main road or the one that went through the forest. The one through the forest was shorter, and the main advantage was that it was cool during the day because of its vegetation. I took the route until I reached a spot I had chosen to have my picnic all by myself. I sat down and opened my food, starting with the bread. I took out the butter and spread it on my bread, then added the liver polony and cheese. Before I could start eating, I thanked God for protecting me until now, and I thanked Him for giving me the food that I wished for as long as I could remember.

I ate my food slowly to enjoy it to my satisfaction. It was delicious, and I thought and admired those children who ate this type of food every day. I wondered if they really enjoyed it the way I did at that moment. I think I took an hour to finish all the food and I must say I was really full and satisfied. I enjoyed the Russian sausage and guava juice (which tasted divine) the most. After eating, I picked up the garbage and walked home.

On my arrival, I found comrades playing table tennis and I joined them. I must say I was very good at table tennis in the sense that I never lost a game and if my memory serves me well, I was the only female comrade who played table tennis at that stage. Although I was good, I had a few comrades who really gave me a tough time, playing with them was a real challenge.

Throughout my life, my weakest point was fear of failure, and because of this, I avoided situations where there was even the slightest possibility of failure from my side. I only realised later in my life that I had a very serious problem, which emanated from my upbringing, where I had to prove to my family, especially Mama, that I was not a failure. I think even at school, it was not the question of me being intelligent, but I worked harder so that there could be something that Mama recognised in me and maybe would learn to love me.

There is a saying that *'One can take away everything from you, but nobody can take away your intellect and knowledge'*. I said earlier that I was an A-student and every time I gave my report to Mama she would always say, "Iris can also get the same results maybe even do better," but it never happened. Instead, she dropped out of school when she was in standard seven (grade nine) because she fell pregnant.

So, I did the same with table tennis. I always made sure that I won; if I lost a game, which was seldom, it would really pain me, and I would stop playing for a few days until I gathered my confidence again. I enjoyed playing table tennis with all my heart. If I was not playing table tennis, I was reading books about the ANC, the history of the then Soviet Union, and books on Marxism and Leninism. As a result, it was easy for me to discuss politics comfortably with other comrades, which was really stimulating. Political discussions from morning to late at night dominated our lives at the camp. The funny thing about it was the fact that even though we would be playing tennis or chess, we were still analysing the political situation in South Africa and throughout the world. The most interesting part to me was when we discussed dialectical materialism and *No Middle Road* by Joe Slovo.

It was at the refugee camp during one of the political discussions where I met Sechudi from Rocklands in Bloemfontein, and although he stayed in Sebaboleng with other comrades, he was always at the camp. Sechudi came across as a very intelligent and honest man; he was light in complexion, with green eyes and well-built body, and he was a real charmer. I loved his sense of humour, arrogance, sense of fashion and his taste of music. He was into reggae, which was also my favourite. We spend a lot of time together, and I was beginning to fall in love with him.

Sechudi left South Africa in 1979 and became a refugee in Lesotho. He was an only child but grew up with his cousins in his grandmother's house as a big family. He had everything that he needed because his mother did everything for him, I was even made to understand that she bought him a car and brought it to him in Lesotho, but he refused it, and his mother had to take it back to South Africa.

That is how much his mother loved him, and I did not understand why he left the country when life was good for him. Although I knew that the ANC was a mass movement, I also thought that if I was loved and cared for, I would not have a reason to leave the country at the age of fourteen. We continued to be together until he left for military training in Angola.

Although it was nice at the camp, I hated it when people fought each other. We had rules, and one of them was that when a comrade misbehaved everybody residing at the camp would punish him or her. We called the punishment 'Iyo', which was in the form of whippings with anything that one could lay his or her hands on. During the beatings, the transgressor would have blood all over his body. I hated this with all my heart. To me, it indicated that we lacked compassion and comradeship, and what we were doing was not different from what we did when we dealt with identified informants back home. I was once forced to partake, and I could not sleep for the whole week because I had flashbacks of what happened to the poor comrade.

It was during this period that Kgabi, Fellow and his girlfriend joined us in exile forced by the security situation. Fellow and her girlfriend stayed at the refugee camp, and Kgabi stayed somewhere in Sea Point. I might not have known the reasons why he stayed outside the camp, but I thought it was because he worked longer for the ANC underground than us and the comrades he worked with had organised a place for him. Even though he stayed outside the camp, he usually came to the camp to visit us.

One morning a knock at the door woke me up, which really surprised me because it was not normal for comrades to knock, and my conclusion was that the person who was knocking was a visitor. I quickly went to the door because all the comrades were still asleep. I opened it, and to my surprise, there stood Mama. I did not know how to react; I just greeted and let her in.

I guess she was surprised to see me opening the door. Something makes me wonder whether I was human because I always made someone feel comfortable, no matter what that person did to me. Other people may interpret it as being pretentious, but I think it means that I'm true to myself because I believe that when you hold grudges, you only make yourself sick; the person who has hurt you does not give a damn about you. To me, life goes on, and I will not treat somebody bad because she or he had hurt me, except the comrade who raped me when I arrived in Lesotho.

I invited her to my room and made her some tea. While she was drinking it, I asked her how she and the rest of the family were doing. She told me that everybody was fine except for Pinkie who seemed not to accept the fact that I left. The first thing that Mama asked me was about the poem she found under the carpet at home. I was honest with her, and I told her about how she treated me, about her discussion with the woman from Theunissen, which I overheard. I did not hide anything, but despite what I said to her, she did not show any remorse. Mama told me that she left home two days ago and the first night, she almost slept under a stationary bus, but fortunately, a lady who was passing by took her to her house.

Mama said it was that woman who gave her directions to the camp. When I asked her as to how she found out about me being in Lesotho, she said the police told her two days after I had left, and they persuaded her to fetch me with the promise not to prosecute.

I listened with keen interest, and I was wondering if she came to look for me as a mother or if she was forced by the Special Branch. With Mama, anything was possible, but I still gave her the benefit of the doubt. She told me that the police came on the morning of Saturday around midnight (remember, I left the Friday).

"When they arrived, they kicked the doors, knocked on the windows and woke everybody who was in the yard. When they finally got into the house, they said they wanted you in connection with the murder of a police officer and guns found near our house. When I said I did not know where you were, in fact, I was actually looking for you myself because you left during the day in my absence, they said I was lying and that I knew where you were. They then pushed everybody outside and started searching the whole house, and that was when I realised that there were other police officers in and outside the yard. There was a lot of commotion as the police were coming in and out of the yard. I remember that at a certain stage, two police officers came out of the house with a paper bag, and they threw all the contents on the ground calling each other to come and look. I did not know what was in the paper bag until they called me to come and look at what my daughter was capable of doing.

To my surprise, I saw your photos, which I had never seen before. In those photos, I saw what seemed to be cuttings from newspapers of which the people on those I did not recognise. They asked me if I knew the people in those newspapers and I said no. They said it was Steve Biko, the other one was the president of the terrorist organisation, and the rest was the terrorists who were involved in killing the people in Soweto. I said to them that was my first time seeing those people and I did not even know that there were such pictures in the house.

They told me that if you came back home or called me, I must inform them as soon as possible. Failure of which there will be a charge of obstruction of justice against me. One of them, who said he was the captain, gave me the number to call. Then they left, and I think they left after three hours of searching and interrogating each one of us. The most unfortunate one was your cousin, Nthabiseng. For some reason, they thought she was you because she was as skinny as you. When they left, I thought they would never come back, but they kept on returning. The last time they came was two weeks ago when they told me that they knew where you were and that I must come and convince you to come back. That is what happened since you left. As for me, I am heartbroken and if there is something that I did, please forgive me and come back home."

I looked at her and thought, "*Woman, you have the nerve to come here and tell me to come home, because some police officer told you to fetch me, now you are standing here telling me to go back home. You must be mad!*"

When she said that I must go home with her, it did not surprise me, I knew deep down in my heart that she was capable of sacrificing me to the Special Branch. If she had her way, she would kidnap me right there and hand me over to them because she was wicked.

I just looked at her and thought, "*Go now, you have seen me, and I am alive and happy now that I am on my own,*" but I just kept quiet. By this time, everybody was up, and I thought this was very good because I was going to introduce her to my comrades and at least it will give her a chance to talk to other people.

"Mama, the comrades are up now. Let's go to them, I want to introduce you," I said. After the introduction, she suggested that we go to the woman who accommodated her. I agreed, but I told the comrades that if anything bad happened to me, they must know that my mother was responsible for it.

We left for Maseru West, where the woman was staying. In fact, the lady was actually a domestic worker, and she was staying in the back yard of her boss' house. On arrival, we found the lady with her two children. They looked like a happy family; they were very friendly and kind, and I think she accommodated Mama because of her kind heart.

They were very happy to see me, and they had actually prepared a nice lunch for us. We ate and were engaged in some discussions about Lesotho and issues in general. I must say I enjoyed the discussions because it was something different from the day-to-day discussions at the camp. We stayed there until around 18:00 pm and Mama left with me because she wanted to spend her last night in Lesotho with me.

The following day, Ntosh and I took her to the border gate. We said our goodbyes and returned to the camp. On our way back, Ntosh asked me if I was not feeling homesick. I said no because I was as happy as a refugee could be; I was surrounded by people whom I share the same ideology with and who loved me for me.

I told Ntosh about what Mama told me about the police and their request to her. I actually told her about my feelings on the same issue; the whole thing puzzled her, but she told me not to worry because they cannot do anything to me while I am in Lesotho.

Ntosh was a real friend, and even though she was from Port Elizabeth where they spoke Xhosa, she understood a bit of Sotho, and she tried to converse in broken Sotho, and we all understood her. We got along very well, and although she was not staying at the camp, she made sure that she visited me almost every day. She was a sister that I have never had and most of all she was my comrade.

The ANC as a liberation movement, accommodated everyone, including petty criminals, and this was evident in Lesotho. During my stay at the camp, I would get beautiful watches, bracelets and golden chains given to me by some comrades. Every time I tried to find out from them as to where they got those things from, they just laughed and said I deserved to be spoiled. That was where my love for beautiful watches started. Even today, I am still addicted to beautiful watches, which I put on my right wrist, though I am right-handed, which is not normal for right-handed people.

On Saturdays, they would take me to Lancers Inn or Victoria Hotel for a treat. They would be in the casinos, and I would be watching TV or playing games. They took turns buying me cooldrinks and food, and they treated me like their young sister, especially those who were from Bloemfontein. It was during those trips to the casinos that I established where those watches were actually coming from ...

One Saturday I was playing games with Susan, the daughter of a certain comrade, when she saw my watch and said to me, "Mpoetsi, your watch is so beautiful, let me see it." I took it off my wrist and gave it to her. She looked at it, examined it, and after some minutes, she said, "I knew I recognised this watch from somewhere. Where did you get it?"

"Comrades at the camp gave it to me," I told her.

She looked at me suspiciously, but said nothing and just gave back the watch. We continued playing as if we never had discussed the watch issue. As we were busy playing, Comrades Tex and Oupa brought me food and a cooldrink, without realising that I was playing with Susan whom they did not bring anything to drink or eat.

They greeted her and apologised for not bringing her anything but promised to make it up to her. True to their word, they brought her something, and she thanked them. After they had left, she told me that we should go to the casino when we're done eating because she wanted to show me something.

I agreed, and we went to the casino, which was, and still is, not my favourite place. We just walked around watching the people who were gambling when suddenly Susan grabbed my hand and pointed at two figures not far from us.

"Just look there at those two figures," she said.

I looked to where she was pointing and saw Fish Monger snatching a handbag from a woman and running away before she could even scream. I was very shocked because I did not expect him to do something like that. I trusted him with my life and was very disappointed in him.

"You see, that watch of yours was snatched from a South African lady, who was on holiday here. I was with her when her watch was snatched, that is why I asked you to show it to me because it resembled her watch. That was not the first time I saw them snatching things from tourists."

I did not know what to say because as far as I knew this behaviour was not tolerated by the ANC, but I was certain about one thing; I was not going to be the one who was going to expose those comrades and their activities. I just left it at that, but I ceased to go with them to those places because I did not want to be associated with people who were involved in criminal activities.

Not long after the incident at the casino, about seven comrades got themselves arrested in Lesotho and deported back to South Africa. That was when I knew that some of them left the country because of criminal activities, and some of them worked for the Special Branch to infiltrate the ANC. Their main mission, as stated, was to cause confusion within the organisation and put the ANC in disrepute. What was puzzling to me was the fact that most of those comrades who were deported were politically matured. They understood what the ANC stood for, they were able to engage one in political discussions, and their arguments would be very valid and consistent with the ANC's policies and processes. When they were deported, the ANC could not intervene because they were charged under the Lesotho Criminal Law.

I left the refugee camp and went to stay with Comrades Bongiwe, Noxolo (Xolelwa Victoria Shosha), Ntosh and Phindiwe. We rented a room at a place called 'Ha Seoli'. The room was big enough to accommodate five sponge mattresses, a Primus stove, suitcases and a cabinet where we stored our food. The place was comfortable and secured. We had house rules, which we followed to the letter; there was no compromise when it came to the rules. Bongiwe was the head of the house, and everybody was accountable to her. She was responsible for the logistics, discipline and everything else. She was a real authoritarian; her no meant NO, and no one could ever make her change her mind. One of the rules of the house was that no one was allowed to come home after 21:00 pm and if you were out of the house at that time, you were supposed to sleep where you were.

I cannot remember how I met S'thembiso and ended up being his girlfriend, but I remember that we had a good relationship, and what I liked about him was that we could engage politically. There was never a dull moment. The thing which I realised as an adult, was that as a teenager, I was always a one-man woman. I wanted stability and security, and as a result, I saw my boyfriend at any given time as a potential husband. From a psychological point of view, I think I saw father figures in my boyfriends, and I did not want to be like my mother.

One day Ntosh and I went out with our boyfriends to watch a documentary about Solomon Mahlangu and his comrades who were with him in Goch Street. The documentary was so stimulating because we saw the interview of our late President OR Tambo, Thabo Mbeki, and the survivor George Mazibuko from Goch Street in Zambia. We watched the documentary with keen interest because it showed how Comrade Solly sacrificed his own life to rescue his comrade. It also showed courage and determination by members of MK to fight for the liberation of our country. Looking at this documentary made me feel that I wanted to join the ranks of Umkhonto weSizwe, the liberation army. I felt that if I did not join MK, I would have failed the people of South Africa. I was just imagining myself in a military uniform and holding my AK-47.

The four of us left together because we were almost going to the same location. It was almost 20:00 pm and Ntosh and I had already decided that we were not going home. S'thembiso and I were walking behind Ntosh and Nokuthula (Gift). I remember S'the and I were talking about the Palestinian liberation struggle when I saw a girl in front of us. To me, she seemed to have been talking to Thulas and Ntosh, but to my surprise, I saw them passing her. As we were passing her, she called S'the in Xhosa, and he excused himself and went to speak to her. I just walked away because I thought their discussions would not be that long.

To my surprise, it took so long that I even arrived at his residence without him, which was about twelve kilometres from where we were. I went into his room and sat on his mattress, still thinking that he would enter any time. I waited for him for more than two hours until I decided to go home, and even though I knew they would never open for me because it was long after the curfew time, I thought I was better off at home than there.

I called Monwabisi, Noxolo's boyfriend, to take me home, and although he was reluctant, he did take me home. On the way, I explained to him what happened and how disappointed I was that S'the chose that girl over me and did not have the decency to take me home and then go back to that girl. Monwabisi tried to convince me that everything would be fine and that it was just a little misunderstanding. He also said that he knew the girl I was talking about and that there was nothing between her and S'thembiso.

Whatever Monwabisi said did not convince me because I did not have self-confidence; I always told myself that everybody was better than I was. There was something in me that thought that if a person had to choose between someone else and me, they would always choose the other person. Even at that moment, I told myself that S'the had chosen that girl over me, and it was the end of the relationship.

We arrived home, and I knocked on the door. "Who are you, this time of the night?" Bongiwe asked.

"It is me," I said.

"Did you see what time it is? It is obviously after curfew. Where is S'thembiso? Go back to him," she said.

"Please open for me. I cannot go back there; you can even give me my blanket. I will sleep in the old car," I begged.

There was a scrapped car in the yard, which I was prepared to sleep in rather than wait for S'thembiso. As I was begging Bongiwe to open the door, I heard Noxolo saying to her that she must open the door because maybe I had a problem and that is why I came back home.

"Go and open the door for her and this will be the last time I open the door after curfew," I heard Bongiwe tell Noxolo. As the door opened, I heard footsteps, and when I turned around, I saw S'thembiso coming towards me. I just looked at him and went into the room. I was about to close the door when he called my name. I did not know whether to go and listen to his side of the story or just lock the door behind me. My intuition told me to lock the door of which I did. I left him there with Noxolo's boyfriend, Monwabisi.

Everybody was now up waiting to hear what happened and I told them about the Xhosa girl and how I waited for S'thembiso for more than two hours. Everybody was so furious with him; they suggested that I should leave him and that if he did not respect my feelings, he was not worth fighting for. Noxolo said she knew the girl because at a certain stage, she was after Monwabisi and she confronted her by telling her to stop chasing her man, and according to Noxolo, it seemed as if she stopped, but she was not sure. I was heartbroken, but at least I managed to sleep. Early the next morning, S'thembiso was at the door knocking. Bongiwe opened the door but said nothing to him. I went outside to talk to him because I had made the decision to end the relationship. I did not even listen to his explanation because to me, he did not exist anymore. I told him that it was over between us, which made him very angry.

I think if we were not at our place, he would have slapped me. The only reason he did not was the fact that all the girls were in the room and he knew how they would have reacted to that. S'the was a short-tempered, egoistic and arrogant person and I think that is what attracted me to him, but that day it did not work for him. I forgot about the things I like about him because I felt betrayed. On the other hand, I was not blaming him because my subconscious mind was saying how anyone could love me when my own mother never loved me.

S'thembiso tried to convince me to continue with the relationship, but I stood by my decision. He even called Ntosh and Noxolo to talk to me, but they did not help him either. The relationship that I enjoyed ended just like that which was unfortunate because we were two people who enjoyed the same things in life and shared many common dreams, but regrettably, those remained just dreams. Even after the relationship ended, we remained comrades and friends. He used to visit me, and we would discuss politics and share information on books we read, which convinced some people that we were still together, but we knew the truth. I think we parted at the right time because two months later he was in the first group of comrades who left for school at Solomon Mahlangu Freedom College (SOMAFCO) in Morogoro, Tanzania. That group included Comrades Bongiwe, Ntosh and Phindiwe. Noxolo and I decided to join the military wing of the ANC, Umkhonto weSizwe.

– Ruth Mantile –

A day before their departure to Tanzania, S'the came to our place to say goodbye, and after he said goodbye to the girls, he asked to see me outside. "Mpoetsi, I'm so sorry for what happened to us, but you must know that I will always cherish what we had," he said, wishing me all the best in my endeavours. I also wished him well until we meet again, which was, of course, theoretical because in exile, we did not know what the future held for us. We parted on a very positive note with no hard feelings.

Noxolo and I stayed behind, waiting for our turn to leave. The situation was so dull now that everybody had left, but we did our best to stay focused. It was also during this time when the devastating news of Comrade Kgabi's passing was announced; it was the worst news I could ever have expected. The worst part was that it was not clear how he died, and we only heard that he was beaten to death by a Lesotho man who found Kgabi with his wife. I was not convinced because Kgabi was not that into women, worse of all somebody else's wife. I was convinced that it was the work of the enemy because he did many things against the system, but they were not aware of it until he left the country. Killing him was their only option. Kgabi was buried by the United Nations High Commissioner for Refugees (UNHCR) in Lesotho, and I had the honour to attend his funeral with some of the comrades, and I think with some of his family members as well.

One day the comrades who were renting in the same yard called us for a meeting. When we arrived at their house, we were met by other comrades who were not staying there. It was a surprise to me because I thought it was a meeting between those other comrades and us. Nevertheless, we sat down and were eager to hear what it was all about. The chairperson was Comrade Xolile who stayed somewhere in Lithabaneng. He opened the meeting by saying that they got a letter from the president of the ANC, Comrade Tambo, who wanted to know what our grievances were since he received complaints that we were not treated equally by the senior comrades in Lesotho.

This was a real surprise because I did not understand who he was referring to when he said, "We have received a letter."

I did not understand it because I did not know who was being treated better. It really confused me because I had stayed in the refugee camp for a long time, and some comrades rented houses outside the camp, which was never an issue. I asked the chairperson about this, but he was evasive, and I just left it at that. Issues like the preferential treatment trained comrades received over untrained ones were raised by some comrade, but to me, it was irrelevant and nonsensical. This issue did not bother me because we were still refugees and UNHCR took care of us, although we were members of the ANC. Those trained comrades were in Lesotho probably illegal, and they could not declare themselves to the UNHCR as refugees, and that was why the ANC had to take care of them.

That was my understanding, and that is what I explained to the comrades. The meeting continued; people raised their issues, and I felt I did not want to be part of this. I then told Noxolo that we should leave, and she agreed. Those meetings continued day after day, but we did not attend them again and instead went to watch movies in town, and I think that assisted us a lot because one day as we arrived at home, we found the cars of the senior comrades in our yard and other cars parked outside in the street.

We looked at each other, but said nothing and just went straight to our room to prepare dinner. We were about to eat when there was a knock at the door. Noxolo opened and saw Comrade Socks standing there. "May I come in?" he asked Noxolo. She opened the door for him, only to find that he was with three other comrades from Mbokotho. They greeted us and sat down.

"Do you two know about the meetings that have been taking place here in your yard?" Comrade Socks asked.

"Yes, we know about the meetings; we were invited to the first one, which we did attend, but we left in the middle of it, and we have never attended any of the meetings again," we said.

"You were supposed to inform us about the meetings, but anyway, it was a good decision not to attend them again. We do not know your reasons, but it was a wise decision. Look, there are enemy agents who have infiltrated the organisation to cause confusion within our ranks. This has resulted in cases where comrades were being poisoned by enemy agents in the camps in Angola, but fortunately, we did not lose anyone. However, it had a negative effect on the morale of the comrades. The objective of the enemy at this stage is to cause confusion and mistrust amongst the comrades in the Frontline States. We have come to you to ask of you to be extra vigilant and report anything that seems to be un-procedural," Comrade Gunnie said.

"Yes, we will," we agreed, and they thanked us and left.

I was no longer happy in Lesotho; it was actually very boring because we had to be vigilant against enemy agents we did not even know. We started treating people with caution because one did not know what to say and to whom. We were just waiting for the day we could leave the Kingdom of Lesotho. As we were waiting, Comrades Gunnie and Stocks came to our place and told me that my mother was around and that she wanted to see me. This was her third visit and fortunately the last because I left soon after that. I took Noxolo with me to see her at Lancers Inn, and she seemed to be very happy to see us. We greeted her and sat with her in the lobby, and she told us about the situation at home and the continued boycotts. We were with her until very late that night, and when we left, we decided to take her with us. It was very interesting to see how Mama pretended when she saw outsiders; she gave everybody the impression that I was her princess, and that nobody mattered to her but me.

You know, before, I used to be so angry at her behaviour, but after some time I did not really mind if it satisfied her because it was fine by me. The other thing was that I used to never talk about my family because of what they had put me through, and that is why her pretence never bothered me. She asked us about Ntosh and for some reason we did not tell her that she left for Tanzania because we thought she would assume that I was to leave Lesotho as well, and we did not want her to know that. We just said that she was visiting some comrades. The other reason was that she requested me not to leave Lesotho because at least she could come and visit me and that if I left, she would not be able to see me again. I thought it was better not to hurt her by not telling her the whole truth.

The following day, we woke up, had our breakfast and left for the Maseru border. When we arrived, we were lucky to catch a taxi that was about to leave, so my mother boarded after we said goodbye to each other. She did not know that this would be our last goodbye because I was due to leave Lesotho soon after her visit.

The taxi left, and I just looked at it until I could not see it anymore. I did not know why I suddenly felt so sad when she left. Maybe it was because there was starting to develop a bond between us, but again, maybe it was just a passing phase.

We went back to our house and had a discussion about family values. I knew Noxolo loved her mother with all her heart, and she would do anything for her mother. They had a very strong bond; a bond that only a mother and daughter can share. She told me that she loved her mother because she was one of those women who were fragile; she would not even hurt a fly, but unfortunately, she got married to a very abusive husband who always hit her and verbally abused her. Noxolo grew up knowing that her mother was defenceless against her abusive father, and because of this abuse at home, Noxolo grew up to be a physically strong woman so that she could be able to defend her mother and her little sister. She loved to do physical training, and her physique reflected it. One could actually mistake her for a man. She was also a very intelligent woman, and I saw this when we discussed dialectical materialism. She would go on and on about the law of the negation of the negation, and she was really admired by many. Noxolo was from East London. I remember the first time she said she was from East London, I thought she meant she was from Great Britain and she said to me, "No, East London is in Ciskei." She was so amused and said, "How are you going to fight inside the country when you do not know your geography?" That was Noxolo for you; she would really make fun of people but without malice.

The time came for us to leave. This information overwhelmed us, but we could not share it with anyone because of security reasons. Noxolo and I bought ourselves essential things like cosmetics, underwear, training shoes and some tracksuits. We really prepared ourselves for the worst, and we did not want to arrive in Angola and be short of sanitary pads or panties. We were ready for any eventuality in the unknown world of 'guerrillas', as MK soldiers liked to call themselves.

The day of our departure ultimately came. We were to board a flight to Swaziland through South Africa then to Mozambique because that was our destination. The flight was scheduled for 9:00 am. We boarded, and I think we were about fifteen people who were on a plane for the first time. We all felt very uncomfortable, and we were not sure if it was the way the plane was flying, or because it was our first time on a plane. We were in Bloemfontein in less than an hour. As we landed, we saw a lot of police officers, traffic cops and soldiers on the tarmac. We did not say anything to each other, but our silence and body language said a lot. We just remained calm, and subconsciously we were saying that if anything happened to us, it would happen; we could do nothing about it. Nobody came near the plane, except the staff working at the airport to fetch the luggage of the passengers. We were in South Africa for less than an hour, and once we took off for Swaziland, we finally started to relax. From there, we proceeded to Mozambique.

NINE

The best decision and a new identity

WE ARRIVED IN MOZAMBIQUE in the afternoon, and a comrade took us from the airport to a residence in Matola. It's important to remember that we arrived in Mozambique not long after the Matola raid, and therefore everybody was concerned about our security and those of other comrades residing in the country.

The situation was a bit tense at the residence, and no one except the trained personnel could leave. This was rather different from the situation in Lesotho where we were free to go anywhere we wanted to, but this was understandable because it was just a few months after the Matola raid where twelve comrades and a Portuguese electrician died from a brutal attack by the racist and fascist apartheid regime.

At the Matola residence, we were surrounded by trained personnel. There was Comrade Billy Dambuza, who seemed to be the commander, and Comrade Klaus Maphepha, who was said to be the commissar. I remember Comrade Mabaso because he was so militant, and his morale was always high. He was also a good motivator and morale booster and such a sweetheart and very enthusiastic about the struggle and the ANC.

There was a duty roster for cooking, but I was not on it because I was young. My only task was to wash dishes with which I did not have a problem with because some comrades volunteered to assist me.

After breakfast, we were required to assemble in what looked like a hall where we would have political discussions, and comrade Mabaso would teach us how to do the 'toyi-toyi' and sing revolutionary songs. The toyi-toyi we were doing was different from the one we normally did in Lesotho; this one was more physical than anything else. You had to raise your feet knee-level, and hold your hands as if you were holding a gun, which exerted a lot of pressure to the body. It really felt as if you were engaged in physical exercise, but I must say that it was very exciting! We would do that until almost lunchtime, and by the time we were done, we would be so tired, and our bodies would be aching.

I admired Comrade Klaus Maphepha a lot because he was eloquent and looked humble. He could explain a concept in such a way that one would never forget it. I thought he was a great man, the calibre that the ANC could never do without. He would put things in perspective and was able to explain concepts that we considered complex, like dialectical materialism. Comrade Maphepha was one of those comrades who made me respect the leadership of the ANC even more, because of how they related to the people on the ground. I remember at a certain stage, I told Noxolo that I wanted to be as intelligent and humble as Comrade Maphepha. To me, he was an extraordinary comrade and the epitome of a revolutionary soldier.

During our second week in Mozambique, we went through interviews where we had to decide whether we were going to join MK or go to school. Comrade Shingler, after I had told him that I wanted to join the gallant army, Umkhonto weSizwe, gave me the name Ruth Mantile as my combat name. I loved the name because it was the name of the greatest women of our time. Ruth First, the wife of Joe

Slovo, was a revolutionary; an intellectual in her own right. The apartheid regime sent her a parcel bomb that killed her in 1982 in Maputo, where she was working at the time. The other powerful woman with the same name was Mme Ruth Mompati, who was beautiful and humble. Mantile was the name of one of our comrades who was from Bloemfontein. I liked the combination of the two names because both represented the most amazing women in our liberation struggle.

During the interview, I realised that Comrade Shingler was also from Bloemfontein, although he did not say it in so many words. The fact that he was happy for me joining MK, as well as for mentioning in passing that I would be the first female from Bloemfontein to join MK, convinced me that he was my homeboy. Even the language that he used told me that we were from the same place. Remember, for security reasons, one was not supposed to tell where he or she came from or expose where other comrades came from. The difference with the groups from Lesotho was that we lived together for a long time and because of that, we knew each other very well.

After the interview, he wished me luck and told me that I was going to meet some comrades from Bloemfontein and that I should make sure to exert discipline and good behaviour throughout my stay in the camps. I thanked him and promised to behave as expected.

After staying in Mozambique for about three weeks, it was time for us to leave. Before we left, a certain senior comrade by the name of Tata uHlokolo called me and asked me to consider going to school because I was too young to join MK. He suggested that I go to SOMAFCO and then move on to MK after completing my studies.

He said he was advising me as a father. I knew he was concerned about me, but I had already made a decision to join the ranks of our glorious army, Umkhonto weSizwe.

"I understand your concern, but at this stage, I want to go to Angola," I said.

He extended his hand and said that he wished me luck. I thanked him and got into the car.

When we arrived at the airport, we saw Comrade Maphepha and other comrades. As we were offloading our luggage from the vehicle, we saw Comrade President Tambo. Everybody in our group was so excited, and some wanted to go to him but were not allowed to do so by his security personnel. They were not harsh; they just said the president would talk to us during the flight to Angola. We were very excited because we were going to be on the same flight as the president of our movement! We boarded the flight, and everybody wanted to have a seat near him, but I just wanted a seat by the window so that I could look at nature because I really admired nature. To me, the beauty of a country laid in its vegetation. I knew deep down in my heart that I would really want to hear Comrade President say something, but I was not prepared to fight for a seat next to him, and if it happened, it would be a bonus. I got a seat next to a window, and everybody else was still standing, probably waiting to see where Comrade President was going to sit.

Besides from me, a man was sitting at the back of the plane who seemed not to care about the excitement that was taking place all around us. I was a bit concerned about him; to me, he was either part of the security of Comrade President or some spy, but if he was a spy, how did he pass security to be on the same plane with our Comrade President? After my analysis, I thought I was just getting paranoid or reading too much into the situation and therefore decided to keep cool about it and relax.

Comrade President boarded the flight, and the comrades started singing freedom songs like "Tambo u Ingwe" (Tambo, you are a tiger). He did not smile when he looked at the comrades who were so happy to see him. He greeted all of us by touching our hands, and I felt honoured to have touched his hand. When Comrade OR, as we knew him, sat down, everybody else sat down in his or her allocated seats. The man at the back was still sitting where he was before, keeping to himself. I thought, *"If he is part of the security of the president, then this is a good choice because he displays a high level of discipline. If he did not, he will react to the excited comrades and thus expose himself."*

The flight to Angola was a very long one. Night had fallen, and as a result, I did not manage to see the vegetation I was so excited to see. The crew finally announced that we were a few kilometres from Lusaka, the capital of Zambia.

"I think there are people who will disembark in Lusaka, and after that, the flight will continue to Angola. We will probably arrive there in the morning," Noxolo said. We landed in Lusaka where we saw people disembarking, including the president, but the man sitting at the back stayed in his seat. We left Zambia shortly after we sang to our president.

TEN

Joining the altruistic army

WE ARRIVED AT THE airport in Angola at dawn, disembarked, and the quiet man at the back of the plane got off with us. As we were waiting for our luggage, I saw him coming towards us with two other men. "Comrades, after getting your luggage, you will follow these two comrades," he instructed. What a surprise! I concluded that he was probably safeguarding us from Mozambique to Angola. We got our luggage and followed the two comrades as instructed. Outside the airport, the two comrades directed us to two vehicles standing near the exit. After we got into the vehicles, the comrade who was driving us indicated that he was taking us to an MK transit camp. Noxolo and I looked at each other but said nothing.

On arrival at the transit camp, we were welcomed by our own soldiers. Some of them wore military uniforms while others were in civilian clothes, but all of them carried AK-47's. Two comrades drew my attention because their skin was so dark. For a minute, I thought we were at a SWAPO camp until I heard one of them talking Zulu to someone. The instruction came that we needed to stand in the formation while waiting for the National Commissar to address and welcome us.

"COMPANY. ATTENTION! AT EASE."

"Good morning comrades, welcome to the transit camp of Umkhonto weSizwe. My name is Andrew Masonto; I am the National Commissar of Umkhonto weSizwe. I hope all of you joined MK voluntarily without duress and if that is the case, then consider yourselves members of this glorious army. I expect high discipline and morale from you; you are going to eat, sleep, walk and talk discipline. In fact, in Lesotho, you went through political education, and by now I expect all of you to know what the ANC stands for and that you know the Freedom Charter by heart like you know 'Muskietejag'. Another thing is that I know some of you participated in some kind of illegal gatherings demanding to see our president. Let me warn you: we are not going to tolerate that because we consider it as counterrevolutionary behaviour.

We know that the enemy has sent their agents and instigators to cause disruptions and confusion within our ranks, but they will not succeed because we are fighting a just war and for that matter, we have a tried and tested leadership. Those people who claimed that the president of the ANC wanted to know your grievances were enemy agents and we have managed to apprehend them before they could do more damage to the ANC. Therefore, I tell all of you that you should know that we are not going to tolerate and compromise when it comes to enemy agents. Anyone who is an enemy agent must come forward now and confess to our security personnel. It is better to confess now because if you do not and we find out, you will be in big trouble. Comrades, it is now 3:30 am; it is time for you to go and sleep in places which the chief of staff has chosen for you. The bell will wake you at 5:00 am. When the bell rings, everybody should run to the formation in tracksuits and training shoes; actually, all of you should be ready for physical training, which demands strength and determination.

As you all know that our terrain inside the country demands that one should be physically strong because some of you may operate in the rural areas where there is no adequate public transport and one can walk long distances. In some instances, because of security circumstances, one can take long walks. Therefore, we want to prepare you for such eventualities. "COMPANY. ATTENTION! Takeover, Chief of Staff."

While we walked to our tents, I thought about what Masondo said about the Freedom Charter and the poem 'Muskietejag'. I wondered how he could associate our programme with a poem that made us hate going to school because if one could not recite that poem, the schoolmistress would clobber the poor pupil as if he killed somebody. The poem went like this:

> Jou vabond, wag ek sal jou kry,
> Van jou sal net 'n bloedkol bly
> Hier op my kamermure ...
> Deur jou gebyt en plaery
> Kon ek nie slaap vir ure ...
> ... Daar gaan hy weer!
> Maar dóód sal hy, sowaar ek sweer –
> My naam is Van der Merwe.

(Mosquito Hunt: You rascal, wait I will get you. Of you shall only remain a bloodstain on my bedroom walls. Because of your disturbance, I could not sleep for hours. There he goes again, but he shall die; indeed, I swear my name is Van der Merwe).

The address by the National Commissar was worrisome to me, and I thought, "*God, the place I was in was not where I wanted to be,*" and I actually remembered the old man in Mozambique who advised me to go to school. What I hated most was the arrogance which the National Commissar displayed; he was different from the comrades we met in

Mozambique. I lay in bed not able to fall asleep just thinking about the bell, formation, and physical training, and God knows what else. My main worry was that I grew up sucking my thumb because it helped me in my solitude. There were nothing and no one who was able to make me quit the habit because I grew up a very lonely child. At that moment, I did not know what I was going to do about it because one had to live as you were told and not as you deemed fit. Finally, I fell asleep, and the bell woke me a little bit later. I jumped out of bed and ran to the formation waiting for the new orders.

"ATTENTION!" a voice came from the front, and the person who was calling marched forward, facing the chief of staff. I saw everybody in the formation freeze, and the chief of staff standing at attention.

"Comrade Chief of Staff, all the members are present except for six comrades who are still on guard duty. The company is ready and waiting for your next order," he said.

"At ease!" the chief of staff responded.

"Company at ease," ordered the person I assumed to be the commander, and I saw the comrades relaxing.

"Good morning, comrades," said the chief of staff.

"Good morning, Comrade Chief of Staff," the comrades responded.

"You can all see that we have new comrades today. They had a briefing with the National Commissar on their arrival in the early morning. Our request to all the trained personnel is to give the new comrades guidance in terms of the rules and regulations governing our army. To the new comrades: no one is to leave this camp unless per instruction from the commanding staff and you will only leave under supervision. Secondly, you must never make any contact with the locals, meaning no contact with Angolans or any foreigner living in Angola.

Thirdly, you have commanders; if there is anything that you want to raise, you must raise it with your commander.

Fourthly, you are not allowed to use dagga or any drugs whatsoever unless it is a prescription from the medical staff.

Lastly, theft is a criminal offence; therefore, you must all know there is harsh punishment if found stealing. In fact, all the things I have mentioned are punishable."

The chief of staff asked if there were any questions. We all kept quiet.

"If there are no questions, then take over Commander," said the chief of staff.

"Company attention" instructed the commander. Then the chief of staff walked away.

"At ease!" Then we relaxed.

"All the new comrades stand aside. All the other members, dismissed," the command came, and all the trained personnel left the formation.

"Attention! Comrades, it is now 5:30 am and time for your physical training. The comrades standing there will be your instructors until you leave Vienna. We expect your full corporation from now on. You will get other instructions when you come back. Instructors, take over," the commander said.

"Platoon, attention! At ease! Attention! At ease!" one of the staff members called out.

"Itoyi-itoyi itoyi!" That was the song we sang running out of the camp to some remote place where we did exercises and continued to do stationary toyi-toyi. The place was so sandy to the extent that one could not see his or her feet when covered with sand. The experience of the physical training was overwhelming; it was very tough, and I asked myself that if the training in the transit camp was so tough, what about the actual training in the bush? How rigorous would it be?

After the morning exercises, we ran back to the camp where the staff members took us around the vicinity, especially the toilets, which were about two hundred metres away from the building, but within the camp. The female toilet was a very deep hole. Actually, it reminded me of the bucket system back home, but this one had a seat that looked comfortable. I could see maggots swimming in the waste. I looked at those maggots, and I wondered what the possibility was of us getting infections or even maggots in our vaginas. Anyway, I guess it was part of the struggle, which we needed to endure. After the sightseeing, we went to our room and got water to wash from a tank situated near the gate. We washed and got ready for our breakfast, which consisted of soft porridge. As we were eating, somebody screamed that there were maggots in his porridge. That was a very disgusting thing to say while people were eating, but immediately after that everybody was complaining of seeing maggots in their porridge. I continued eating because I was hungry, and to me, those maggots were not an issue as long as I had something in my stomach.

After breakfast, they instructed us to pick up the fallen leaves around the camp. The painful thing about it was that there was no way you could say you were finished with the task because the leaves kept on falling throughout the day. Therefore, it meant that you had to pick up leaves all the time. Sometimes you were lucky in the sense that you were required to assist in the kitchen. There you had to clean fish, and I preferred that over picking up leaves.

In Vienna, we found many trained female comrades doing different duties. I remember a Comrade Christina, who was dark in complexion, but beautiful, very eloquent, and intelligent. She was working at Radio Freedom, and throughout our stay in Vienna, I never heard that Comrade Christina was involved in petty issues or gossips like you would hear about at Mzana. Comrade Dimakatso was also in Vienna with her little beautiful baby girl, Puna, who we all adored. She never struggled with Puna because everybody was prepared to babysit her while she was at work at the printers.

On the other hand, we had comrades from the Amandla group, who only came to Vienna to sleep because throughout the day they were rehearsing or performing outside Angola. The females were the only people who were in Vienna, and I presumed their male counterparts were staying where they were rehearsing, which I later learned that it was at 'eholweni', meaning the hall.

I found Vienna to be enjoyable, especially during jazz hour where we sang revolutionary songs in what was then a swimming pool, where everybody would gather. The songs caused you to imagine how it would be when you went back to South Africa as a trained MK cadre. The other thing which was boosting my morale was to see trained comrades from other camps, the Frontline States, and others from inside the country. They would be in transit for further training or in need of medical attention.

The amazing thing about those comrades was the fact that they were all so humble; they did not boast about what they did inside the country, and they behaved very normal as if what they did during their missions at home did not matter. I sensed that they took it as part of their responsibility to liberate the country and that they did not want to be glorified for what they did. On the other hand, I thought it might be for their own security, which is why they did not talk about their activities. We only knew about their military activities because some of them told us about them what they did, and I could see that they felt proud of their courage and dedication to our struggle.

I only realised later that they were actually required to behave acceptably as MK members, and that was after I had studied the Manifesto of Umkhonto weSizwe. The Preamble stated the following:

Recognising that our army, Umkhonto weSizwe, must define its aims and objectives in clear and precise terms. The rights and duties of each member should be likewise defined without ambiguity. The Politico-military Council, acting on behalf of the African National Congress of South Africa, has adopted, and hereby decrees, this code for the guidance of members in cell positions.

The manifesto stressed the following:

People's War: Umkhonto weSizwe as the People's Army.

MK soldiers should display high standards of selfless devotion to the revolution on the part of all its members. MK soldiers should have revolutionary discipline and consciousness.

In the manifesto, there were also general regulations like, for example:

"All army units shall preserve and safeguard political and military and organisational information relating to the army's security and well-being.

All combatants must defend the ANC and be loyal to it, the army and the revolution.

Combatants shall act in such a manner that the people will put their trust in the army, recognise it as their protector, and accept the liberation movement as their legitimate and authentic representative.

Combatants shall protect the leadership and property of the ANC.

Combatants are required to have the permission of a competent authority to travel, move from one place to another or leave a camp, base or residence to which they are assigned.

Combatants and members of the ANC and Umkhonto weSizwe shall observe an adequate sense of responsibility."

The manifesto stated clearly that it would be an offence to do the following:

Smoking of dagga and other harmful drugs.

Neglecting one's duties.

Drinking on duty or in public.

The regulations and the manifesto made MK soldiers the most disciplined soldiers because they understood their purpose – that of liberating the oppressed masses of South Africa.

In Vienna, we had the commissariat, which was responsible for political education in MK. They were responsible for listening to international broadcasters like the BBC, etc. After listening to the broadcasters, we had news analysis, and during this, everybody was required to contribute or share their analysis with the other comrades. One thing I really admired about the MK cadres was the fact that one was not judged for one's opinion, especially when it came to political analysis. If someone did not agree with your analysis, they did not make you feel inferior or anything of that sort. They would just raise their opinion, and it would depend on an individual if he or she agreed with the opinion or not.

The other positive thing was that we were taught to understand issues holistically and that we had to be able to form an opinion at the same time. That is why, even today, comrades understand politics as they understood them in 1961, for example. Another good thing about the education in MK was the fact that it did not matter whether you were literate or not because everyone understood complex issues at the same level.

There were many more activities in Vienna than picking up the leaves or having political discussions. We were involved in the choir, especially the females. I cannot remember why it was compulsory for women to be part of the choir, but what I do remember is that it was an order from Comrade President Tambo that all females should take part in the choir. I remember saying that I sang in a church choir but could not really sing.

One day, someone said to me, "Where have you ever seen an asthmatic person sing?" I felt insulted because I really loved singing, but I guess it was never one of my talents. There were comrades, both females and males, who had beautiful voices, and I really admired them. During practice, I listened and looked at them with admiration and thought, *"God, why can't I sing like them?"* You know, listening to them was like listening to birds singing. I know in fact that our leadership, especially Comrade OR, was very proud to have such dynamic soldiers.

We also had 'Indlamu' (A Zulu traditional dance), which different cultural groups took part in. The amazing thing about this was the fact that you would have expected that only comrades who were Zulu-speaking would be involved in this but no! Even the comrades from Bloemfontein participated in Indlamu!

I remember that the late Comrade Steve (Hola) loved Indlamu with his whole heart. He was tall and big, but when he raised his leg, you totally forgot that he was big! He always received applause from the audience, and the comrades used to be so excited to see him dance. Everybody participated in cultural activities, and there was never a dull moment in the transit camp. Another fun activity was gumboot dancing. It was amazing to see comrades doing this, and one would think that they once worked in the mines because it was my understanding that mainly miners performed the dance. The person I used to admire the most was Comrade Joseph (Computer) because of his skills in soccer. He was, and still is, my hero. The shy ones used to participate in 'ditsamaya-naga' which translates to 'those who travel the country' and they would perform and sing 'isicathamiya'.

Vienna prepared us for military training and discipline. We did everything by order; you had to ask permission to go to the toilet, permission to consult a medical practitioner, permission to do everything, especially if you were in the formation. Every single one of us had to report to the section commander or commissar. I remember Comrade Mdanda, who was from East London and one hell of a comrade, during one of his malicious behaviours say, "What kind of a place is this where one has to sing before he gets food?" This was very amusing to all of us (the trainees), but the commanding staff of the camp was not impressed at all. They scolded him and promised to punish him if he did it again, but from our side, it was funny. The thing that made it funnier was the fact that we indeed used to sing before we got food. We would sing while standing in the formation, and section by section we would receive our food from the kitchen. This we did from breakfast to supper, but you know, before Mdanda mentioned it, we did not find it abnormal and actually enjoyed the singing because we thought it was part of the discipline in the MK. But, after he mentioned it, we took notice and found it funny although we could do nothing about it. This is just an example of the type of culture that existed in MK.

We stayed in Vienna for about two months, and by then we knew the comrades by their names, from the camp commander to the section commander, but did not dare call them by their names. There was a particular comrade by the name of Doctor; dark in complexion, tall, handsome and very quiet. He always walked between the staff room and the kitchen and looked very lonely. I loved his character because he also had something in him; he displayed high discipline, integrity, and selflessness, and he was one of those comrades you could not miss in the crowd because of his dignity. One day as we were engaged in our normal activities, we heard a gunshot coming from the administration side and as we ran to our positions, but before we even arrived, an 'all clear' bell rang. We ran to the formation, where we were told that Comrade Doctor had just committed suicide. No reasons were given, and I felt so sad about his passing, and even today, I still wonder what made him take his own life at that crucial moment of our struggle.

The commanding staff of Vienna was very humble; they all demanded respect, and I think all the trainees admired them. In turn, all of them treated us with respect, and I cannot remember one incident where we felt belittled by them. Because of this, most of us developed what I can refer to as 'conscious discipline' whereby one does something consciously. It was difficult for some comrades to adhere to discipline, but because it was a military requirement, they did not have a choice. Some comrades were naturally stubborn, and unfortunately, that was construed as being ill-disciplined, and in some cases, some comrades were labelled as enemy agents because of their negative attitude towards discipline and their stubbornness.

One evening, the camp commander informed us of our imminent move to the training camp the following morning, which excited us because we were already at Vienna for over two months. They only told us that we would leave at 3:00 am and nothing else was said except that were not allowed to tell anyone about our departure.

ELEVEN

The family I never had

WE FINALLY ARRIVED AT the training camp in the eastern part of Angola after a very long journey. The trip was enjoyable because we sang and ate throughout the journey. The journey by truck was comfortable, but I still did not enjoy travelling in trucks because it reminded me of the vans we used for funerals back home. I think it was more a phobia for vans or trucks than anything else because, in those days, one would be in a van with comrades, singing and chanting slogans, when all of a sudden the police would be throwing teargas at us, and we had to jump out of the moving vans to get water. That experience made me hate getting into vans, and I preferred walking to those funerals because at least one was free to run away from the threats.

The drivers were good at what they were doing, and I think what fascinated them the most was the songs, excitement and high morale we displayed throughout the journey. We got off, and the commander of the truck, Comrade Babes, reported to the chief of staff.

"Company, attention! Eyes front. Comrade Chief of Staff, the company is ready and waiting for your next order."

"Good afternoon, comrades," said Comrade Chief of Staff.

"Good afternoon, Comrade Chief of Staff," we responded.

"At ease!" he said. We stood at ease. He was dark in complexion and looked handsome in his Cuban uniform.

"Comrades welcome to Kamalundi; this is the camp that you will be part of throughout your training. As you all know, we expect maximum discipline in our ranks. We have the camp commander, Comrade Timothy Mokoena, the camp commissar, Comrade 'Che', and I am the chief of staff and my name is Goodman Soweto. This is the chief of ordinance, Comrade Ben Litchi, and chief of logistics, Comrade Sipho. We also have Comrades Limpopo, Lux and Talks as members of the camp administration. The camp also has members of staff who are going to be your instructors, and they have their commander, Comrade Sixteen.

You, as trainees, have the company commander, Comrade Jaguar and company commissar, Comrade Mondlana. You also have platoon commanders, and that is Comrade Dan Xaba for Platoon One and Comrade Sidney Mpila for Platoon Two. For Platoon One, the commissar will be Comrade Moropa, and Platoon Two, your commissar will be Comrade Hamba Zondi. All these comrades will be introduced to you in due cause. What is going to happen now is for you to get your military uniforms at the stores and after that, the comrades responsible will take to your different places for accommodation. Company, attention! Commander, take over."

"Company, attention! We are now going to the stores to get your uniforms," said the commander.

"Company, attention! Forward march."

We all marched forward as commanded. We arrived at the stores and two tough-looking comrades, who we later got to know as Comrades Bizzar Matsogo and Peter, welcomed us. They were very cute in their uniforms, and they had great personalities. They gave us two pairs of khaki uniforms with golden buttons, a matching khaki hat, and a pair of boots. We also received a pair of red, white and blue training shoes, but I could not get the shoes because of size problems. We were all very excited to receive our MK uniforms. After this, Comrade Peter took the females to a building adjacent to the guardhouse, but opposite a big kitchen. There, we found bunk beds, showers and toilets.

It was quite different from Vienna, where, if you wanted to wash, you had to fetch water with a bucket from a tanker outside the building. At Kamalundi, everything was within reach, and you could actually see the difference between the two camps.

Comrade Peter told us to choose our beds, and I chose a bed near the door and on top because this made it easy for me to be first at the door during a combat situation. There were five females in our group; Noxolo, Beauty, Nonkululeko, Patience and me. Beauty and Patience were from Tanzania and were older than the rest of us; I remember Beauty was already married to a comrade by then. I was the youngest in our company, or rather in the whole camp.

The camp was so quiet, you could hear a pin drop, and it was also spotlessly clean. I was disappointed about one thing though; the fact that the camp was not in the bush as I had expected it to be. I expected that we were going to stay in the bush where there was no civilisation, and this was the only thing I did not like about that camp.

We were relaxing in our room when we heard the sounds of people singing outside, and as we looked out of the windows, we saw a group of exhausted-looking people performing toyi-toyi. They were soaked in what looked like mud and seemed very tired, but despite this, their morale was very high. You could see this by the way they picked up their legs when they did the toyi-toyi. We watched them until we could not see them anymore, but from where we were, we could still hear them singing.

Suddenly, we heard the command, "Dismissed!" and six female comrades entered the building. They were dirty, and looked very tired, but managed to greet us with smiles. Their combats smelled terrible, and I could not figure out why. They actually smelled like shit or cow dung which made me nauseous. They were so dirty that we could not make out if they were male or female and from a distance, they all looked like males to me. After they had washed, they came to introduce themselves. They were Comrades Sello, Kuki, Edith, Amanda, Thobeka and Vera. I knew Comrade Kuki from Lesotho; she was one of those females who were very intelligent and was from a very good family of intellectuals. I wondered how she ended up in MK because to me, she was a fragile female who could not even kill a fly, but as it was, she made her choice.

The comrades looked very friendly and accommodating. "Welcome to MK. We hope that you are going to enjoy it here. Make yourselves comfortable," said Comrade Sello, who was said to be the commander of Mzana. After their welcome, we had a conversation with them about the situation at home, and they were surprised that most of us left the country some time ago and could not really tell them much of what was going on in South Africa, except for what we heard in the news.

The bell rang, and we did not move because we did not know what it meant. "Let's go to the formation. It is supper time," said Comrade Sello. We ran to the formation and found our group already there with our commanders and commissars who we met for the first time.

Our platoon commander and commissar were not as cute as the comrades we met earlier; they looked shabby and arrogant, especially our commissar who did not shave his beard or comb his hair. What was even worse was the fact that they both wore the same uniform as us, so we could not see the difference between them and us. Maybe I was too subjective, but they did not look attractive at all!

While we were waiting for our turn to get food, we sang as we did at Vienna. The comrades who were singing were those we saw with the female comrades. One could tell that they had been around for some time because of the perfect way they marched. You know, when they marched, you only saw the first, and the last comrade's legs and hands and their actions were so coordinated that you could not see the rest. It was beautiful to see them marching, and their coordination fascinated me. Section by section, they went to the dining hall until it was our turn to go. I was in Platoon Two, section one.

My section commander was Comrade Johnson, and the commissar was the late Comrade Fana. I knew both comrades from Lesotho, and although they left Lesotho before us, we ended up training together. Their group left Lesotho with other groups, but I do not know how they ended up in Tanzania instead of Angola. They actually stayed in Tanzania for close to a year. This group included comrades like Joseph, Mshengu, Sidwell, General, Bonono, Mazolo, Fana, Mdiliya, Mdidiyeli and a lot of others.

It was now our turn to go to the dining hall, and we went there with a song that was led by Comrade Joseph Mokwena (Computer). He sang, "Sizo ba shiya bazali ekhaya" (We are going to leave our parents at home). This was one of Comrade Mokwena's favourite songs and a very emotional one because it said that we are going to leave our parents at home and go to faraway countries our parents did not know about.

We went into the dining hall with a song. The kitchen staff gave us our food, which consisted of rice, vegetables and something that looked like corned meat. The food was delicious! The ANC taught me something that I will cherish for the rest of my life, and I will never forget as long as I shall live. In the ANC, no matter what we ate, we were always sure of our three meals a day. This was not the case at home; we used to eat a 'proper' meal in the evening that consisted of pap and cabbage or something like that, but in the ANC, and now MK, the situation was so different. The

ANC really took care of us! I always wondered where they got fresh vegetables from.

We ate our food in silence, and you could see that we were really enjoying it, especially me because it was the first time I ate corned meat. I remember that they mixed the corned meat with potatoes and tomato. It was delicious! I even went for a second serving, which, in MK, we called 'ambush'. I think all the females were a bit surprised that I actually went for ambush because most of them were older and they were women still concerned about their figures, but at that stage, I did not really care about my looks. I ate my food comfortably until I was done. After eating, I would go with the boys to discuss the political situation back at home and how we were going to make sure that we enjoyed our training and go back home to fight, not knowing what awaited us.

After the roll call, we were dismissed for the night and went to our barrack and discussed camp life, especially for the females. The other group told us that training was a bit tough, especially for the females because they were expected to do whatever the males were doing with no exception. They also told us about 'ema-gojini', the insolent and strict physical training instructors who were part of the group who were trained by the Zimbabwe People's Revolutionary Army (ZIPRA). Some of them even fought along ZIPRA during the last part of their military battles. They spoke especially about Comrade Shakes, who was very rude, but kind in some cases. We talked until curfew time when the lights were switched off.

In the middle of the night, I heard something that sounded like people barking like dogs, and I was a bit puzzled by that because I never imagined that people would be training in the middle of the night. I listened to the songs until I fell asleep.

The following morning, we were woken up by a bell and jumped out of our beds to the formation. After the roll call, we went back to our barracks to wash and make our beds. We were then called to the formation again for breakfast. We stood there singing revolutionary songs while waiting for our turn to go into the hall.

Our turn came to get our food, which consisted of oats with maggots floating in it. It was really disgusting, but I ate it without any problem because I thought that we only had a few minutes to eat and that I'm was not going to waste my time trying to spoon maggots out of my oats. After breakfast, we went to the formation again where we were given hoes and ordered to go and dig our own trenches which we were going to use in case of a ground-air attack by the regime. This was a strange thing, but it made sense. We went to the place allocated to our platoons and started digging the trenches. I cannot remember how deep we were supposed to dig, but I do recall that we had to dig a trench that we could fit in. This carried on for over a week in very hot conditions, but we did it with high morale.

"Did you hear people singing during the night?" I asked the group. They confirmed it. "We asked, and we were told that those comrades were serving punishment for smoking dagga," Comrade Mdanda said.

It made sense to me because I remember in the manifesto it was categorically said that smoking dagga and other illegal substances were a punishable offence in MK. I told myself that they deserved to be punished, but I didn't verbalise this and kept my opinion to myself because it might have come out as if I was a cruel person or a reactionary. Remember, I did not know any better and just believed in the regulations that governed MK. Days passed by without any incident, but three days after our discussion, we saw the three punished comrades fastened to trees, which really shocked us, but I thought it had nothing to do with me. My experience in Lesotho taught me to stay away from things that had nothing to do with me. Again, I felt that comrades should own up to their mistakes.

What I am going to say now might sound controversial to some people who do not believe in the truth. It baffles me today to hear people talking about the ANC and MK leadership as if it was a group of anarchists who did not believe in the rule of law. MK had a manifesto which we had to adhere to, and besides this, there were also security issues that were to be considered. There were incidents of poisoning in the camps. Our camps in Angola were attacked, and innocent students in Tanzania were poisoned. What about the secret meetings in Lesotho I mentioned in a previous chapter? Were they coincidences or did they just happen?

It is a fact that the ANC was highly infiltrated by the enemy from the lowest ranks to the highest echelons; we cannot run away from that. Even during the Truth and Reconciliation Commission's hearings, there were things mentioned that emphasised the fact that there were enemy agents and moles within the ANC and MK.

Yes, we as the ANC might have used the wrong methodologies, but what option did we have under the circumstances? Again, I am not saying that everything that was done in the camps of MK was right, and we certainly made mistakes, but I think the leadership owned up to it.

After we completed the trenches, we were taught how to use them during an attack. The demonstrations were at first theoretical and were held during the day. After this, we felt very tired, and I thought I was going to sleep like a child, but at around midnight we were woken up by the noise of people, trucks, gunshots and bombs. I jumped from my bed, thinking that the camp was under attack. The first thing that came to my mind was the lesson we were taught during the day that if there is an attack, everybody should make sure that he has his full uniform on, including the boots, before leaving the barracks. This rule ensured the combat readiness of the soldiers.

Dressed in full uniform, I left the barrack very scared, and when I opened the door, there was a big fire in front of it. It did not deter me, and I just wanted to reach my position, and that is exactly what I did. I was now safe in my trench just waiting for the next order when I heard people screaming, and trucks being revved. The situation was chaotic, and I was getting anxious and more convinced that we were under attack.

After about ten minutes, I heard the all-clear signal, and I started to relax. All the commanders were checking on their personnel, and after everybody was accounted for, we were called to the formation, where the commanders reported to the chief of staff, who then reported to the camp commander. He stood in front of us, and even though it was at night, I could see that he was a man of dignity. I looked at him when he saluted; he stood there with the seriousness and composure of a real soldier fighting for a just cause.

"Battalion, Attention! Eyes front! Comrade Camp Commander, all the comrades have been accounted for; those who are not in the formation are on guard duties. Otherwise, everybody is here waiting for your next order," reported the chief of staff.

"At ease!" said the camp commander.

"Battalion, at ease!" said the chief of staff.

"Comrades, chief of staff, members of staff, company commander and commissar, platoon commanders and commissars: Comrades, today we have demonstrated that we are not ready for deployment in case of an attack; this has been demonstrated by the time you took to deploy from your barracks to the trenches. I am especially referring to the trained comrades. I was looking at some members of staff who left their barracks with their boots still unfastened. What are you teaching the new trainees? I am not going to tolerate this situation! Comrade Chief of Staff, you must punish all the members of staff, including their commander, for being reluctant to respond as required. Comrades, I want everyone to always be ready for combat.

We should get as little casualties as possible in case of a real attack, but as I looked at the situation today, all of us could have been killed here. Therefore, I want us to rectify the situation. Comrade Chief of Staff, take over," the camp commander instructed.

"Battalion, attention! At ease. Commanders, take over," instructed the chief of staff.

We were immediately dismissed after the chief of staff had left. We went to our barrack and fell asleep again, but I slept in my boots and uniform in case there was going to be a mock attack again. The next morning after breakfast, we were taken to the vegetable garden where we worked throughout the day. The garden was full of vegetables and fruits like watermelons, tomatoes, cabbages, eggplants, etc. and I particularly enjoyed eating raw tomatoes. Our task was to clean the garden and get rid of weeds. The garden was a symbol of self-sufficiency; it demonstrated that even under abnormal circumstances, people will always be able to make the best of the situation. The ANC taught me that one should not always wait for handouts when you have hands you can use to work the land.

We continued working in the garden for a very long time, and I was actually afraid that we were already deployed there, but that was not true. After we performed our duties in the garden, we always took part in cultural activities like in Vienna. All the females went to the choir, as it was required. Choir practice was two hours long, and I used to get very bored. If I had a choice, I would have liked to participate in 'ditsamaya-naga' because the advantage there was that they always covered themselves with blankets like the Basotho men, so you were not exposed to the audience.

One day, while I was walking towards our barrack, Noxolo told me that Comrade Current was looking for me.

"Who is Current?" I asked her with surprise in my voice because I did not know anyone by that name. She whispered in my ear so that no one could hear his real name and I was shocked to hear his real identity.

"You are lying! Swear to me that you are telling the truth!" I said.

"It is the truth," said Noxolo.

The person she was referring to was Sechudi, my first boyfriend in Lesotho. We sort of parted ways just before he left for Angola because of his infidelities. I could not stand his womanising because of my own insecurities. Yes, I admit we had good times together, and sometimes I wished that one day we could get married and have children, but I think I was ambitious; we were too young to think about marriage at that stage. He was a very charming young man and goal-driven. He knew what he wanted in life in terms of the struggle and because of his commitment, I really enjoyed discussing politics with him.

His political maturity surpassed everything else, but he was a bit of a spoilt brat as well as arrogant. He loved music, especially reggae, so we shared some common interest as I loved reggae too. We parted ways, and as the saying goes, it was nice while it lasted. I did not understand why he was looking for me; maybe he just wanted to see me as a comrade and as a homegirl because we were both from Bloemfontein.

I did not know if I wanted to see him or not. Days passed without hearing anything from him until one day. I was going to the clinic because my knee was giving me problems, and I bumped into him just outside the clinic.

"Hi, how are you?" he asked.

"I'm fine, thank you, how are you?" I asked. He said he was fine, but that he had been so busy with training that he did not get time to see me, but he really wanted to.

"You look so beautiful and much more mature," he said.

I just smiled at him feeling really flattered because he never said anything like that to me before. He asked me why I was not with my platoon, and I told him that I was going to the clinic because of my painful knee. He said it was good to see me again after such a long time. I said the same to him, and he kissed me on the cheek and left. "What was that for?" I asked myself. The medical officer on duty looked at my knee and gave me rubbing stuff, which smelled terrible, but I took it anyway.

During supper, I met with Current again, and he told me that he heard that one of the instructors was interested in me. He did not want me to have a relationship with instructors because he still loved me, and I did not know what to make of this.

"Are you declaring your love for me now because somebody wants to make advances?" I asked him?

"No, I love you, and I have always loved you. I was not ready to commit then, but now I have grown up, and I think you are the only woman for me," he said. I just laughed at him and said nothing.

We stood there discussing politics and camp life until roll call. After we were dismissed, I went to my barrack still wondering about what Current said. I mean, when he was serious about me, he would not have waited for a month to tell me that. I knew it was one of his tricks to get me back; he always did that in the past, but not anymore if I could help it. I was tired of being second-best.

We met occasionally, and for some reason, everybody concluded that we were a couple. I did not have a problem with talking to him, but I did not want him back because I knew he was going to hurt me again. Therefore, I made it clear to him that I would only consider dating him again once we were both outside the camp. That would assure me that he had changed. In the camp, it was possible for him to date only me because women were scarce, but in the real world, he would go back to his old ways. The saying, 'a leopard never changes his spots' described him perfectly. Like I said, I did not have a problem meeting him, but I was getting tired of the insinuations about us, and it seemed as if he enjoyed it. What made the situation worse was when I was slapped by the chief of staff for cheating on Current, which was a real shock to me and an insult to what I stood for. We had a good relationship with the chief of staff, and this originated from the fact that he was dating one of the female comrades who adored me like a younger sister. She was very protective of me, so I think it was the same for the chief of staff. After slapping me, he told me that the chief of tactics, Comrade Junior Limpopo, told them during supper that we were an item.

I got the shock of my life, and even as I am writing this book after twenty-seven years, I still get goosebumps. "What? Tell me it is not true," I asked the chief of staff. That is what he said in front of everybody. You know I think I would not have had a problem with being accused of cheating, but I took exception because the person they were referring to was never in my thoughts. (May his soul rest in peace.) I admired him in terms of his knowledge of guerrilla warfare, but no, I did not even know what to tell Goodman because I did not even know that we were an item. It just did not make sense to me. I do not even want to describe what kind of a person I am talking about here because I respect the dead. So, let him remain dead.

After this incident, I knew I had to be careful to whom I smiled at because it seemed that comrades confused being nice and friendly with flattering. I considered the situation as a difficult one because some of us were natural charmers. I tried to stay away from situations that could land me in trouble, but it did not last long ... One day, I was coming from the clinic, where I got treatment for my sore knee. It was very painful, and I was limping. As I was walking past the staff barracks, I saw one of the instructors coming from the barrack. As a rule, I was supposed to have marched and saluted him, but because of my knee, I only managed to salute him. He stopped me and asked me why I was not marching before saluting him. I told him that I had a problem with my knee, which he understood and after he left, I went to our barrack.

I did not take notice of him until I met him again. He was very smart and cute and looked like a total gentleman. The way he wore his uniform, was as if it was made especially for him. He used to wear his Cuban uniform, which suited him perfectly; actually, the uniform complemented his walk. He had a unique walk, which reflected a lot of confidence, but if I knew then what I know now, I would not have looked at him twice …

I was wondering where I had met him before, but I could not place him. One morning after breakfast, he walked towards me and greeted me, and I responded. He told me his name, which I truly forgot immediately. I told him mine. "May we meet later on today?" he asked. I did know what to say, and I remember saying to him that I was going to rehearsals, and there was no way I could see him that day.

He said it was fine and that he would see me when it was convenient for me. For some reason, everybody made a fuss about this. I did not understand why, and I think it was because of this pressure that I ultimately dated him. We became the Romeo and Juliet (or even the Beyoncé and Jay-Z) of the camp. I was happy with the choice I made, and I think it has always been in me to fall in love with a person that is not approved by others. Maybe it was a cry for independence from my side because for as long as I can remember, I have always hated it, and still do when someone wants to control me.

Although we had our limitations, the relationship was good, and I enjoyed every adventurous moment of it. Fortunately, we started the relationship before we started training. I thought that was an advantage because by the time we started with our training we were used to each other, and I knew how to behave in his class. Unfortunately, our happiness was short-lived because we had to move to different bases because of security reasons. We were told that there were plans by the South African regime to attack our training camp. Apparently, the decision was made that two bases should be opened not far from the camp. We were separated but met during rehearsals, which was fine with me because I enjoyed my freedom very much. Our separation did not last long; for some reason, we had to join the other comrades in the other base, and that is when we met again.

***

It was December 16, 1981, the twentieth anniversary of the formation of MK. The camp had organised the celebrations, which was our first since we arrived in Angola. There was food, liquor, cooldrinks and cakes.

On that occasion, which I will never forget, we were visited by the late Comrade Moses Mabhida (May his soul rest in peace), and the then General Secretary of the Communist Party. Comrade Mabhida delivered a message which was part of a speech for the twentieth anniversary of the formation of Umkhonto by the then president of the ANC, and the commander-in-chief of MK, Comrade OR. The message went as follows:

"*Fellow countrymen and Comrades,*

Militants of the People's Army, Umkhonto weSizwe (Spear of the Nation). Lerumo la Sechaba.

December 16, 1981, marks the 20th anniversary of our glorious army, Umkhonto weSizwe, the Spear of the oppressed black people of our land. This year on Heroes Day, we look back with pride over 20 years of arduous struggle and forward with resolve and determination to the battles ahead.

We look back firstly, to December 16th, 1961, when Umkhonto weSizwe was born. Born out of a mighty mass movement led by the ANC, which had united people in every corner of our land against white minority rule. Born out of decades of peaceful struggles for freedom and justice, which brought nothing, but in-

creased violence and oppression; born finally, out of the people's realisation that the violence of the white racists would have to be met with the revolutionary violence of the masses."

Comrade OR in his message quoted from the manifesto of Umkhonto weSizwe, which stated the following:

"The time comes in the life of any nation when there remain only two choices: submit or fight. That time has now come to South Africa. We shall not submit, and we have no choice but to hit back by all means within our power in defence of our people, our future and our freedom."

"On this national day of commemoration and rededication, the ANC calls on all patriots of our land, regardless of race, creed or social stratum, to close ranks in a mass struggle for a non-racial and democratic South Africa, now."

Comrade OR was a giant and sometimes I wished that if I were to be allowed to decide whom I would choose to be immortal, without any doubts in my mind, I would have definitely chosen OR. To me, he was the father I never had, a comrade, also a president. He was everything to me. Comrade OR was a man of honour, a distinguished man and an icon to the liberation of humankind. I never doubted his Christian values, which he demonstrated through his warm and loving personality.

The celebrations were going well, and we had a terrific time until the camp's commander, Bra T, announced that our training was to start the following day. That came as a shock to all of us because most of the comrades were drunk. The worst part was that our first class was four hours of physical training and two hours of politics. To me, that information alone would have made anyone who was drunk sober.

As I am writing this now, I am laughing just as I laughed that day when we realised that we had four hours of physical training. I might have been wrong, but I am sure I saw the surprise in the eyes of the comrades, and some of them even wondered, "*Why today?*" I watched the situation with interest because I knew that nothing would change the decision taken.

The following day we woke up, had our breakfast and off we went to our first training. All the comrades who drank the previous day looked sick, and I really felt very sorry for them. As we were waiting for the next order, we saw Comrades Shakes, Maria and Viva coming towards us. I prayed that each of them had a hangover so that we could miss the physical training, but to my disappointment, they were full of energy. It is true! I was laughing at the comrades who were drinking the previous night, but I was actually very scared of the four hours of physical training.

"Hey wena povu, four mankhase lapho" (Hey, you civilians, form four lines), shouted Comrade Shakes. We quickly formed four lines and stood very still. Comrade Shakes was a hell of a comrade, and in South Africa, we would have referred to him as 'lepantsula' or something very close to a thug because of the way he used to wear his uniform. His trousers used to hang almost on his bum, and his gun always hung loosely over his shoulders as if it was heavy for him to carry. He had big, red, threatening eyes, which he really used to intimidate us. I could never predict his moods during my stay at the camp. He was very unpredictable; one minute, he would be laughing, and the next, he would be very angry and insolent.

"Attentioner! Attentioner! Phakamisa ijambo, killer man, phakamisa ijambo nyamazana" (Attention! Attention! Lift your feet, killer man, lift your feet, tiger), he started singing, and we were supposed to lift our feet and go very slowly from one foot to another. We did that for almost twenty minutes before we could start running after him.

We ran for almost five kilometres before he stopped, but we continued singing while doing stationary running. He then said, "Exercise number nine, position take." By that, he meant that we had to do the frog jump. We took our positions, and he instructed, "Move and bark like a dog!"

We started moving and barked like dogs. "Hawu, hawu, hawu." It was a very tough exercise, especially after running, because one's legs would have cramps, which made it difficult to do the exercise, but we had to do it. At first, I thought it was going to be for a short distance like we did in Vienna, but I was wrong! Some comrades did it faster than others, and they were sometimes about a kilometre in front of us. That certainly demoralised the rest of us because we knew we still had quite a distance to go. I thought they would let us walk to those comrades, but no! Comrade Shakes would be with the comrades in front of us, and we would be left with Comrades Maria and Viva. At least they tried to encourage us to move, and we really tried because, in MK, there was an unwritten rule that we had to move with the pace of the slowest. Unfortunately, that rule did not apply during physical training, especially for Comrade Shakes!

I forgot to mention that our commanders and commissars were with us during classes. They also had to run, but at least they were spared from doing 'exercise number nine'. Luckily, I was always in the middle, which was better for me because if one was in front, you had to wait for the comrades in a squatting position until the very last one. When you were in the middle, it would not take long to wait for those who were behind because they would be forced to roll until they reached the whole group. Rolling was the worst thing that one could do. Remember, it was very hot in Angola and rolling made you feel nauseous, and some comrades even threw up from this. I think we covered about one to two kilometres doing 'exercise number nine' at a time and after that, we would be required to run again. In an hour, we would cover about ten kilometres running while doing 'exercise number nine'!

Sometimes, depending on the mood of Comrade Shakes, he made us all roll, crawl, run and do 'exercise number nine' with intervals of thirty minutes in between. During this, we would also be singing. I used to admire the morale of comrades like Computer, Mazolo, Babsy, Pitlo, Bonono, Mazolane, Noxolo, Pudi e Kgaotse, Mdiliya, Mdidieli, Mosala, Fana, Johnson, Theron, Jabulani, Patience, John, Mdanda, Hubert and many others who were always the best in 'number nine'. (May the souls of those who have passed on rest in peace.)

After four hours of physical training on our first day, we returned to the camp, still running and doing the dreaded 'exercise number nine'. When we eventually reached the camp, I felt like sleeping because I was so tired and very hungry. The amazing thing was that nobody wanted to eat, and we just wanted to sleep. We had our lunch, and after that, we had our first political class, which was two hours long. There we were introduced to our instructors who were the late Comrade Aluko and Comrade Edwin Mabitse. (May their souls rest in peace.) Both comrades were very good at what they did, and they were very eloquent. I remember that even though we were very tired after the physical training, none of us dozed off because the class was really stimulating.

Their presentation was on class struggle, which was a very interesting topic for those who stayed in Lesotho longer because we always had discussions about the different classes in society and their struggles, especially the struggle of the working class. That is why we were able to contribute in class and asked for clarifications from the instructors.

What I admired about those comrades the most was the fact that they did not make us feel inferior. They accommodated our opinions, and it did not matter how wrong the argument was from their own point of view. They just gave their perspective, and that was it. Those two were the Maphepha type; one of a kind.

We continued with our classes from Monday to Saturday, raining or not. There was a saying in MK that *'there was no rain in the army'* and that was true. If we had physical training and it happened to be raining, we continued as if there nothing was happening. What was funny was the fact that we did not get the flu or anything like that under those rough conditions because, for some reason, our immune systems accommodated it.

The other subject was Firearm Training. The instructors were Comrades Khaya Mdaweni, Curtis, and Sipho who were later joined by Comrade James, whom I saw in Lesotho during his detention. I loved firearms, but the amazing thing about it was that throughout my training, I was never able to shoot at a target. It was even worse when I missed a target using an RPG-7. This was embarrassing because everybody was saying that throughout the history of MK, I was the first female to miss targets. You know, all the female comrades were snipers except for me, but for some reason, it never bothered me, and I was cool about it. Given the circumstances, I always consoled myself by saying that my mission inside the country was mass mobilisation through political work. Therefore, I would not be required to carry a gun, but that was not true, and I knew it.

I must say that I enjoyed the theory behind firearms more than the practical; I remember that we had to run eighteen kilometres to and from the shooting range during firearm practice. As if that was not enough, we would have all the instructors with us, including tactics and physical instructors, who ensured that we did their core businesses in the process of going and coming back from the shooting range. We would crawl, roll, do tactical manoeuvres and the terrible 'exercise number nine'. I always thought the eighteen kilometres was not a problem; the actual problem was the exercises, but those were the rules.

We were also taught topography, which was very interesting. Our instructors were Comrades, Refiloe and Erick, and I particularly enjoyed Comrade Refiloe's classes because he was a no-nonsense comrade. He was very serious, especially when he had to deal with Mzana. I used to laugh at him because nothing would make him compromise. You know, sometimes we would take chances and ask for breaks, and other instructors would give us breaks, but with Comrade Raff, as he was called, it was a different ballgame altogether. Amazingly, even Caroline's smile and Nonkululeko's sexy eyes did not have any impact on him. I respected him for that.

Military Tactics was one of my favourite subjects. My fellow comrades did not understand why I liked it so much, and to them, it was because the head instructor was my boyfriend. This was a very narrow assumption; I loved tactics because, for me, it was something that prepared you for any eventuality in the country. Tactics was a means of survival under very hostile conditions, and that was why I loved it.

During our training, something happened that really worried us. Comrade Erasmus Mshengu (May his soul rest in peace), became sick. He was vomiting, had a headache, and his temperature was very high. He also had joint pains and was shivering, although it was very hot. The medical officer said he was going to be fine because he would be given malaria treatment, as malaria was the cause of his health problem. That was very worrisome to us because of what we were told about malaria and how fatal it could be. It was confirmed to be malaria, and we were assured that the treatment would help him. We were still not convinced, and as a result, we checked on him after classes just to make sure that he was fine. After a week or so, he got better and continued with the training.

After Mshengu, there was a stage where five to ten comrades would have malaria at the same time, but fortunately, they all survived. During his treatment, Mshengu had some big pimples on his back and hands, and the worst thing was that they were itching and made him feel very uncomfortable. One day I was with him in their tent, and I decided to squeeze the pimples but was shocked to see a worm coming out of what I thought was a pimple! I got so scared and went to the clinic to inform the medical officer about it. He laughed at me and said, "There are flies around here that lay their eggs on fabrics, and if one does not iron his or her clothes, those eggs penetrate the skin, and because of the body heat they hatch and become worms. Those worms stay under the skin, and as they grow, you will notice something like a pimple, but when you squeeze it, the worm comes out. The worms are not dangerous, but they can cause discomfort. There is nothing wrong with Comrade Mshengu. You will get them too if you do not iron your clothes," he laughed. I went back to Comrade Mshengu and explained the situation the way it was explained to me.

Other subjects we had to take during our course were Tactics, Topography, March and Drill, Engineering and Radio Communications. We had different instructors for different subjects, and all of them were very good at what they were doing. I enjoyed and passed everything, but I made sure that I failed Radio Communications because I realised that most of the female comrades were deployed in communications after their training. Also, when I read books about international guerrilla warfare, the Second World War and the Russian Intelligence, women were always used in communications. In all those books, there was one common denominator, and that was the fact that females were always used as radio operators. Because of that, I had a negative attitude towards all those stereotypes, including secretariat and administration jobs. My favourite subject was Politics because I realised that I could convince people about the just war the ANC was fighting in, and because of my experience inside the country, people believed in me. I thought I would be in a better position to mobilise the youth to join the ranks of MK, better still, to create underground cells inside the country, which would unleash attacks on the enemy within.

During training I got sick. Fortunately, it was not malaria, but flu, so I had to stay in bed for the afternoon. After supper, all the comrades went for rehearsals and around 20:00 pm, I went to the clinic to get an injection and went straight back to the tent. As I was about to climb onto my stretcher, I got the shock of my life! I saw a shining thing next to the stretcher and realised it was a snake. I slowly walked back by 'bouncing' to the entrance. I was so scared, and I still do not know how I managed to climb the steps! I ran to another tent and went inside without asking for permission to enter.

"There is a big snake under my stretcher! Please come and kill it," I said to the occupants who were members of my platoon.

"Mantile, calm down, where is the snake?" Mdanda asked.

"It is under my stretcher, please hurry!" I was so scared and confused, I actually said the snake was under my stretcher instead of saying it was next to it. At that stage, we did not carry guns because we were 'povu draai'. As 'krusants' we only carried 'izigodo' (tree stems), which were fastened with a sting and we had to pretend as if we were carrying guns. The worst thing was that we had to carry this 'weapon' with care like a real gun. If your gun fell, you had to fall like it yourself. That's how difficult it was with 'ombobo wa bantu' as it was called. Anyway, Mdanda went out to call the OD, who asked three other trained comrades to accompany him. I was waiting outside when I heard a round of fire coming from the tent, which really attracted a lot of attention in the camp. People started to deploy, and I presumed they thought it was a mock attack, but they were told to go back to their tents. Comrades came running to our dwelling and found a tired or sated python who did not move, and they shot it.

After this, I was actually afraid to be left alone in the tent, and I had to go and sit with the members of my platoon until curfew when the other female comrades were back from rehearsals. The snake was cleaned, and I was made to understand that they got something in its tummy, but I cannot remember what it was.

At a certain stage during our training, we were ordered to put everything (our training) on hold to move our base from Kamalundi to Caculama in Malanje, also in the eastern part of Angola. We were moved immediately, and the new camp was only a bush because we were the first MK soldiers to occupy the campsite, which was left by ZIPRA forces back in 1980.

I must say that Caculama was the place I was longing for since I joined MK. It was wild, and you could hear the sounds of baboons and hyenas, and you could actually see where the snakes passed in the sand. The campsite was green with trees all over. It looked like the Garden of Eden, and the only difference was that it did not have apples; otherwise, we would have been in trouble, especially with snakes all over the place! We were in direct contact with nature, and I loved it to bits. We had to start from scratch to make it habitable; we started by digging our dwellings, which was hard work. The dwellings had to be dug downwards like fortresses; the roof was at the level of the ground, covered with military tents. After we completed our dwellings, we started with the trenches, and our training commenced as well. We used to attend classes, and after lunch, we continued the digging of trenches. I think we were able to make the place habitable in a matter of three months.

I forgot to mention that a week before we left Kamalundi we were joined by two platoons which went with us to Caculama. There was only one female in those platoons which brought the number of females in the camp to seven. Her name was Comrade Caroline Busuku, and she later died in an ambush in Cacuso in the eastern part of Angola. (May her soul rest in peace.) Heritage was part of this platoon together with Knox, Senaoana, Manzini, Linda, Raymond, Mlamli, David, Radinyeka, and others.

We were almost done with our training, and most of the comrades had left the camp, which we used to call 'ba dliwe NGU Mchina'. This concept meant a lot of things – from here, you either had to go for further training, changed camps, go to Lusaka, the Frontline States, or even home, which was unlikely as we later come to realise. It is equally important to mention that comrades who trained with me did not enter the country immediately after their general training. Most of them went for further training before they entered the country. I thought that it was a good thing because, after general training, we were wild and excited. It would definitely not have worked out if they sent a person like that into the country! It would have resulted in chaos, and although there were comrades who were mature enough to handle the situation, those were the exceptions.

During this time, we received new recruits, and we knew most of them because they were from Lesotho. There were a lot of females in this group, and their commander was Comrade Moscow. I remember Kate, Seipati, Dodos, Marilyn, Joyce Jones, and Rebecca, who became Moscow's wife. It was nice to have more females in the camp. Other comrades I remember from this group were Lloyd, Mayibuye Thabang, Lucky, Lesheleshele, Reggie, Mokete, Papase, Admiral, Mzwandile and others.

In my platoon, I was known as mischievous, especially by Commander 26. I did not consider myself as such and just got amusement from pranking people. I looked at the new comrades, and I thought of a plan to prank them. During my planning, I decided that I was going to pretend as if I was one of the members of staff in the camp so that they can salute me. There was a river between HQ, the kitchen and Moscow's base, and the company had to fetch water or food every day by crossing the river. Therefore, there was no way that I could not be saluted once or twice a day. The following morning after breakfast and after I had completed my chores, I went to the kitchen to get to the river without anyone from the staff seeing me. On my arrival, I greeted Comrade Bernard (May his soul rest in peace), and I pretended to be helping him with something. The moment he started concentrating on something else, I left the kitchen and crossed the river to Moscow's base, where I tried to conceal myself amongst the trees. I stood there for almost thirty minutes without any movement except for the monkeys running around. I was getting tired of waiting when suddenly I heard a song, "Siyo ba Shiya Bazale Khaya", and I knew they were marching towards the river and not running because if they ran, it would have been awkward for me to stop them. I patiently waited until they almost reached the riverbank, and when the last section of the platoon was about to cross the river, I called out and said, "Stoi (Stop) about, turn forward, march."

"What do you think you are doing? Were you not told to salute your officers?" I asked.

"We are sorry comrade, we did not see you," one of the section commanders apologised.

"Then do the right thing," I said. They went back and came towards me drilling and giving me a salute. I let them drill up to a certain distance, then shouted, "At ease, comrades." I did that for days until I was caught out by one of the commanders who knew me. By now, there was no need for me to remind them; they saluted me wherever they saw me, and that was when I was caught. What was nice about it was the fact that I enjoyed the status.

A lot of comrades thought I was very naughty because for a long time I was the youngest and everybody had a soft spot for me. As a result, I was a bit spoilt, but in a good way. You know, when we were in the formation, we were supposed to be quiet, and the comrades stood very still without making a sound. That was until I pinched them or put insects like red ants into their combats! The insects bit them, and you would just hear someone screaming, and I would crack up with laughter.

Where our company used to gather, there were small snakes, which I used to play with (they were less than thirty centimetres long, and they did not have eyes). I realised that they were blind because they could not see my fingers as I tried to entice them to bite me, and they just moved by instinct. One day I decided that I was going to grab one and put it in Mahlobo's combats. As we stood in the formation, I grabbed a snake and threw it inside his combat.

At first, he did not feel it, but I think it started moving because he suddenly jumped out of the formation screaming and everybody was surprised as to what was happening to Mahlobo. For some reason, the company commander came to me, shouting, "Mantile, what did you do? I know it was you! This ugly thing; you just look beautiful because you are light in complexion. If you were dark, we would see the devil himself!" he said. Everybody was laughing at me, and I just looked at him and said nothing.

By then, Mahlobo was almost naked, and that is when they saw the snake as it was about to enter his boots. Everybody wanted to run away, but I just took it and threw it aside. Afterwards, I told them that the snake only wanted the warmth of a human's anus, and surprisingly, they believed me! I cannot remember how many times I was punished. The worst time was when I had to wear a big Russian jacket and a hat with temperatures running between forty-five to forty-eight degrees Celsius.

Once I stole cigarettes for my comrades from a 'krusant' who had just joined us. You know, in the camps, almost everything was scarce, and as a result, comrades smoked something they called 'Makanya'. When this woman arrived at the camp from Lusaka, I heard that her parents were also in exile there. She had two cartons of Rothmans, and when I saw them, I thought, *"How can a new recruit smoke real cigarettes when officers do not have cigarettes?"* and I decided to steal the whole carton and give it to Computer with clear instructions that they should not smoke in front of other comrades. He took the carton and went to their dwelling. I do not know what I was thinking because eventually, someone was going to find out that comrades were smoking real cigarettes.

The woman reported the theft to our company commander and apparently, an investigation was conducted without me knowing. Computer and the others went through interrogation, and I do not know who, between Mahlobo and Mshengu, told the truth, but that is how I was exposed. I was punished, but to tell the truth, I felt so humiliated. Despite all these things, I remained their 'rooimier' (red ant) as they used to call me, because of my skin's complexion.

It was during this time I noticed something about myself. Whenever I was hungry, I felt very sick and weak, and I could not understand why. I only understood later in my life when I was diagnosed with diabetes. Before that, comrades thought I was a spoilt brat, but others took it very seriously, and as a result, they used to sacrifice their bread for me so that I could eat before lunch. Some comrades would actually go and ask for 'ambush' so that they could put away some for me because I really felt awful when I was hungry, and this really touched me to be shown such unconditional love.

We stayed in the camp for more than a year, and this was really getting to me. I remember thinking that maybe we were seen as enemy agents, and that is why they kept us in the camp, but that was not the case as I would later learn. The ANC, and MK, in particular, showed me that it was important to know what you were *supposed* to know and not what you *wanted* to know. The reason for this was that if you were arrested by any chance, it was almost impossible to talk about things you did not know about. Therefore, it minimalised the extent of torture when you were incarcerated. As we were wondering when we would leave the camp, some people knew, but no one said anything to us.

One day, I think through frustration, I wanted to pee, but I was not in the mood to go to the toilet, which was a bit far from our dwelling. I just slept on my stretcher and pissed on it. Remember, we had our clothes and the uniforms because we used stretchers to iron our clothes. You know, I totally forgot about that incident until the day I was told that I was leaving the camp. As I was about to pack my things, I realised that all my clothes had urine stains on it and that I could not wear them anymore, so I had to throw all of it away because I knew I would get new clothes. That is how much the ANC took care of us.

I travelled to Luanda with Noxolo, Patience and eight male comrades very early in the morning. I looked at the combination of the group and realised that there was nothing common between us in terms of maybe being sent home or something like that. Nobody said anything except that we needed to pack our clothes to leave for Luanda the following morning. We arrived in Vienna before sunset, and everything was the same except for some changes in the commanding staff. We were given accommodation and remember, we were now fully-fledged guerrillas, so we were treated with respect except for the fact that we were not saluted by anyone. I was really disappointed by this because that was the one thing I liked in MK. Maybe I was obsessed with being saluted?

We were in Vienna for more than a week, and still, nobody said anything about where we were going. It was as if we were part of the staff, and that made me scared, but I continued to keep my cool. After two weeks, I met Comrade Peter. (May his soul rest in peace.) We became good friends, and I even forgot about my worries because we used to discuss politics and social issues during my free time. He was one of the members of the staff; handsome, tall, very nice, humble and intelligent, and if I had my way, I would have told him to marry me. Do not get me wrong, we did not have a romantic relationship, but I really enjoyed his company, and I was the one who was harbouring illusions.

We were told that we would be leaving Vienna for East Germany, and we promised each other that we would meet up again after the year I would stay there. He even accompanied us to the airport, and gave me a hug and kissed me on the cheek. He smiled and told me that he wished that I could stay longer so that we could get to know each other better. I never understood what he meant, and God knows how much I wished to know.

TWELFTH

Turned into a young Marxist

WE TRAVELLED FOR ALMOST fourteen hours from Angola to the German Democratic Republic (GDR), which was a very tiring flight. We arrived in Germany and were fetched by two old men and an interpreter. They greeted us in English and fetched our luggage, and we left the airport in a microbus. We were all very quiet during the drive from the airport and finally reached what looked like a college of some sort in Magdeburg County where we were shown our rooms and told to meet in the foyer at 13:00 pm. In my assigned room, I found an African woman whom I greeted and introduced myself to, and she did likewise. She told me that she was Lydia from Tanzania. I was very surprised because I thought it would only be us there, but I just kept quiet, and she showed me my drawers and the bathroom. I thanked her and started unpacking and afterwards took a shower because I thought I needed it after our long journey. I had never used a shower before, and I really enjoyed it!

After the glorious shower, it was time to meet in the foyer. Everybody was already there, and the interpreter told me that the group was only waiting for me because we were going to lunch.

In the dining hall, we found some African men and I thought they were also from Tanzania. We introduced ourselves and went to get our food, which consisted of boiled potatoes, pork, green beans and gravy. The food tasted delicious, and I was wondering if we were allowed to have 'ambush', but I thought it was too much to ask for that. After our meal, we had chocolate cake with cream as dessert, which was absolutely wonderful!

We then had a tour of the college and were taken to our lecture room to meet the members of the staff and lecturers. They also gave us a briefing on the programme as well as the rules and regulations of the college. Everything was fine except for one regulation that prevented us from accessing other floors of the college. We were all staying on the first floor and were not allowed to go the other floors. Everyone shared a room which had two beds, two desks with side lamps, wardrobes and an en suite bathroom with a toilet. Every room also had a water heater. Remember, it was my first experience with such comfort, and as a result, everything fascinated me!

The lectures began, and we started with the subject Historical Materialism. The Germans did not speak English, and we had to use an interpreter. Our lecturer, an old man called 'Genosse' (Comrade) Rudi, presented the subject. He was one of the young people who joined the Communist Party in his teens before the end of the Second World War and was very jolly and funny.

The lecture on Historical Materialism dealt with the existence of living human individuals, their physical organisation and their consequent relation to the rest of nature. It also dealt with the fact that consciousness was one thing that distinguishes human beings from animals, and this came about when human beings began to produce their own means of subsistence, which was influenced by their physical organisation. By creating their own livelihood, they were indirectly producing their destination as human beings who were different from animals. This was a very interesting subject because, in essence, it meant that a human being developed from evolution. We were with Genosse Rudi for almost three months. I really enjoyed his presentations because he spoke with passion, and he was able to illustrate complex issues.

During this period, we also dealt with different social classes and class struggles. This topic dealt with the relationship between the working class and the bourgeoisie and their relationship with the means of production and lead us to discuss the manifesto of the Communist Party, which stated the following: "The history of hitherto existing society is the history of class struggles. The modern bourgeois society that has sprouted from the ruins of the feudal society has not done away with class antagonisms; it has but established new classes, new conditions of oppression, and new forms of struggle in place of the old ones. All previous historical movements were movements of minorities, or in the interests of minorities. The proletarian movement is the self-conscious, independent movement of the immense majority, in the interest of the immense majority."

These discussions were very interesting, especially when one looked at the working class in South Africa; they worked in the mines and were paid only for their subsistence which they had to share with their families back at home. When we were not in class we would go for excursions, and most of the time we visited factories, museums and various restaurants, and as you now know, that was the part I enjoyed the most.

One day we were taken to Buchenwald concentration camp, which was in Weimar. The camp was constructed in 1937, and it was liberated by the US Army in April 1945. When the camp was first established, there were about one thousand prisoners of war, but when they were liberated, the population of prisoners was more than 80,000, and this is where some of the cruellest activities of the Nazi SS happened.

They killed people as if they were killing wild animals, and we were shown the 'souvenirs' they made with shrunken heads of the prisoners. We also saw lampshades made of human skin. The SS killed prisoners in the most horrific ways. They used to make them work to their death, and thousands of prisoners died during the construction of a road leading from the foot of Ettersberg to the entry of the concentration camp, and as a result, prisoners ended up calling it 'Blood Street'. The SS killed many Soviet prisoners of war through lethal injections, and they used prisoners for medical experiments.

The tour through Buchenwald was so depressing that I could not eat that day, and I was heartbroken about what I had experienced. The way they were killed was so unimaginable, and I could not understand how another human being could have the guts to do that to another, but it was a lesson to me that you should never trust just anyone because people look so innocent from outside, but what they do privately is shocking.

Before we went to Buchenwald, I read a novel by Bruno Apitz, titled, *Naked Among Wolves*. The novel was based on the true story of a Polish prisoner who arrived at the concentration camp carrying a suitcase, which had a small Jewish boy inside. The Polish prisoner had this boy with him for some time and did not tell anyone about him, because he wanted to protect him from danger. The boy stayed in that suitcase until he was discovered by other prisoners who were working in the storage room. Those male prisoners endangered their lives by protecting the boy from the SS. The presence of the boy posed a threat to the inmates, especially those who were involved in the underground cells of the Communist Party mobilising inmates to join the resistance organisation. I cannot remember how many times I read the novel, but I did not believe what was written about Buchenwald until we visited the camp. It was very sad, indeed.

We continued with our studies, and after lectures on Historical Materialism, we started with the subject Dialectical Materialism, which we were taught by Genosse Otto. Otto looked older than Rudi, but they had a lot in common; they believed in communism, and both were members of the Communist Party for a very long time. He was married with three kids. After the introduction, the lecture started with Otto introducing the topic as one of the three components of Marxism. He elaborated by saying the following, "Dialectical materialism is the essential prerequisite to understanding the doctrine of Marxism. Dialectical materialism is the philosophy of Marxism, which provides us with a scientific and comprehensive world outlook. It is the method on which the whole of the Marxist doctrine is founded."

He continued by quoting Engels on dialectics when he said, "'Our best working tool and our sharpest weapon', and for us also, it is a guide to action and our activities within the working-class movement. It is similar to a compass or a map which allows us to get our bearings in the turmoil of events and permits us to understand the underlying processes that shape our world."

Otto then said, "Whether we believe it or not, or are conscious of it, or not, everyone has a philosophy." He also told us that philosophy is a way of looking at the world in its entirety, "Dialectical materialism explains the laws of evolution and change which see the world not as a complex of ready-made things, but as a complex of processes, which go through an uninterrupted transformation of coming into being and passing away."

That was a very complex topic to understand because besides the fact that we had to read many books written by Karl Marx, Friedrich Engels and Vladimir Lenin, I grew up knowing that God existed and that He was the Creator of heaven and earth, and now I was being told that the earth always existed and was not created by any supernatural being. For a moment I recalled a situation at school where we were taught that matter is "everything that has weight and occupies space", but according to dialectics, matter is a "continuous evolution towards the formulation of ever more complex beings like atoms, molecules, living cells, plants, men and society". Lenin explained matter as a "philosophical category serving to indicate objective reality". In essence, it meant that matter is not a product of the mind or consciousness, but the mind itself is the highest product of matter. Engels stated that "all ideas are taken from experience, are reflection – true or distorted – of reality". Marx reiterated this by saying that "life is not determined by consciousness, but consciousness by life".

To tell the truth, at first, I did not understand all these things. They did not make sense to me, and I found them to be very complex concepts, but through our informal discussions, I started to understand. Remember, I said in MK we moved with the pace of the slowest, but not of the laziest.

During weekends we were the only ones at the college because all the German students went home on Fridays and came back on Mondays. Although we had the liberty to go to town on our own, we still had to come back to a very quiet college. I used to go to the cinema (what we called the bioscope back then) to watch movies because at the college, we were not allowed to watch the channels of the 'West' because they were afraid that we would be indoctrinated. *Welcome Home* was one movie I really loved to watch. It was about a British prince who went to war and came back because he had injured his spine and was paralysed. He told his wife that she was at liberty to leave him because he was not going to be able to make love to her anymore due to his condition. The wife was adamant that she would not leave him, and after some time, she saw one of their employees who looked after the pigs, taking a shower. She suddenly felt attracted to him and made a move. She finally managed to convince the poor employee that he was doing the right thing by making love to her. At that stage, she was not aware that she was constantly being monitored by her husband. She fell pregnant and got the shock of her life when she saw her husband standing on his two legs and telling her that he knew about her infidelity. He then chased her away from the palace and fired the employee. What I learned from that movie was that a man will never forgive a woman her infidelity, but that a woman will forever protect and cover her husband's ill deeds.

Another movie I really liked was *How the Steel was Tempered*, based on a novel by Nikolai Ostrovsky. The novel was about one of the heroes of the October Revolution in Russia, Pavel Korchagin. He was a Bolshevik, and during the battle, he decided to be a determined steel soldier who believed that personal business must yield to the collective interest. It was during that time, after his arrests and torture, that he became paralysed and lost his eyesight, but because he was a determined man, he did not let all those things distract him. Instead, he took his pen and wrote about experiences in life and his stories inspired many people across the world. This story became my inspiration throughout my revolutionary life.

One Monday morning, we received the *Sechaba Journal*, and when I went through it, I saw Comrade Peter's photo and his obituary. I was devastated to read that he had passed away and according to the obituary he was involved in a motorbike accident with Comrade David Nkadimeng, and he (Peter) died instantly. I thought, *"God, Peter should have told me what he wanted to say before I left Angola,"* but on the other hand, maybe it was good that he did not tell me because as it was I felt so empty at that moment and maybe it would have been worse if I knew how he felt about me. My whole week was ruined, and the other comrades did not understand why I was so miserable. The worst part was that I could not say anything about Peter to anyone because I had never said anything to anyone about him. The other problem was that I was not going to be able to bury him because I was just too far from Angola and there was no way that I would be allowed to go and bury a comrade who was not my husband or relative. I tried to console myself that maybe we were not meant to be together and that maybe one day, I would meet a person who was meant for me. Deep down my heart, I knew that Peter was a good man.

We continued with our classes in Dialectical Materialism. Otto, in his lecture, told us that "the world is not only materialistic, but it is also dialectical". To clarify this, he quoted Engels in his book, *Anti-Duhring* when he said, "Dialectics is nothing more than a science of the general laws of motion and development of nature, human society and thought". My understanding was that "it should be obvious to us that the world is not static, everything in the world is always changing". That is why Engels said, "Motion is the mode of existence of matter. There has never been anywhere where there has been matter without motion, nor can there be". My understanding of the whole concept was that there is nothing in the world that is static; the earth itself is not static; therefore, it means death is inevitable. To me, this meant that everything on earth is changing, moving or developing, but if the change or development seizes to happen, that thing dies because there is no more development or movement.

Lenin said, "Dialectics is the teaching which shows how opposites can be and how they become identical - under what conditions they are identical, becoming transformed into one another – why the human mind should grasp these opposites not as dead, rigid, but living, conditional, mobile, becoming transformed into one another."

We also dealt with the unity of opposites where Otto explained that "the world is a unity of opposites or a unity of contradictions, e.g. where there is life there will also be death, things are positive or negative. The unity of opposite is that two opposing things can co-exist as long as their contradictions are non-antagonistic". He continued by saying that "motion, space and time are nothing else, but the mode of existence of matter, motion itself is a contradiction, and it is a unity of opposites". He quoted Hegel when he said, "Movement means to be in this place and not to be in it; this is continuity of space and time –and it is this which first makes motion possible."

Otto went on explaining the unity and struggle of opposites by saying that in Marxist philosophy, the unity and struggle of opposite is a fundamental methodological principle. He said that Lenin considered it important to investigate the unity and struggle of opposite as a law of cognition and a law of the objective world.

I thought I understood what Otto was saying, just to realise that I was very confused. It was when he started to explain these issues that I finally understood. He quoted Lenin, when he said, "*Dialectics* is the teaching which shows how *Opposites* can be and how they happen to be (how they become) *identical* – under what conditions they are identical, becoming transformed into one another – why the human mind should grasp these opposites not as dead, rigid, but as living, conditional, mobile, becoming transformed into one another." Otto continued dealing with the negation of the negation, and said, "Generally, historical development is not straight, but is a very complex interaction in which each step forward will only be achieved by moving a step backwards. The regression brings about development." I looked at him, and I think he realised that I was confused because he looked at me and said, "Ruth, you look confused, take it easy. You will understand why I am saying that." I just looked at him and smiled.

"There is a constant struggle between form and content and content and form, which results in the shattering of the old form and the transformation of the content."

My understanding was that the law of the negation of the negation explained the repetition of certain features at a higher level and properties of the lower level and the return of the past features. Otto then quoted Marx when he said, "The capitalist method of appropriation, which springs from the capitalist method of production, and therefore capitalist private property, is the first negation of individual private property based on one's own labour. However, capitalist production begets the inevitableness of a natural process its own negation. It is the negation of the negation".

I enjoyed staying in the GDR because we used to eat delicious food, especially pork, and for dessert I enjoyed fresh strawberry cake, which I still miss even today. We ate potatoes every day, and maybe I ate too much because I think that was the reason I gained weight even though we exercised. During our free time, we used to play table tennis, volleyball, and handball. Although the winter was freezing cold, I really enjoyed it. We played outside and created baby dolls from the snow and threw each other with snowballs. You know, what used to amaze me was that although most of the people in our class were far older than myself, they used to play with me and found it to be fun, especially Comrade Castro (Vic Hoho). We used to go for walks in town, and we would meet people from Libya, Palestine, Cuba, Russia, Egypt, and many other countries. Remember, in Arab countries, like Libya, Egypt, you find people with different complexions. There were those with a lighter complexion and those who were very dark, and most of them (who were very dark) were racist. During our stay in the GDR, they were the ones who would make funny comments about Africa. (As if they were not Africans?)

One day we went to a restaurant, and on arrival, we found Cubans, Mozambicans, Angolans and some Arabs. There were three of us, and we got a table just behind the Cubans. While we were waiting for a waiter, an Arab who looked Egyptian came to us and asked us in German, "Weist du nicht, wo Affen essen?" (Don't you know where monkeys eat?) I was shocked, and thought, *"Oh my gosh! No! He didn't just say that!"* I was so furious that I wanted to punch him, but before I could even look at him, he was already on the floor! I was confused as to who hit him until I saw a tall, black Cuban on top of him. It seemed as if the Cuban heard him insulting us, jumped over his table and clobbered him so hard that I could not see where the blood was coming from. After leaving the Arab on the floor, he came to us and asked, "Are you South Africans?"

"Yes," we said.

"My name is Fidel, and these are my comrades. We are from Cuba. Come and join us," he said.

We went and sat with them. After a brief introduction, they told us that the person was from Egypt and that he was very notorious for making other Africans feel out of place or inferior in Magdeburg, but he did not do it with Cubans and other people from Latin America.

This incident taught me that racism was an issue all over the world and that it does not matter what the social system is. We sat with the comrades from Cuba until past midnight, eating and listening to stories about the history and social life of their country. They told us that education was free and that Cuba also had free, and the best, medical services. Everyone had shelter, and the people (except for those who still wanted to go to the United States of America) were happy about the way the government, under the leadership of Comrade Fidel Castro, ran the country. The discussions were very interesting, especially when we looked at it from a working-class point of view.

One could see that the working class had taken their historical position to govern their own country and that they made sure that they controlled the means of production. Cuba was able to assist many liberation movements, including the ANC and the People's Movement for the Liberation of Angola (MPLA). We talked about the Cubans who were in Angola offering military and medical assistance. I was very impressed by the good work the Cubans were doing, and it was indeed the reflection of the international working class uniting against international imperialism. I must say that the discussions with the Cubans were very stimulating, and they gave me a new perspective in terms of the working class and their role in society.

Monday morning, we started with Political Economy, which Herbert presented. Herbert was a staunch member of the Communist Party; he was also part of Otto's group who joined the Communist Party just before the Second World War. He was a very dynamic individual with a sense of style in terms of fashion. I used to look at him in his jeans and beautiful T-shirts, and the only problem was that he could not speak English at all. Maybe he was pretending?

He told us that he was not going to talk much about other issues because they were covered by lectures on Historical and Dialectical Materialism. He continued by saying that Political Economy was one of the sources and components of Marxism. He quoted Karl Marx in *Das Capital*, volume one, when he said, "By classical political economy, I understand that economy which, since the time of W. Petty, has investigated the real relations of production in the bourgeois society, in contradistinction to vulgar economy, which deals with appearances only, ruminates without ceasing on the materials long since provided by scientific economy, and there seeks plausible explanations of the most obtrusive phenomena, for bourgeois daily use. But for the rest confines itself to systematising in a pedantic way, and proclaiming for everlasting truths, trite ideas held by self-complacent bourgeois with regard to their own world, to them the best of all possible worlds".

Herbert continued by talking about the relationship between labour and capital: "The labourer sells his labour to the capitalist who then gives him a subsistence allowance which is going to sustain the labourer for that period, and he will be forced to come back to the capitalist to work because he needs to survive – not only him but with the rest of his family." He also said that "the relationship between the labour-power and capital is not a homogenous one because the rise in wages presupposes a rapid growth of productive capital and the rapid growth of productive capital leads to the growth of wealth which in turn leads to social pleasures and enjoying all sort of luxuries. Although the labourer seems to enjoy all the luxuries, he is far from enjoying what the capitalist is enjoying. Therefore, you cannot compare the two because the labourer does not own the means of production, but the capitalist does".

Political Economy was also very interesting, especially when one looked at how the workers were being exploited by the bourgeois. To stress his point, Hebert took us to factories around Magdeburg and Dresden, just to see how the labour was organised in a socialist country. The problem with this was that I had never been to a factory and did not know what to expect, but thought it would be interesting just to see how they did it.

Amazingly enough, the people who were working in those factories were young people. We were told that most of them were struggling academically and they were taken to vocational colleges and actually made it there. I found it fascinating because I remembered back at home where a friend failed grade two six times. No one thought that she might have a learning problem, and they just let her repeat the same class year after year instead of taking her to a vocational school or something like that. These outings helped us to understand socialism as a system that had the interest of the working class at heart.

Besides excursions, we were able to see how the people of the GDR enjoyed life. Most of the people did not have cars, but public transport was readily available, and no one had to stand at the bus terminal for more than five minutes without getting transport. There was transport going to town and back every five minutes, and as a result, you would think that it was not necessary to have a car. I really admired the government of that country.

One day we were playing table tennis with some German students, and it just happened that our course leader was also there. As I was waiting for my turn, I saw him laughing and wondered why but did not ask him. Some Tanzanian fellows were conversing in Kiswahili, and I do not know what they were talking about, but they were laughing, and they seemed to be enjoying whatever they said to each other. I realised that King was laughing at what they were saying and looked at him and asked, "I know you know Kiswahili, why are you hiding that?"

"Ruth, don't ever tell anyone about it! Look, I stayed in Tanzania for more than ten years as an operative, so I know Kiswahili, but I do not want them to know that because if they know they will never use Kiswahili and if that is the case, we will not be able to know what they are saying. So, please do not tell anyone about this conversation, do you understand?" he asked, and I told him that I understood. That day I learned something which I still use: If you arrive in a foreign country or at a place where they speak a language that you know, it will not hurt to pretend as if you do not know the language. By doing this, you can operate smoothly without being detected.

Herbert, in continuing with Political Economy, said that Marx explained that "Political Economy came into being as a natural result of the expansion of trade, and with its appearance elementary, unscientific huckstering was replaced by a developed system of licensed fraud, an entire science of enrichment". He continued by saying that Marx was excellent in understanding Political Economy, in fact, he was an economist himself, and that is why he was in the position to explain in detail how the proletariat was being exploited by the bourgeois.

He talked about Marx's book, *A Contribution to the Critique of Political Economy* where Marx said, "In the social production of their existence, men inevitably enter into definite relations, which are independent of their will, namely, relations of production appropriate to a given stage in the development of their material forces of production. The totality of these relations of production constitutes the economic structure of society, the real foundation, on which arises a legal and political superstructure and to which correspond definite forms of social consciousness. The mode of production of material life conditions, the general process of social, political and intellectual life. It is not the consciousness of men that determined the existence, but their social existence that determines their consciousness".

This subject was very interesting because it showed the relationship between labour and capital and how the capitalists made a profit. It also intended to show the importance of the working-class struggle against exploitation. South Africa had a unique situation because the working class did not only struggle against exploitation but also against oppression. The working class was divided according to race, and because of this, the majority of the white working-class could not participate in the class struggle because they felt they were better off than their black counterparts. The colonialism in South Africa was special because the oppressor and the oppressed were living in the same country, unlike other countries where the colonisers lived in their countries of origin.

The course was almost coming to an end, and we were preparing to go back home. I must say that I really enjoyed my stay in the GDR. Yes, I sometimes felt nostalgic, but the strange thing is that I never missed my family in South Africa; I missed Angola and my comrades there more. I remember that there was a stage during which I was eating nice food, and I would always think of them. I know we were provided with food in Angola, but there were no chocolates, cakes, puddings, etc. and here I could eat what I wanted to eat.

After our farewell party, we were taken to the airport, and for some reason, I started crying. Everybody was concerned about me, but I just could not explain myself. I remember Comrade Castro saying, "Shame, she is crying for the good food that she will never taste again." Everybody laughed. We flew out of East Berlin around 18:00 pm that night, and I must say that it was a very long flight back to Angola.

THIRTEEN

A taste of the battlefield

WE ARRIVED IN LUANDA during the early hours of the morning and Comrade Spokes, who was the driver in Luanda, fetched us from the airport. He drove us to Vienna, where the chief of staff, Comrade Richard, welcomed us. The commander of Vienna allocated places to each one of us, and I had to share a tent with two female comrades. They told me that they trained in 1978 and that they were on their way to Lusaka. According to them, they were in Vienna for two months already, and they were worried when they would leave Luanda. While they were telling me this, I became concerned about my own situation. I liked Vienna, but just the thought of staying there for two months made me feel a little bit uncomfortable. My ambition was not to stay in Vienna; I wanted to go to the front to fight as soon as I could. I think this was a sentiment of every 'guerrilla'.

The next morning, we woke up and went to the formation where we were given tasks for the day. As I was busy with my tasks, I heard someone calling my name, and when I looked up, I saw my Romeo from the camp. He rushed to me and gave me a warm hug; I must say I was happy to see him again after such a long time, but remember, it was not like before, because when I left the camp, we had drifted apart even though we did not say it was over between us.

Maybe this was a chance to mend the relationship? I was not enthusiastic about it anymore, but maybe time would tell. He assisted me with my chores, which was to clean around the swimming pool. We quickly finished the job and sat under the mango trees trying to catch up. My Romeo told me that he just got circumcised, which shocked me because all along I thought he was circumcised! I guess it was my ignorance of some of those things ...

For some reason, I asked him what led him to circumcise, and in response, he said he contracted a venereal disease from one of the female comrades I knew. The sore was so septic, and he was advised to circumcise. When he told me that story, I felt that he was still a womaniser who would never change. I immediately lost interest, and I told him that it was over between us. I left him there to join Noxolo who was sitting at the kitchen with some comrades.

That evening, Noxolo called me from the swimming pool where I was playing table tennis to tell me that Current was looking for me. After two games, I went to meet with him in one of the tents. I was happy to see him, and something in him looked different from before. He looked happy and content; he was his old self, the charmer. We sat down and talked about everything from politics to social things, but not about the two of us.

As we were talking, we heard a knock, and without waiting for a response, the person came into the tent. Remember, there was no electricity in the tents, so we used diesel lamps, which made the tent dimmer. I only realised who it was when he greeted us.

"Comrade Ruth, I was looking for you and was told that you were here. Comrade Current, as you know, Comrade Ruth is my girlfriend, and I love her very much. Yes, we had some problems, but I'm prepared to sort them out with her. I want her back because she means everything to me, and you know that. I don't think I can live without her, and I know she feels the same. She even bought me shoes from the GDR," my Romeo from the camp said. I was furious at him for declaring his love for me in this manner, especially after he had told me about his infidelities just hours ago. I looked at Current and then at this comrade and I did not know what to say. We were quiet, and you could feel the tension in the tent until Current decided to say something which really took me by surprise, "Comrade, I understand what you are saying, but remember that we are now in Luanda and I am now a trained soldier. You are not my instructor anymore so I can say whatever I want to say to you. You took my girlfriend because you had time on your side of which I did not have because of training, but today we are on equal grounds. I am not going to listen to you, now or ever."

I did not say anything because I knew in my heart that I did not love any of them for the hurt they both caused me.

"Let her choose who she wants between us," my Romeo said.

"I do not want any of you. Both of you have equally hurt me so I can be friends with you and nothing more," I said and left the tent, leaving both behind. I was happy and proud of myself for ultimately closing that chapter of my life with the two men I thought I loved.

The day seemed to be very long because Noxolo and I were very eager to leave Angola after we received information that the South African Congress of Trade Unions (SACTU) had arranged for us to operate from Lesotho. This was really a surprise, but we played it very cool because we had learned that in MK, one plus one does not always equal two and that things could change at any time. What made me happy was the fact that at least someone still remembered us!

After a week in Vienna, I was asked to work with a team of comrades who were broadcasting for Radio Freedom. My task was to broadcast in Sesotho for viewers at home. The experience was overwhelming because I worked with the most intelligent and dynamic comrades. One of them was Comrade Diliza, whom I got to know personally. He had worked in the office of the late President OR Tambo, the Tiger himself. I understood that he was at a certain stage responsible for writing his speeches, but I really did not know the reasons that brought him back to Angola. Diliza was a soft-spoken and down to earth comrade; I do not remember him saying anything about himself, and he always had praise for others.

I spent every day with this energetic and gifted team of comrades, who assisted me in growing politically, and strengthened what I learned in the GDR. Comrade Reggie Mpongo was responsible for my slot, which was at 16:00 pm, but throughout the day, Comrades Diliza, Zama and Bhekimpi would coach me on presentation skills and work on my confidence. They taught me the skills to convince my listeners in understanding the purpose and the objective of the liberation struggle. I must say this was a mammoth task for them because for a long time I convinced myself that I was a shy person, so they had to unlock that part of me, and help me believe in myself and gain confidence.

Comrades Christina and Busi were also part of the team. Both comrades were kind, caring and non-assuming, and I learned a lot from them by listening to their presentations on air. Chrissie, as I called her, was confident and extroverted and displayed more political maturity and dynamism. She would engage those male comrades as her equals, and her analogy was out of this world. I really admired her, and I wish we could meet again so that I could tell her that she was my inspiration. I really enjoyed working at Radio Freedom, although at that stage I felt I was not confident enough, but everybody else was saying I was doing well. I wish I could go back and listen to my presentations so that I could hear how I fulfilled my task on the radio.

We would go back to Vienna every evening, and unfortunately, as part of the staff, we would be on guard duty. One night I was on guard doing the 20:00 pm to 22:00 pm shift while posted at the back of the camp near the pigsty. It was very dark and scary, and you could only hear the noise of the pigs (Oink! Oink!) which were irritating and frustrating because it was easy to mistake that noise with the noise that is made by the wild pigs. As I was standing there listening to those pigs, I think I fell asleep because I just heard somebody saying, "You are sleeping on duty; I'm going to punish you!" I opened my eyes and saw Comrade Super, who was the officer on duty (OD), standing beside me looking very angry. I told him that I was actually thinking and not sleeping, but he just looked at me and left without saying a word. I understood why he was angry; sleeping on duty was a serious offence in MK because the lives of all the comrades in the camp depended on you. Therefore, it was expected of you to be very vigilant during guard duty because scientifically, it was said that a person could only concentrate and exercise vigilance for two hours at a time.

I was now wide-awake because I did not want to get into trouble again. I was just waiting to go off duty so that I could rest before I resumed my duty at 2:00 am to 4:00 am the next morning. For me, being on guard duty was the time I used to reflect on things I did during the day, whether right or wrong. It was a time of introspection, especially about what I wanted to be and where I wanted to be in a year's time. I would think about the things I had done wrong and how to remedy the situation. During this time, I also thought about the positive things I had done and how I could improve on it.

As I was standing there dreaming about my future, I did not even realise that it was already 22:00 pm, and just saw the person who was to relieve me standing in front of me. I just gave him the tactical security situation, wished him luck, and left. I went straight to my tent and fell asleep immediately. At 2:00 am, the officer on duty came to fetch me for my guard duty, and I went to the same post near the pigsty where the OD left me without saying anything. When he left, I just stood there thinking about my own things like going to the front to fight the enemy. I do not know how long I stood there thinking when suddenly I heard footsteps, and as I looked behind me, I realised that it was the OD. I just looked at him and turned back to where I was standing without saying anything. He followed me and stood beside me, saying nothing. After a while, I heard him saying, "If you make a noise, I am going to kill you." I looked at him, saw an AK-47 hanging from his shoulder, and thought, *"My God, not again!"* I tried to be cool and pretended as if I did not hear him. This guy was tall and tough; my height was then 1.72 m, and he was about 1.80 m, and I could not fight him. From the moment he threatened me, I was thinking about a lot of possibilities that would get me out of this situation.

As I was thinking, he grabbed me by my neck with his two hands, choked me and I struggled to breathe. As I was gasping for air, he let free his other hand and started to unzip my trousers, but his other hand was still on my throat, and the grip was very strong. He loosened my belt, pulled down my trousers, and let go of his other hand. As I was trying to breathe, he pushed me on the ground and raped me.

He was so rough and did it with such vengeance as if I owed him something. This person was like a wild animal; he was so angry, and I could not understand why because I had never seen such anger in my life. After he was done, he helped me to my feet, pulled up my trousers, and left without saying a word. I stood there not knowing what to do next, and while I was still deciding, he came back. I thought he was coming back for some more, but to my surprise, he said, "Go and sleep. I will stand for you." I left my post and went straight to my tent. There, I just went straight to my bed. I laid there thinking about what had just happened. My predicament was that although I wanted to report him, I did not know if the comrades will believe me or think I'm a counterrevolutionary who wanted to destroy another comrade. I did not know what to do and slept without thinking much about it because it seemed that the curse followed wherever I went ...

I was woken up by Nompumelelo who told me it was time for the roll call. I felt a sharp pain in my private parts, and I thought I could not go to the roll call like that. I asked Mpumi to report to the OD that I was not feeling well. That day I did not go to work because I was nursing my bruised private parts and ego. I felt so down, and I did not know what to do. I just slept the whole day. When I woke in the afternoon, Mpumi told me that the bastard came looking for me, but she told him that I was asleep, and she was not going to wake me up. He promised to come back. I thought, *"Thank God Mpumi did not wake me up,"* because I did not know how I would have reacted seeing him after what he did to me. For a week, I was not able to go to work because for some reason, I was feeling very tired, and I had terrible stomach pains, which I could not explain. I went to the clinic, and the diagnosis given by the medical officer was that I had peptic ulcers. He gave me some antacid tablets and told me that I had to relax and that everything would be fine. I tried to relax as much as I could, so I spend almost all my time reading books on class struggle, and the journals *Dawn* and *Sechaba*.

I remember there were articles in those two journals written by dynamic comrades and intellectuals of our struggle who included Comrade 'Mzala' (Jabulani Nxumalo), who wrote several articles using names like Sisa Majola or Khumalo (May his soul rest in peace), Klaus Maphepha, ANC Khumalo and Peter Mayibuye to mention just a few.

During that time, I compared what I had learned from the party school, arguments in the articles, and the objective situation inside the country. I then realised that South Africa would never be a socialist country – at least not in my lifetime – because I realised that the country was slowly, but surely, developing into an imperialist country where the monopoly of the economy was in the hands of only a few. I also thought of the possibility of the development of the black bourgeois in the country because of the very nature of capitalism of divide and rule.

In my mind, developing the black bourgeois was the only way to divide our people further. Although the black bourgeois would not be in the majority, and they would not own the majority of the means of production in our country, they would not be part of the working class either. Therefore, they would not engage themselves in the struggle against exploitation, but they might fight against discrimination in business to secure their individual interests or even use the workers to fight their battles against the monopoly capitalists exploiting the race card.

During this period, I was really focusing and reflecting on my purpose in life and most importantly, my purpose in the struggle. I did not want to dwell much on what had happened to me. I thought I must concentrate on things that are more positive and I actually decided that I was going back to Radio Freedom and put my ideas forth and I knew that the comrades were going to assist me in being what I wanted to be. For some reason, when I thought of becoming something in MK, I always thought I wanted to be like Comrade Klaus Maphepha; politically powerful, yet humble.

Comrade Itumeleng requested me to be a bodyguard for Comrade Gertrude Shope, who was coming to Angola for the celebrations of Women's Day. I agreed, and he gave me a 9 mm pistol and a combat to be ready to be the bodyguard of a very powerful woman of our liberation struggle. I was supposed to be with her 24/7 to make sure that she was safe. This was really an incredible time because I felt that by protecting one of our leaders, I was doing something very special. For some reason, we had many things to discuss with Mme Ma-Shope, including politics and sports, and she even asked me who my boyfriend was, which was embarrassing.

During her stay in Angola, she visited several camps, and I accompanied her and some of the comrades, including Current, who was working at Res One at that stage. We spent a lot of time together, but we never discussed our feelings for each other; we only talked about the political situation inside the country and the international situation, which I really enjoyed.

After Ma-Shope's departure, I again kept to myself until one day, on my way from the toilet, I met a certain comrade who was tall, dark, and handsome. As I was about to pass him, he said, "Excuse me, comrade, may I talk to you for a minute?" I stood there, mesmerised by his wonderful, hoarse voice. I turned and looked at him; he was standing there with a killer smile, and I thought to myself, "*Where does he come from being so handsome and so humble?*" He looked at me and said, "My name is AB, and I am from Pango Camp. We arrived yesterday afternoon, and I think I will be here for some time. Is it possible for me to see you later today?"

In my heart, I knew I wanted to say yes, but something inside me was refusing, and I stuttered something that I, myself, could not even understand. As a result, he had to come closer to me so that he could hear what I was saying. As he came closer, I could feel his heartbeat and his trembling hands as he touched mine. What I felt made me feel so uneasy, but at the same time it felt very good, I just wished that the feeling would never stop. He said something to me that I did not hear, so I had to get closer to him to hear what he was saying. As I got closer to him, the more I felt something like electrical shocks running all over my body!

As I was still enjoying the feeling, I heard a very warm, hoarse voice saying, "Are you able to see me later today?"

I looked at him and said, "I am definitely going to see you today." I left him standing there, and when I looked back at him, I found him looking at me with a broad smile on his face. I waved him goodbye and went into my tent.

I just lay on my bed thinking about this person and the overwhelming feelings I had while standing beside him. The other thing that baffled me was the extent of pain that I felt in my abdomen when I was near him. I felt this sharp pain, which I thought was part of the electric shock I felt when he was whispering some 'words of wisdom' to me. For some reason, the pain was still there, but not as acute as before. At that moment, my only wish was to have this pain gone before meeting with Comrade AB, as I called him.

It was 16:30 pm and time to meet Comrade AB just outside my tent. I went outside and there he was, standing by the swimming pool, which was directly opposite my tent. I went straight to him and sat next to him. After the greetings, he said to me, "The reason I wanted to see you is that when I saw you yesterday, I felt something inside me, but I could not approach you there and then. I thought I would get an opportunity to meet you in person and talk to you. Just to be honest with you, I love you, and I do not have any other way to say this. Please make me part of your life; I can do everything to make you happy. I do not want to say to you I want to marry you now, but I am sure if you agree to be mine, everything will fall in place as time goes by. Please tell me you love me too."

I looked at him, and I could see his eyes were wet as if he was crying, and before I could say anything, I saw tears rolling from his eyes. It was the first time I experienced such emotions from a man who was declaring his undying love for me, and I must say that I was touched.

Although I felt the urge to touch his hand, I just could not bring myself to do it because of what happened to me.

After the last rape, I did not want to be touched or touch anyone, and for some reason, I thought it was for my own protection. I just ended up saying, "I am so sorry. I cannot have a relationship with you. I think you are a wonderful man and you deserve better. I do not think I am good enough for you. Please look around – I am sure you will get somebody you deserve." As I was saying this, I was hurting inside because I looked at this comrade and I thought he was too good for me. He deserved a person with no rape baggage; someone still 'pure'. You know, I felt that I had lost the power to make decisions, and I think this feeling came from the experience of repeatedly being violated.

At that stage, I was experiencing extreme disrespect for my wishes and feelings, and I felt that my feelings and wishes were not important anymore. There is no sane man who would decide to have a woman who was raped four times in her life as his lover, or wife, for that matter. *"What good will come out of that relationship?"* I thought. We looked at each other without saying anything. Fortunately, it was time for supper, so we had to go to the formation without concluding our discussion. As I stood at the formation, I was thinking about this man, and I knew that I loved him more than I wanted to admit. I decided that I would tell him how I felt and stop putting my life on hold because of my insecurities. I felt I wanted to take charge of my life and put all the negative feelings behind me by telling AB that I was ready to be his girlfriend.

During supper, he came to sit with me but said nothing until we had finished our food. "Ruth, please love me, I do not want anything else from you, and I promise I will never hurt you, ever," he said. I looked at him and said, "I love you too."

"What are you saying? Do you love me?"

"Yes, I love you!" He held my hand very tightly and pulled me towards him, saying, "And thank you for loving me. I promise I will be true to you until I die, and this is a promise I am making to you today." I looked at him and felt contented. I responded by giving him a hug, for which he kissed me with such passion that I ended up feeling very dizzy and overwhelmed. We were now an item. The love we felt for each was real; no one and nothing would come between us, and I think that had been the problem with me. If I am in love with a person, I give that relationship my all. I am one hundred percent in the relationship, and my mistake has always been that if I am one hundred percent in a relationship, I expect my partner to be in that relationship one hundred percent too. I realised later in my life that I was not realistic in terms of how most people perceive relationships.

The majority of men can be so much in love with a woman, but they will have another one. This really confused me for a long time. I was happy with AB because he was a very opened-minded person with a sense of humour. He was my pillar of strength during those trying times. I do not know what I would have done without him.

***

I was in my tent when I heard a bell ringing. I rushed to the formation and found other comrades already there, just waiting for the next order. We stood there wondering as to what was happening because it was 10:30 am in the morning.

"ATTENTION! About turn! Eyes front," I heard the chief of staff's voice coming from behind. Comrade Commander, the company is ready and waiting for your next order. Five comrades are sick, and eight comrades are on guard duty."

"Good morning, comrades," said Comrade Bra T.

"Good morning, Comrade Commander," we responded.

"COMPANY, ATTENTION! Eyes front! Comrade Army Commander, the company is ready and waiting for your next order. All comrades have reported to the formation except for five comrades who are sick and eight comrades are on guard duties."

"AT EASE COMRADES," the late Comrade Joe Modise responded.

"AT EASE COMRADES," said Comrade Commander Timothy Mokoena.

"Amandla," said the army commander.

"Nga wethu we," responded.

"Comrades, it gives me pleasure to see how quickly you respond to emergencies. I must say it is reflective of our combat readiness. Comrades, I want all of us to be always combat-ready because we do not know what the enemy is planning at this moment. You ought to know that the UNITA (National Union for the Total Liberation of Angola) bandits have moved from the southern part of Angola to the eastern part, and that is an indication that MK might be the focus of the enemy at this stage because comrades, as you all know, we have a training camp in the east. Therefore, it means that as the enemy advances towards Malanje town, it is inevitable that we are going to be the target in that area. I've got a list of names here, and I want everyone who is on the list to come forward and stand in front."

By now I was wondering what was happening, and I was really praying that my name should be on the list because for some reason I thought the list would be for comrades who were going home.

"Ruth Mantile."

"Ja." That was how we were expected to respond. I went to the front wondering what was next, but I was convinced that I was going home for a mission. Although I was convinced that I was on my way home, I was also worried that Noxolo was not on the list with me and I was wondering what would happen if I went to the country alone without her. The only female who was with me on the list was Joyce Mudau, who was part of the group of comrades who attended the party school in East Germany before us.

"Comrades, you must all get your combats and your weapons with ammunition and be ready by 13:00 pm, when we will be moving from this camp. Comrade Commander, take over," instructed the army commander.

"Company, attention!" said Comrade Bra T. When the commander had left, Bra T shouted, "AT EASE!" Then we stood at ease.

"Comrades. I am going to dismiss you, but just make sure that you have all you need for the war situation. I want each one of you who is on the list to be ready by 12:45 pm when I ring the combat bell. We are leaving at 13:00 pm. Do we understand each other?"

"Yes, Comrade Commander," we said, and the company was dismissed.

After we were dismissed, I did not know where to start looking for military gear. While I was still wondering Comrade Mbuso (Pule Wesi), whom I was engaged to years later (May his soul rest in peace), brought me a full uniform and a nap-sack.

"Take this and put it on, you should be ready by 12:45 pm. Listen, I expect you to do your best in the battle. Be disciplined and exercise vigilance all the time. Remember, you are there to ensure that the people of South Africa and Africa are free from all kinds of exploitation and oppression of the South African regime. Make me and our people proud." He shook my hand and left me standing there, not knowing what to say. As I was standing there, comrades came and told me how proud they were, and wished me well.

AB came running to me and gave me a big hug and a passionate kiss. I was so excited knowing that I would be with him on this mission. "Chunku," as he used to call me, "I understand that you together with Joyce, Bra T and a few commanders will be flying to Malanje, and we will be driving from here tomorrow morning. I think we will be together by tomorrow evening," he said.

I felt a little bit disappointed, but I did not want to show him how I really felt. As he was talking, it dawned on me that we were not going home, but to Malanje to protect our camps against the UNITA bandits who were now targeting the eastern part of Angola. I looked at him and felt that sharp pain in my abdomen, which I usually felt when I was with him.

I almost knelt because it was so unbearable. "Chunku, what's wrong? Did I say something that upset you?" he asked while holding my hand. I just shook my head and held his hand tight, and we walked to my tent without saying anything to each other. The pain was still there, but not so severe anymore. We were still relaxing when the bell rang; we kissed each other and ran to the formation.

"Company, attention!" Commanded Bra T said. We stood at attention.

"AT EASE!" he said.

"All the comrades who are not on the list: dismissed," he commanded, and all the comrades who were not on the list dispersed. We just stood there waiting for the next order.

"Comrades, as you all stand here, you must know that you are going to the east to assist FAPLA (People's Armed Forces for the Liberation of Angola) and MPLA to fight and drive out the UNITA bandits who are now occupying some strategic position in the east. Our intelligence reported that Battalion 32 is with the UNITA units in the east. Therefore, it is imperative now than ever before that we should come together as revolutionary forces and fight the enemy together. Comrades, we are going to leave Luanda today, and by tomorrow evening all of us should be in Malanje ready for deployment," he said.

"Attention! Comrade Chief of Staff, take over," he said.

"Attention! Dismissed," the chief of staff said.

"Comrades Ruth and Joyce, come here please," he then said.

We turned around and went to him. We saluted, and he said, "If you are ready, just go and get your things and wait here for the vehicle that is going to take you to the airport for a helicopter that is taking to you to Malanje."

We arrived at the airport, and I was still confused by the whole thing. The worst part was that Joyce and I were not acquaintances, so we did not have much to say to each other. We stood there waiting and finally got into the Russian helicopter with two Russian pilots, the late Comrades Rogers Nkadimeng, 'Mthakathi' (May their souls rest in peace), and Comrade Lennox.

The take-off was okay, but it was so uncomfortable in there that I just wished for a safe and speedy flight to Malanje. We had ammunition in big boxes and food. There wasn't much space left in the helicopter, and you couldn't even stretch your legs. I was really uncomfortable, and I made a decision that from that day I would never use a helicopter in my life again.

The landing was swift, and I felt happy to have landed safely in Malanje. We disembarked, and the People's Liberation Army of Namibia (PLAN) forces welcomed us at the airport. After military formalities, we all got into a Land Rover that was waiting for us. We left the airport and went straight to our residence in Malanje, where we were given food. After eating, we sat around the residence listening to music and just relaxing. So far, the briefing was that we were waiting for the comrades who were driving to Malanje and who were expected to arrive by 18:00 pm.

Feelings of boredom and anxiety had cast their shadow over me because I did not know what was going to happen when the trucks arrived and whether we were going straight to the camp or were going to sleep at the residence, which seemed to be impossible because of the number of comrades who were expected. The only option was to go to Caculama camp, sleep there and wait for the next order. As I was thinking about the possibilities, one truck arrived, driven by Comrade Mafela, a very handsome and humorous comrade. (May his soul rest in peace.) He arrived with only a few comrades because his truck was loaded with ammunition, food and weapons. I was so disappointed because I thought AB would be in that truck. Mafela told me that they were on their way, and he had sent his love. I do not know if he thought he was consoling me by telling me that, but anyway, I was happy to know that he was actually thinking about me.

"Comrade Ruth, Ben and I are going to visit a certain Angolan family, do you mind joining us?" Comrade Mafela asked.

"It is fine, I don't mind," I said. Comrade Ben was one of the two comrades who were responsible for the residence in Malanje, so it meant that he had made many friends around the residence. We walked two streets from our residence and arrived at a house, which had a beautiful garden. We knocked, and the door was opened by a young, lovely couple, who welcomed us. Fortunately, they could speak English, which made me comfortable. The wife offered us drinks and food, which comprised of chicken stew and what looked like pap, but was not as white as our pap in South Africa, because it looked brown. I looked at it, and I think Comrades Ben and Mafela realised that I was a bit disturbed by the colour. They reassured me that the pap was fine and that it was brown because it was made of cassava and not maize meal.

I started eating, and I somehow enjoyed the meal. Although it was different from what we ate in the camps, it was palatable. After the meal, more beers were brought, and I could see that the comrades were enjoying themselves. I felt relaxed because it was my first time having close contact with Angolans, and I must say it brought another perspective of how I looked at them. Before this encounter, I looked at them as unfriendly people, but that night, I realised that they were not different from us. We stayed there until at 21:00 pm, and we said our goodbyes and left for our residence.

On our arrival, I was told that we had to go and sleep at the camp because it was not safe at the residence. We left for the camp and Joy went with us. At night the camp looked and felt strange. The place was no longer the same, even though I knew it for more than two years. All the memories of this camp came rushing into my head, but there was no physical reflection of those memories. The place had changed; it was no more the bush I was used to, no smell of potatoes, which indicated that there were pythons nearby.

Anyway, I slept without any incident, and the next morning, I took a bath and went for breakfast. I realised that there were still comrades I knew. I must mention though that many comrades had left the camp. I was very happy to see familiar faces, but I felt deep in my heart that this was not the place for me. It was as if I knew what was coming. We were talking with some of the comrades when I was called by the camp's commander, Comrade Sipho. After the usual military protocols, he told me that I was appointed the commissar for the 'mzana' in the camp. I was very shocked and told him there and then that there was no way I was going to stay in the camp, especially because that was not the reason I was in the camp in the first place. I requested him to speak to Comrade Chris Hani (May his soul rest in peace) because I was there as part of the comrades who were going to the Eastern Front not based at the camp. I told him that if he wanted me at the camp, he should have made it known before I was selected to go to the east. Comrade Sipho just looked at me, laughed, and said, "You haven't changed a bit; you are still as stubborn. Let's wait for Comrade Chris, who will be here at 10:00 am. Ruth, please, I want you here, and I am going to make sure that you stay. Go to your dwelling, and I will call for you when he arrives."

All I could say was "Thank you."

As I was leaving the administration, I met some comrades who were very happy to see me. We stood there talking about the political situation at home and the developments in international politics. Our focus, of course, was the role of America, especially the Central Intelligence Agency (CIA) in Southern Africa. While we were debating these issues, we heard, "ATTENTION! Eyes front!"

We all stood at attention, not knowing who just arrived at the camp. We were more excited than surprised to see Comrade Chris, especially me because I last saw him in Lesotho in 1981. After all the military protocols, he started going around shaking hands with comrades. He finally came around where I was standing, and in my heart, I thought he would not recognise me, but to my surprise, he looked at me, shook my hand and said, "Mpoetsi, is it you; you have grown so much since I last saw you. How are you doing?"

I was so embarrassed that he actually remembered me and used my real name; fortunately, I realised that the comrades who were with me did not pick up the name. Comrade Chris held my hand and asked me how I was doing, but now more in private. I told him that I had just returned from party school and I was one of the comrades who were selected to come to the Eastern Front, but I was just told that I must stay at the camp to be the commissar of Mzana and I was not prepared to stay in the camp. Comrade Chris promised to go and speak to the camp commander about this, and he continued by saying, "Mpoetsi, I was talking to Comrade Gazi in Lusaka, and he told me that you and Xolelwa are going to be deployed in Lesotho by SACTU. Your mission there will be to create political cells and mobilise the workers inside the country from Lesotho. Are you aware of that?"

"Yes, Comrade Chris, I have been briefed by Xolelwa. We are still waiting for an order," I said.

"That is fine, we shall talk again," Comrade Chris said, and he went with Bra T and the camp commander to the HQ of the camp.

After my talk with Comrade Chris, I went to my dwelling to pack my things because I knew I was not going to stay in the camp. I must say I did not have a problem staying in the camp per se, but my problem was that one had to be psychologically prepared to stay, and not 'ambushed' into it. Deployment in the camp might be for two months, one year or for a lifetime; thus, it needed some form of preparedness, which I did not have at that stage.

The other issue, which concerned to me, was the fact that I was going to be the commissar for Mzana only. Not even platoon commissar for that matter, meaning that I would stay in the camp and be responsible for females and their issues. To me, that was not appealing, and I knew I was too smart to be stuck in the camp dealing with such issues.

The dilemma I was in actually reminded me of the president's speech during the Women's Day celebration 1981 in Angola. President OR Tambo said, *"Women in the ANC should stop behaving as if there was no place for them above the level of certain categories of involvement. They have a duty to liberate us men from antique concepts and attitudes about the place and role of women in society and in the development and direction of our revolutionary struggle"*.

I felt like those women who needed to prove to their male counterparts that we were more capable of doing whatever men could do to liberate our country. Therefore, I decided there and then that I was not going to be pushed to stay in the camp, especially in that position.

As I was packing my clothes, I heard a knock, and as I was approaching the entrance, I saw AB standing there. I was so excited to see him after what seemed to me like a month. He got inside and gave me a very passionate and warm hug. There was no explanation for what we felt for each other; it was out of this world. We clung to each other as if our hearts and souls were intertwined; unfortunately, we were rudely interrupted by a knock. (Don't you just hate it when that happens?)

"Comrade Ruth, the OD has sent for you," the person said.

"Thank you, comrade, I am on my way," I said, giggling like a teenager. We held each other and kissed before we went to see the OD, who was one of the comrades I trained with. We greeted each other, and he told me that the camp commander wanted to see me. I thanked him and went to see Comrade Sipho. I saluted him, and he let me in his dwelling while AB stood outside.

"Comrade Ruth, you have won for now, but I am telling you that in two months you will be back here as commissar for Mzana. You can go and fetch your luggage; your transport will be waiting for you. Good luck," he said.

I thanked him and left his dwelling with a lot of excitement. I reached for AB's hand and went back to the dwelling. I took my luggage, and we went back to the guardhouse where the Land Rover 110 was waiting for me. We kissed and said our goodbyes with the belief that we were going to meet again soon.

We drove through Malanje and left it far behind until we reached Cacuso. The town not only looked weird and spooky, it felt that way, and for some reason, I was not comfortable. We arrived at a residence, which was to be our HQ where the military commanders stayed. After the formalities, we were taken to where we were going to stay, which happened to be caravans, which were just about five hundred metres from our HQ.

Each of us had a room which was furnished with a bed, fridge and some kind of wardrobe. The toilet was outside the caravans, almost one hundred metres away. The place was relatively comfortable, and the arrangement was that we would eat at the camp, which was about five hundred metres from the caravans. Everything was organised in such a way that we would have ample time to respond to any emergency.

We unpacked our clothes and walked to the camp, just to do some scanning of the place. As we were walking back, we met our trucks full of comrades, which really felt better because when we arrived, we were so few and I think it was because of that, that I felt scared. As the comrades were disembarking from the trucks, we realised that there were two additional females in the group and that was Comrade Caroline (my friend from Caculama) and Comrade Dimakatso, who became my friend and partner in the Eastern Front.

We immediately took the two comrades to our place, and we organised two other beds for them. I shared with Dimakatso and Joyce shared with Caroline. We made ourselves comfortable as much as we could. After we cleaned and made ourselves comfortable, it was time for supper, which we had to get from the camp. We walked to the camp and had our supper there.

The following day we woke up, bathed and went to have our breakfast. During the breakfast, it was announced that we should get ready to go to Kwanza-Sul, a province of Angola, where our comrades were ambushed after the truck they were travelling in had driven over a minefield. Two comrades were badly injured, and three FAPLA soldiers were killed. We all left our food and hurried to the trucks, which were outside ready to leave. We left the camp and drove for more than two hours without any incident until we arrived at the scene of the accident. What I saw there was terrifying. There were comrades and FAPLA soldiers lying everywhere, crying in agony with blood and pieces of human flesh all over the place. My knees felt weak, and I had trouble breathing because the situation was so overwhelming.

We jumped out of the trucks and began looking at ways to assist the medical team that came with us. Unfortunately, there was nothing we could do, and we just had to wait for the medical team's prognosis. I made sure that I stood far away from the victims of this terrible attack because I could not bear to see their pain and hear their cries. As I stood there, I felt a shiver down my spine and a tight hand around my waist. When I turned around, it was AB with his masculine arms. Seeing him made me feel safe and in control of my fears, and we stood there looking at each saying nothing.

I did not know where he was until then. He explained to me that he was part of the reconnaissance group that heard the shots, but that they were too far from the scene to help. On their arrival at the scene, it was already too late because the comrades were by now in the minefield and their two trucks were already blown to pieces. He also told me that two comrades had lost their legs in the blast. This was a tragedy, but I was somehow grateful that AB survived.

The dead were put into a Land Rover, and the injured were carefully transported in a separate vehicle, which took them to Malanje where they were going to be airlifted to Luanda by helicopter. Comrade Mthakathi, who was the overall commander of this unit, instructed us to patrol the whole area to see if we could identify any group of people or funny movements around Kwanza-Sul. We patrolled the area for about six hours and found nothing suspicious. Around 19:00 pm, we were told to go back to our camp in Cacuso. We drove to the camp in silence, but we were all very vigilant because we could not rule out another possible surprise attack.

As we were driving towards Cacuso, we saw a truck in front of us, but before the commander could decide on what to do next, we were showered with bullets from the truck. We were luckily armed to the teeth, with RPG-7's, AK's, LMG's and other artillery, and retaliated by firing back. For a moment, I felt as if I was in Beirut; there were gunshots everywhere. I took cover because I realised that my gun jammed, and I could not take a chance to expose my position to the enemy. The shooting continued for more than forty minutes, and I was really scared for my life and those of my comrades. After a while, the shooting stopped, and I raised my head and found that all the comrades were still alive, and I could see the excitement of victory on their faces.

Suddenly the shooting started again, but this time it was from our truck to the enemy. At first, I could not see what was happening, until I saw three UNITA bandits jumping out of the enemy's truck, which was not far from our own. By the look of things, the driver of the truck died from a bullet wound to his forehead before the truck hit a nearby tree. All three bandits died after a volley fire from our comrades.

We jumped out of our truck to investigate the enemy's truck, where we discovered sixteen dead bodies and two others nearby with bullet wounds in their backs, which showed that they were running away. It meant we found twenty-one dead bodies and no one from our side. We got back to our trucks and left for our camp where after roll call we went to our different ways.

I went straight to our caravan because I did not want to discuss what transpired during the day because I was upset. I knew and understood the danger the bandits posed to us and the Angolan people, but for me, it was also difficult to accept that we had to retaliate by fire to stop them from killing civilians in Angola. The only consolation was that they were UNITA soldiers who were aided by the South African Defence Force (SADF). This made me see that we had to fight them in any way possible. That night, I slept sound without a care in the world.

The following day I woke up and I found that everybody had left already. I quickly bathed and left for breakfast at the camp where I found my girlfriends having their breakfast. I joined them, and we ate in silence, but I could feel the tension at the table. I could not figure out why they were so tense and after eating, decided to go to AB's place. I was ready to go when Caroline said that she was going to walk with me because she wanted to see her boyfriend, who stayed with AB.

"Mantile, are you aware that you are pregnant?" Caroline asked as we were walking towards the residence. The question shocked me because I was aware of the fact that I did not get my periods for three months, but due to ignorance, I thought I would never get pregnant because of the kind of exercises we used to do.

"What nonsense are you talking about?" I asked.

"Look, Ruth, I have been looking at you for some time now, actually before even coming here. There was a stage whereby you were not eating rice and always felt nauseous, and now I can see that your breasts are becoming bigger and your nipples are black. If you are not aware, those are all signs of pregnancy. I advise you to tell AB, and after that, you must go and see a gynaecologist as soon as possible," Caroline continued. I just looked at her and said nothing because I knew exactly what she was talking about, but how could I be pregnant? What a bombast question!

She was not making sense at all! I thought when a person is pregnant, her tummy becomes big, and my tummy was still flat, and I did not feel sick at all except for the time I had headaches and stomach aches which were diagnosed as ulcers. I was otherwise fine, and there was no way I could be pregnant! We walked in silence until we reached our destination where we just went to our boyfriend's rooms, not saying anything to each other. I did not tell AB about Caroline's insinuations because I knew that if it did not make sense to me, it would not make sense to him too. We just spoke about the war and the best way to come alive from the situation and were still talking when someone knocked on the door. AB opened it, and I recognised Comrade Simpi. (May his soul rest in peace.)

"Hey, Ndoda, we are wanted at the guardhouse, hurry. Mthakathi is waiting for us," he said. AB gave me a kiss on the cheek and ran after Comrade Simpi. I followed them in case they were going away and because I wanted to say goodbye to him. I thought that if death was imminent, I at least knew that I said goodbye and that would make me take his death in stride and it will console me.

As I was approaching the guardhouse, I saw comrades getting into the trucks, and fortunately for me, AB saw me coming, and he ran to me, kissed me passionately and ran back to the truck while leaving me dizzy by the side. After he got into the truck, he blew me a kiss and said, "Chunku, I love you, and you must never forget that." The comrades who were with him laughed and shouted at me saying, "If he dies, it will be too bad! At least you'll have us." I looked at them and felt tears rolling down my cheeks, wondering if I would ever see him alive again. On my way home, I imagined the day I would be told that AB was dead, and I did not know how I would react if that day came.

Days went by with no serious engagement except for patrols around Cacuso, which had its own results. During the patrols, we identified some shady characters, which we took to the guardhouse for questioning. Most of the times, I just stood outside the guardhouse because the questioning was so intense, and I felt that I was strong enough to see somebody going through all that.

Both FAPLA and MK comrades interrogated them. I must say that the results were positive because after those sessions we would know about the modus operandi, capacity and hideouts of UNITA, although sometimes when we tried to follow the leads, we got to a cul-de-sac because we were either fed disinformation or the bandits had relocated. We tried several times to act on information received from the captured bandits, but nothing came from it. I realised that most of the times they were bullshitting us, and this really made me angry, especially because most of the time I felt sorry for them during interrogations.

One day while doing patrols, we stopped a train from Luanda to the south of the country. We got into the train and searched everybody. Even young children, because we understood that the bandits used children to transport arms from one place to another, and therefore, they were potential threats to the security of the country and to ourselves.

As we were searching, we found two boys who were around the age of twelve, sitting next to the toilet. They looked malnourished and a little bit wild. They looked as if they had not eaten and washed for days. Comrade Bubezi became suspicious and called Dimakatso, and after a minute of consultation, I saw them approaching those two kids. They searched their bodies and then instructed them to take out their luggage, which seemed difficult to get. The two pushed those kids aside and looked for their luggage which they found under the seats. As they opened the bag, I saw Dimakatso's body language and concluded that there was something in those bags.

I went closer to Dimakatso and Bubezi, and I confirmed what I saw in Dimakatso's eyes. As if by instinct, Dimakatso jumped to the direction of the two boys screaming, "Tshwarang dintja tseo di seke tsa baleha!" (Stop those dogs, they should not run away!) Everybody ran towards the toilets where those kids were standing, and I just stood there because I wanted to check exactly what was in those three bags.

I opened the bags and found hand grenades, AK's, pistols and some food. By then there was an instruction from the commander of the unit, Comrade Drift (May his soul rest in peace), that Dimakatso and about five comrades should take the two kids to the guardhouse, while the rest of us should thoroughly search the train all over again. We also had to physically search all the people on the train. We again started with the search and after three hours called it off, and the train was free to leave Cacuso. By that time, I was tired and very hungry and just needed to sleep. On our arrival at the guardhouse, we were dismissed for lunch, and I went straight to the barracks where food was served. After eating, I went straight to my caravan, where I immediately fell asleep, only to be woken up by a bell. I quickly put on my boots, took my weapon, and ran to the formation.

"ATTENTION! AT EASE! Comrades, we got a radio message today that there was an attack in the villages around Kwanza-Sul. The bandits have killed civilians and set the villages on fire. Secondly, some of our comrades got in the minefield, and two of them were seriously injured. We are, therefore, required to deploy there for some time and stay in one of the camps, which were occupied by SWAPO. Comrades Ruth and Dimakatso, you will be part of this group of comrades who are going on this mission. I give you twenty minutes to get ready. ATTENTION! DISMISSED," said Commander Mthakathi.

Comrade Dan Petersen, 'Madada', as comrades called him because of his love for goose meat, stood beside Mthakathi as his second in command. All along, when Comrade Mthakathi was talking about the ambush, I was just thinking about AB. I did not even know where he was, and I just wished him to be safe and alive.

We packed our combats and some necessities and left for the guardhouse where we got into a van and drove off. The only problem with this trip was that it was at night and to think that our comrades got into a minefield on the same route. It was really scary, but we were fighting for a just cause, and that was my consolation.

We drove in silence throughout the night without any incidents and only arrived in Kwanza-Sul in the morning around 5:00 am. As we were disembarking from our van, I saw AB from a distance, and I got excited and happy to see him alive. We kissed and hugged, but it was short-lived because he told me that he was going back to Cacuso the same morning. I just sighed, hugged him for the last time, and left him there. He came running behind me.

"Chunku, please do not do this to me, I beg you. You would know that things do not depend on me. It is my wish to be with you every minute of my life, but remember, that will only remain a wish because we are MK soldiers and our lives are not ours, but the people of South Africa's. Please understand that I will never hurt you and seeing you like this hurts me a lot. I beg you, please understand," he said. I just looked at him and said nothing because I understood that our personal feelings are insignificant. The national interests would always take precedence over everything else. I looked at him and said, "I love you so much, and I do not want to stand between you and our mission, the thing is I become worried when you are not with me. I do not want anything bad to happen to you. Please take care of yourself and try not to be 'Matrosov'." He laughed so loud until tears rolled on his cheeks after of which we kissed and said our goodbyes. (Alexander Matveyevich Matrosov was born on February 5, 1924, in Yekaterinnoslav in Russia. He was a Russian infantry soldier during the Great Patriotic War in the Second World War and died on February 22, 1945, when he blocked a German machine gun with his body to protect his country. He was posthumously awarded the title of Hero of the Soviet Union.)

After AB's departure, I went to join Dimakatso and the other comrades who also included FAPLA soldiers. We stood there talking about this and that, and although I did not understand Portuguese that well, I could follow the conversation a little. As we stood there, I saw Bra T, Uncle (Mshengu), and Peter Seiso (Scandal), Rex, Tebogo Kgope (Dimakatso's boyfriend from Duduza in Nigel) and Wiseman. All those comrades formed the commanding staff in that operational area. They greeted us and called us to the barrack where they told us we were going to sleep in the barrack with them because there were only two barracks and the other one was going to be used by all the other soldiers so it would not be appropriate to sleep there. We agreed because I guess we did not have any choice, and anyway, we were all soldiers.

After supper, Dimakatso and I went to our barracks accompanied by some of our comrades and the FAPLA soldiers who were telling us about their experiences in the fight against UNITA in the south and FNLA (National Front for the Liberation of Angola) in the north. As I said – I did not understand a lot of Portuguese, so Dimakatso translated for me, assisted by Comrade Phillip, who was very good in Portuguese and had the physical features of the Angolan people. As a result, I actually thought he was Angolan at a certain stage.

We sat there listening to their stories until very late when we decided to go to sleep. We went inside and found everyone fast asleep, and we just got into bed with our combats and boots on. We had our weapons between our legs. I slept peacefully only to be woken up by terrible heartburn, and I did not know what to do about it. Without fear, I went outside because I had my AK with me.

While I sat there nursing my heartburn, the sun rose in the east, and the horizon looked so beautiful and peaceful. I could also smell the freshness of the trees and soil, and I listened to the birds humming. Come to think about it now that was the most memorable day of my life. I woke Dimakatso and we 'washed' by using water from a two-litre bottle, which was given to us the previous day by Comrade Phillip. We only managed to wash the most vital parts of our bodies, not caring about the rest. We then walked to the kitchen where we were each served a tin of condensed milk and 'soldiers' biscuits'. The 'soldiers' biscuits' were brown and very hard and there were four in a packet. I only learned later that they were supposed to be energy boosters for soldiers, especially during long marches. We ate in silence until we were disturbed by the commanding staff, Bra T and his entourage, whom we had to salute. We finished our meal and waited for the next order.

The bell rang, and we ran to the formation where we were given instructions to go and investigate our operational area to make sure that there were no bandits around. At the camp, we were five platoons, meaning one company and a section, which comprised both MK and FAPLA soldiers. During the briefing, we were told to move by skirmish through the bush covering twenty kilometres from the camp and make our way to the Kwanza River where it was suspected the UNITA bandits operated from. Depending on the speed we were going to take, we would be able to come back to the camp, but if we were slow, it meant that we had to sleep along the riverbank. That meant we needed to take logistics that would cover us for about two days. The commander of the unit was Comrade Tebogo Kgope, who took over from Bra T, with an order that we should go and get our logistics, which included food, water and extra ammunition and gather again after twenty minutes.

"ATTENTION!" instructed Comrade Tebogo. Comrade Phillip translated for the Angolan comrades.

"As we have heard the instruction from the commander, I am not going to waste any more time. ATTENTION! Forward march."

Just after we left the camp, there came an instruction to form a skirmish. We did as told and entered the terrain covered with weeds almost 2 m high. I remember this because, at that stage, I was 1.72 m and could not manage to see anything in front of me. After walking for more than three hours without any incident, we saw in the distance what we thought were barracks. The order came that myself and six other comrades should go as a reconnaissance group and the other comrades should wait for us. Our group's commander was Comrade Rex. We approached this building walking by 'bounds' to avoid detection in case the enemy was in the vicinity. We took ten minutes to get into the abandoned building. The building looked like a big, abandoned house, and after investigating the inside, Comrade Rex called Comrade Tebogo to advance with the rest of the unit. We had a ten-minute rest, and after that break, we continued with our mission.

After we passed the building, we found ourselves in open terrain without any cover. We could be seen from far away, and this was certainly a very big disadvantage for us. The commander thought it was wise to halt for a lunch break so that we could buy time until later in the afternoon when the sun was about to set. Our lunch consisted of one tin of sardines and 'soldiers' biscuits'. I ate in silence because I wanted to nap. I was terribly fatigued, and I could not explain why. After lunch, I took my knapsack, made it a pillow, and with my weapon between my legs, I fell asleep. When I woke after an hour or so, I realised that almost everyone was asleep except for Dimakatso and Comrade Tebogo. I stood up, slung my AK over my shoulder, and fastened my spare ammunition pouch around my waist ready to continue with the revolutionary mission. I looked at the couple with admiration; they looked so happy together. At a certain stage, I saw those two exchanging sexy looks and smiled naughtily at each, which was so wonderful. The two started singing a song I recognised as Aretha Franklin's – if my memory serves me well that song was 'Baby, I love you'. As they sang, they kept on exchanging sexy looks and smiled at each other. Looking at them reminded me of the life I wanted to have with AB; the kind of love that most people thought only existed in James Bond movies. Here I saw that same love in the bushes of Angola, and it was wonderful to see two people so much in love despite the odds. I just sat there thinking about how wonderful love is, especially if you love someone and that person loves you back. I must say that it was rare to see a relationship flourish in Angola because of the constant movement of personnel. Comrades would be involved in a serious relationship, and suddenly, one would be taken away either for further training abroad or to the front, which resulted in frustrations and uncertainties especially to the one who was left behind.

The thing is, if you were sent to the front, there were many possibilities. You could die in battle, be kidnapped and jailed, or even sentenced to death by the regime. We were really faced with some difficult situations, and that is why one could find that after a while, the one who was left behind would be involved with someone else. On the other hand, we should not forget that there were not a lot of women in MK. We had a situation where there were only fifteen women out of approximately two hundred soldiers.

As I was looking at Dimakatso and Tebogo, I thought of one couple I knew back then in Kamalundi. Those two comrades were so in love, and everybody thought they were going to get married, but that never happened. Unfortunately, the female comrade had to leave the camp for Luanda. After a month or so, she wrote a letter to her lover, our instructor at the camp that read, "The silver cup has broken, and love has gone away. From: Your comrade in arms".

The instructor was devastated because he was one of those comrades who were very egoistic, and who thought women would eat out of his hand. I felt very sorry for him, but you know what? Life goes on! This was the most interesting part of life in the MK camps; we tried to make the best of a bad situation. I was worried about the two lovebirds because Dimakatso still had the name of her ex-boyfriend, Comrade Mengistu, tattooed below her belly button and I always wondered how Tebogo felt about it. Anyway, that was their business.

It was almost 15:30 pm when Comrade Rex called us to start moving. We again formed a skirmish, and this time moved faster because it was not so hot anymore. As we moved by 'bouncing', we observed movement about a kilometre away, and the commander instructed that we should stop and send a reconnaissance unit to investigate. Dimakatso was the commander of the unit of eight comrades who included Comrade Zanempi, the one who was one of the comrades who used to help me with my work at Radio Freedom and who later died during the mutiny. The rest of the group remained behind to cover the reconnaissance unit.

As we were waiting for a report, I suddenly developed a craving for lemons, and the craving was so intense that I could not ignore it, no matter how hard I tried. I thought, *"Where am I going to get a lemon in this fucking place?"* I was still trying to understand where the sudden craving came from when I heard the commander say, "Advance with fire!" I came to my senses, looked around, and saw comrades advancing with their guns at hip position. I followed suit with my gun on my hip and in a firing position. All of a sudden, the sound of gunshots were everywhere. We did not wait for an order and fired in every direction the gunshots came from. I was shooting but scared that I might shoot one of my comrades, which often happened in battles like this one where the same unit shoot at each other by mistake, thinking that they are shooting at the enemy. As comrades were firing, I was listening to the sound of their weapons, and it was like listening to a thunderstorm in the middle of the night. Different sounds were coming from different weapons, which included AK's, RPG's and PKM's. The funny part was that the sounds of all these weapons soothed my whole being; the sound camouflaged the danger of the weapons, and it was as if they were not meant to kill. At least that is how it sounded to me.

"Mantile why osa thunyi," (Mantile, why are you not shooting? Are you mad?) I heard Mokete (who later became an Askari) shouting at me. I just looked at him and thought to myself, *"Shoot, if that is what you want to do."* At that stage, I could not imagine myself hurting or killing anyone. The amazing thing was that most of my comrades considered me as being brave, but deep down in my heart, I knew I was very gentle. As we were advancing, we ultimately arrived at what looked like an abandoned church, where we found the reconnaissance group.

The uniforms and the weapons found on the scene were said to be those used by the SADF, and these pieces of evidence proved beyond any reasonable doubt that UNITA was being sponsored by the South African regime. The discovery made me very angry, and I decided there and then that I was not going to show any mercy to the bandits anymore. I think it only dawned on me that we were at war and I only then understood the anger displayed by the comrades when we captured bandits.

As some of us were busy looking at the uniforms, Comrades Rex and Tebogo called, "Nazi le zi nja!" (Here are the dogs!) We all ran to where the comrades were calling from. On arrival, we were met with three hungry-looking men, with big, red eyes. They looked as if they hadn't seen food and water in months. Our unit was very excited because we had finally found them after months of searching. I just stood aside when everyone wanted a piece of flesh to smash even though Comrade Rex was calling for calm. "Comrades, please let us calm down! What we need to do now is to get information about their deployment and where to find them. I assure you, if we beat them, they will never tell us the information we need. Please give me time to talk to them; I intend to persuade them to take us to their base," Comrade Rex pleaded with us. After he spoke, I decided to get a place nearby under a tree and relax, but I think I dozed off because I just heard an order that we should move to the river.

As the battalion followed the tracks of UNITA bandits along the harsh bushy terrain, a huge beehive fell on Comrade Rex who was with the two bandits. It seemed as if one of the bandits disturbed the bees with the long stick he used to open the bush with. As the beehive fell on Comrade

Rex, chaos erupted as everyone scattered to take cover. Comrade Rex became the centre of attraction as the bees stung him all over. The poor comrade did not know what to do, and I remember one comrade and the two bandits helping him out of the situation. It was a very sad state of affairs, but I was laughing at Comrade Rex, especially when he took off his trousers and I saw his penis because I could not tell if it just looked like that or was swollen from the stings! Although Rex was in pain, he remained positive and strong, and we continued with our march led by the two captured bandits.

We finally reached the Kwanza River late in the afternoon and were ordered to relax until the next morning. Dimakatso and I spent two weeks around the Kwanza River hunting down the bandits in the area, and it felt as if it was six months. We got involved in skirmishes with the enemy on several occasions, and even though we had some casualties, it was not as bad as the casualties suffered by UNITA.

One day as we were busy with our mission of pursuing the enemy, we got involved in an unexpected exchange of fire. We intended to go back to the camp when we suddenly heard the beating of drums about two kilometres from the river. From experience, we knew that the enemy had laid an ambush, so we quickly took our positions and waited for the new order. At that stage, I had decided that I was going to shoot at anything that moved and exactly ten minutes after our deployment, we heard two shots not far from us. My weapon was cocked, and my finger was on the trigger, waiting to hear the order "fire". As I was waiting, I heard a volley of fire from about five hundred metres from where I was standing, and I must say that really took me by surprise.

"Fire!" I heard Comrade Tebogo's voice coming from behind me. We opened fire simultaneously, and the sound of it came out like thunder. We were advancing by fire towards where the enemy was, and I was very excited because it was the second time we were directly engaged with the enemy near the Kwanza River.

Before we reached the spot where the fire was coming from, we realised that there was no retaliation anymore from the side of the enemy, which was worrisome. We advanced by 'bounce' until we reached the enemy territory, but still, there was nothing.

At first, we thought it was a trap, but when we realised that the place was quiet, we decided to check it out. There were about thirty dead bodies lying around, and it looked as if it was a camp of some sort with big pots, some foodstuff and water tanks.

While we were investigating the place, I felt a sharp pain in my right leg, and my boot felt a bit wet. I sat down and tried to take my boots off, but my leg was so painful that I felt like I was losing my mind. I managed to unfasten the boot and saw blood running from what seemed to be a wound. The thought of being shot at gave me goosebumps, and I called for assistance. The first comrade to reach me was Comrade Mahero. He slowly took my boot and blood-soaked sock off and said, "Comrade Ruth, you have been shot, but the bullet did not penetrate your leg, it just passed, and I think your boot protected you. Don't worry; I will call Comrade Medico to come and attend to the wound." I sat there waiting for Comrade Jerome, who was busy checking for survivors from the enemy's side. Everybody was so busy examining the camp that no one noticed that I was shot. The pain was excruciating, and it felt as if somebody had penetrated my heart with a spear.

"Fortunately, the bullet passed your leg, Comrade Ruth. For now, let us just stop the bleeding; you will be fine," Comrade Mahero said while we were waiting for Comrade Jerome, who came with his medical kit and cleaned my wound and bandaged it. "Comrade Ruth, you are so fortunate that the bullet scratched you and did not penetrate your leg. Maybe your boot helped? I'm going to give you pain tablets, and I think you will be able to walk to the camp," commented Comrade Jerome. I sat there waiting for the pain to subside while watching what the other Comrades were doing. I realised that all of them were eager to find those bastards.

After our engagement with the enemy, we stayed in the vicinity for another three weeks. Comrades used to cross the river to the other side, but I could not because the first time I tried to cross, I got so anxious that I had to go back to the riverbank. Every time they crossed the river, I was left behind to guard the observer post, and I preferred that over being in the river.

On another occasion, while we were on a skirmish, Comrade Mokete said to me, "Mantile, did you hear that JJ was shot dead by Sugar Ray, our homeboy in Malanje?" I nearly lost a heartbeat. I just stood there and thought about her parents back at home. How were they going to find out that their daughter has been killed by that bastard?

I just kept quiet and did not say anything to Mokete, who looked at me as if he was waiting for an answer. I just looked at him and continued with the march. I was marching, but my mind was on JJ, who was actually Joyce Jones, and if I remember correctly, she was from Port Elizabeth. She was a beautiful and wonderful comrade, who stood her ground, and I especially liked her energy. I remembered her well because at a certain stage there was an issue concerning her in Caculama, where she was in a relationship with Comrade Cool who worked in the kitchen, but she later left him and got involved with Comrade Mbongeni who was in our company.

There was nothing wrong with what JJ did, but the situation turned ugly because other comrades, including my own commissar, Hamba Zondi, turned it into a tribal issue, asking how she could leave 'indoda' (a man) for 'inkwenkwe' (a boy) because Mbongeni was a Zulu from Natal (now the province of KwaZulu-Natal), and it was assumed that they did not go to initiation schools. They then started isolating her. JJ's case reminded me of Noxolo's case in 1982, where Noxolo's boyfriend, Comrade Ellof, left the camp and Noxolo started dating Comrade Parker, who happened to be speaking Sepedi. Noxolo came under fire from the comrades who were from the Eastern Cape.

One day she came running to me saying that Comrades Juba Mfene, Hamba Zondi and Mxaji called her for a meeting where they asked her, "Did Ellof show you your 'sector of fire?'" meaning that he did not tell her whom to fall for within the Xhosa-speaking comrades after his departure.

That really made me mad, and that day I took a vow that I will never date a Xhosa-speaking comrade in my life. The worst thing was that this tribal 'shit' was being done by commissars who were supposed to be politically matured and beyond reproach and to me that was very disappointing.

So, JJ was the second victim of tribalism in the camp that I know of, but you know, I admired her because whatever those comrades said never affected her love for Mbongeni, and she stood by her decision. As we marched, I imagined the joy that was being felt by Hamba Zondi and the gang when they heard that JJ had been killed by her jealous lover, who as another 'inkwenkwe'. (May her soul rest in peace.)

That day we did not go back to our camp and stayed in the bush for two days and two nights. We returned to camp on the third day, stayed a night and then Dimakatso and I was taken back to Cacuso early in the next morning. We arrived in Cacuso and found people waiting for their next instructions. We went to the caravans where we found Caroline and Joyce Mudau relaxing. We greeted each other and went to our room because we desperately wanted to take a bath. We literally did not bath for a whole month, but we were lucky in the sense that we could wash the vital parts of our bodies using two litres of water daily. As I was taking off my clothes, I saw that my body was covered in layers of dirt, which I could not remove with my face cloth.

The only way to remove the dirt was for Dimakatso to get a stone and scrub it off, which was very painful, especially around the wound where the bullet scratched me. I think she took about an hour to scrub off all the dirt! The most amazing thing was that although we were using the same amount of water to wash in at Kwanza-Sul, Dimakatso's body was not infested with the dirt I saw on my body. I actually thought that maybe I did not wash properly before I went to Kwanza-Sul.

After washing, I felt refreshed and very cool, and we went to see Caroline and Joyce. We spoke about our different experiences in battle, because during the period when we were not around, they had their own engagements with the enemy, but they were fortunate to sleep at home most of the time. While we were talking, Caroline looked at me and said that there was something wrong with my breasts. According to her, they looked bigger, and I actually looked fat. Everyone agreed, and Dimakatso said that she was looking at me while bathing and that my breasts around the nipples were black and that she actually wondered if I was not pregnant. They all looked at me, and I thought they were crazy because how could I be pregnant when I did not have a big tummy?

"Mantile, I'm going to Malanje tomorrow. I'm going to bring you something to drink, and you will be fine after you drink it," said Caroline with her naughty smile. Caroline had a smile that made most male comrade's knees go weak, especially after she had lost weight. She was beautiful and kind, with a great sense of humour.

"Mantile, do you understand what I'm saying?" repeated Caroline.

"Yes, I do," I replied. I looked at them and rushed out of the room, not knowing where I was going. I felt so confused about the whole thing regarding the pregnancy; I could not imagine myself having a child – an illegitimate child – and definitely not at that age.

The most important thing to me at that stage was to go home and fight, especially after I was baptised by fire by the UNITA bandits. The confrontations with the bandits made me more eager to go inside the country to fight the enemy. I felt that I was ready to lay down my life for our country more than ever before.

"Hey, Comrade Ruth, what are you doing here?" I looked back and saw Comrades Simpi and China, rushing for me.

"Where am I? What am I doing here?" I asked.

"We do not know. We just saw you walk in here, and we thought the bandits were going to attack you, especially because you were alone. Those people who were admitted are very cruel; they do not have hearts!" Comrade China said.

"Let's get out of here," Comrade Simpi said.

What happened was that I left our caravan and went to a barrack which was used as a clinic, but at that moment, it was used to admit injured bandits. Unconsciously, I just went into the barrack and walked between the beds saying nothing to nobody. I felt so empty inside, and while I was walking around the barrack, I did not think about how dangerous these people were. Even worse, I had left my gun in the caravan and would not have been able to protect myself if anything happened. Even today, I cannot explain what I was doing there, and I still ask myself what could have happened to me if Comrades China and Simpi did not come to my rescue. They took me back to the caravan, where I got into bed and miraculously fell asleep without any hitches.

"Chunku, please wake up. I need to talk to you," I heard AB's voice as if he was talking to me from far away. I tried to open my eyes, but I could not, and I guess I was too tired.

"Chunku, it's me; let's talk, please," I heard him again, only this time I felt his hands touching my forehead. I opened my eyes, and there he was, looking at me with a sad smile on his face.

"Come here; give me a warm hug. Why did you not come to my place when you arrived? China told me that they saw you, and you did not look good at all. They say it looked as if something was bothering you. They actually thought you were losing your mind. What is happening sweetheart? Please tell me!" he pleaded.

I looked at him with no idea on earth what to say. The thing was that I did not know how to explain what I felt inside, but one thing for sure: I was very angry, and my mind could not stop thinking about those bandits in that barrack. I had flashbacks of the engagements with the bandits in Matete and all those dead bodies. I also had flashbacks of the rape in Vienna, which I tried to shake from my mind, but would not go away. It seemed so fresh in my mind as if it happened yesterday.

"Ruth, what's wrong? Come, let's take a walk," AB said. He held my hand, slung my weapon over my shoulder, and closed the door behind him. I only realised then what time it was; it was 15:50 pm. That meant I slept for more than four hours!

"Where are Caroline and the others?" I asked AB, who said they were at the guardhouse. We walked hand in hand, occasionally kissing each other, and I felt so safe with him around. I think we walked for about fifteen minutes before we found a fallen tree trunk where we sat down and talked about my experiences and fears in Matete. While I was busy talking, AB's mind seemed to be very far away, and I wondered what was on his mind. Before I could ask what was wrong, he asked me about the incident at the barrack earlier that day, which I thought he had forgotten about.

"Please tell me what is bothering you?" he asked, and I just looked at him, not knowing what to say.

"AB, I'm not sure what happened, but what I know is that I had a discussion with Caroline and Dimakatso, which upset me. I remember that I left the caravan, not knowing where I was going. As to how I ended up in that barrack, I cannot explain," I said, not looking at him. I guess I did not want him to ask me any further questions.

"I understand, but tell me: what were you talking about that made you *that* upset?" he asked sincerely. That was the question I was avoiding since our meeting started. I felt I did not want to talk about it. Maybe I was pregnant? Two or three weeks before we left Vienna, I had cramps, and I was diagnosed with stomach ulcers. I remember those pains became worse when AB touched me. I remembered the cravings I had for lemons in the middle of God knows where. Maybe those were the signs? Was I in denial? Those were the questions I kept asking myself.

"Caroline and Dimakatso think I am pregnant," I said. I could see the shock and disbelieve in his eyes.

He just held his head in his hands and lowered it as if he wanted to put it between his thighs. I just looked at him without saying anything.

"Chunku, come here," he said and just held me very tight without saying anything further.

"Let's go to my place, I want to talk to Jerome," he said while holding my hand. We walked to his place where we found Comrades Jerome and China eating their supper. After sitting down, Comrade China offered me food, which I ate with difficulty because I did not have an appetite. While I was eating, AB was talking to Comrade Jerome, and I assumed that they were talking about my alleged pregnancy. After eating, I washed the dishes and went to AB's room, where he found me.

"Chunku, I have spoken to Jerome. He has suggested that tomorrow you should be taken to Malanje to see a gynaecologist. I think it is imperative to know in time so that you can be excused from operations," he said. I agreed with him, and he walked me to my room. He kissed me goodnight and off he went. I found Dimakatso fast asleep, and just put my weapon under the pillow, took my boots off, and got into bed wearing my combat gear. I fell asleep immediately and did not waste any time dwelling on issues that I had no control over. My only wish was not to be found pregnant.

We woke up in the morning, washed and went for breakfast. Afterwards, I was called by Comrade El, who informed me that we were going together to the hospital as he had to interpret for me. We left Cacuso for Malanje at around 9:00 am and arrived at the hospital just before 10:00 am. We did not have to wait long, and when I was called in, Comrade El went with me. After greetings, I was given a hospital gown and told to take off my clothes and climb onto the bed.

The gynaecologist ordered me to open my 'by-pots', referring to my legs, and I did. He then inserted an instrument inside me, and for some reason, it felt sore, especially when it felt as if it was rotating inside. The examination took about ten minutes. He took out the instrument and whispered something to Comrade El in Spanish. I relaxed when I saw blood on the instrument, because the blood further convinced me that I was not pregnant, and as a result, I did not even bother to ask Comrade El about the diagnosis because I was sure that I was not pregnant. We arrived in Cacuso, and I went straight to bed without even bothering to see AB.

I only woke up in the morning, had my bath and went up to the barracks for breakfast where we were informed that our meeting with the leadership was going to start at 11:00 am of which we were instructed to clean the barrack that was going to be used as the venue. We cleaned the place thoroughly, and it was spotless. After cleaning, we waited for the leadership outside the barrack singing revolutionary songs.

"Amandla," he said.

"Nga wethu," we responded.

"Long Live Umkhonto weSizwe Long Live."

"Long live," we responded.

"Long live the international proletariat, long live."

"Long live," we responded.

"Long live the spirit of Che Guevara, long live."

"Long live," we again responded.

"Comrades, we are here today to witness the bravery and selflessness of our combatants in the battle against UNITA. This battle, as you know, has culminated from random attacks on civilians by UNITA bandits, who might even attack our training camp. Comrades, the message from the commander-in-chief, Comrade OR Tambo, is that we should ensure that UNITA does not come any nearer to our training camp or our residence in Malanje.

Comrades, I must tell you that we are making progress in international affairs; Comrades OR, Makhathini, Thabo Mbeki and others have done an excellent job to mobilise our friends and comrades against trading with the South African regime. The international working class in America, Britain and other imperialist countries are forcing their countries to stop trading with the apartheid government by demonstrating and waging protest marches.

The workers in those countries have shown their solidarity with the oppressed masses of South Africa by denouncing apartheid and fascism in all their forms. It, therefore, suggests that we should intensify our struggle on all fronts. Comrades, I am accompanied by Comrade Nkadimeng, who is the general secretary of SACTU, and he wants to see for himself the calibre of cadres we have. He intends to recruit some of you to go to the front to advance the workers' struggle against exploitation and colonialism."

I was listening to Comrade Joe Modise with keen interest, especially his coarse voice. I saw in front of me a man who was full of himself; an experienced fighter, but a very egoistic leader. To me, he had Stalin's traits: ruling by fear, and very intimidating. At that stage, I concluded that he was actually an insecure individual who masqueraded as being a no-nonsense man who oozes with confidence. To me, he was the direct opposite of Comrade OR, who was a thoughtful, wise and warm-hearted leader. JM went on and on about the importance of fighting against the bandits, but never spoke about us going to the front, and this really baffled me because our purpose was to liberate South Africa and not to die in the bushes of Angola.

Anyway, after his long speech, it was time for questions and comments. As I was listening to the speech, something happened to me that I could not understand. I had a terrible pain in my tummy whenever AB held my hand; it was a sharp pain, and sometimes it felt as if I had an upset tummy. I could not really explain how I felt, but one thing I knew was that it was damn discomforting.

"Comrade Leader, I have heard loud and clear about us defending our camps because of imminent attacks by UNITA, but the situation is such that our deployment is far away from our camp, how do you explain that? Secondly, we have been here for almost three months; do you realise how many of our comrades have been victims of limpet mines in the operational areas?" asked Comrade Zanempi, and I could see the anger and frustration on his face. The questions that followed were about us infiltrating South Africa and the timelines. Comrade JM answered the questions with a lot of arrogance, telling us that the ANC was not going to be controlled by soldiers; soldiers had to wait for the next order. He further said that there was nothing wrong with dying in Angola because it was part of our international duties. "There are Cubans, Russians, and even Namibians who are sacrificing their lives for the defence of the Angolan revolution. Who do you think you are?" he said while thumping the table with his fists to emphasise what he was saying. He went on and on ridiculing concerns raised by comrades and the meeting adjourned with no clear direction as to where from there.

I must say I was not particularly happy about the turn of events, but I kept my comments to myself because of my experience in Lesotho. We went for lunch, and while eating, Caroline told me that she was going to Malanje with Comrade Benson. We said our goodbyes, and she left immediately after her meal.

After lunch, I was summoned to the guardhouse, where I was instructed to go to the shooting range with Comrade Joe Modise and his entourage. I was so annoyed by this because I was tired. Also, I did not want to embarrass myself by missing the targets in front of everybody, especially in front of the army commander. I got into the vehicle with some comrades who were escorting Comrade Joe to the shooting range. There we found our Angolan counterparts (the infantry units we had been operating with), and the MK commanding staff. I remember that the late Comrades Rogers Nkadimeng and Morris Seabelo were there as well.

After the formalities, Comrade Modise explained the purpose of the activity. In short, he said, "Angolan comrades, today I want to prove to you that witchcraft does not exist in front of a gun – whether you believe it or not. There is no way that a gun can produce water instead of a bullet. I have brought Comrade Ruth, to prove to you that no gun in the whole world can be bewitched."

When he mentioned my name, my knees went weak, and I cannot recall hearing his closing remarks because I just wanted to disappear! I was given different kinds of weapons, from a 9 mm pistol to an RPG-7 rocket launcher, took it, and stood at the firing line. With me was Comrades JM, Rogers, Bra T, Mthakathi, and I cannot remember the rest. We first had to shoot the pistols, which I was comfortable with. I just reminded myself that I needed to inhale before releasing the trigger. I did exactly that, and all my ammunition went straight to the targets for the first time in my life! When the target shooting was done, comrades came to congratulate me, especially Bra T, who knew me to be a bad shooter, and I felt very happy with my achievement.

I went straight to the caravan from the shooting range because I was very tired. I think I must have dozed off because I was woken up by a bell from the guardhouse. I grabbed my AK and ran towards the guardhouse with my unfastened boots. On my arrival, all the comrades were already there.

"Attention comrades! There has been an ambush towards Malanje which involved one of our vehicles driven by Comrade Bernard." When I heard his name, my heart skipped a beat because I knew Caroline left with him. I was very anxious, but could not ask anyone because there was an unwritten rule in MK that you do not ask anything that does not concern you.

"Comrades, let's get in the trucks and move! Attention! Dismissed!" Comrade Mthakathi commanded. We all got into our trucks and drove towards Malanje. I was the only female in our truck, and Dimakatso was with Joyce in another. When we were about thirty kilometres from Cacuso, we saw one of our vehicles passing us very fast but did not think much of it. As we were driving and listening to the tranquillity of the night, we heard something like the beating of drums from about four to five kilometres away.

"Comrades, those are bandits; cock your weapons, but ensure that your safety pins are closed. Expect real engagement," said Comrade Tebogo.

We did as ordered, and we were about to pass a hillock when we heard a volley of fire coming from that direction. Some of the comrades jumped from the trucks and those still on it fired in the direction of the enemy fire. I rolled and crawled towards the hillock, taking advantage of the darkness of the night. As I crawled, I saw about fifteen men shooting towards our trucks. I opened my safety pin and shot at them. Of course, my comrades on the truck did what they knew best, and that was shooting to kill. Remember, we had two heavy machine guns on both trucks, so the fire that came from there and the ground forces would have made the bravest man run for his life!

The exchange of fire lasted for about fifteen minutes, and after that, there was dead silence from behind the hillock. We were then ordered to advance, while covered by the comrades on the trucks. To ensure our safety, we moved by 'bounds' because we did not know the terrain and therefore had to be extra careful and vigilant. As we reached the hillock, we saw about fifteen dead bodies of which most were shot in the back meaning they were running away, which, according to some theories, is a sign of cowardice. Although we were excited about our victory, we were also worried about our comrades who were attacked. We were ordered to get on in the trucks and go back to the camp. As we were getting in the trucks, Comrade Mdanda shouted that he saw movement in the opposite direction from the hillock.

I remember I was just about to settle in the truck when I heard someone shout "fire!" and immediately I heard the sound of AK's and PKM machine guns, (including a Bazooka). The sound itself was like music to my ears, and I just sat down and listened. It was fascinating, and at that very moment, I imagined us fighting like this in our motherland for our freedom. I was sure that all of us were prepared to die for the freedom of our people so that they could be free from fear and want. As I was listening and thinking, I stood up, and as I did, I saw a man hit in the groin by a bullet. I was shocked and actually thought it was a mistake or maybe the person aimed at that part of the body, and if it was his aim, it was terribly cruel! I could just imagine the pain the man experienced, but you know what? We were at war! The man who was hit cried like a baby. In my heart, I felt sorry for him, but when you are at war, you cannot display affection and sympathy.

Comrades got out of the truck to look for injured bandits, and they brought back five of them including the one I felt sorry for. They were covered in so much blood that one could not see where the bullet wounds were. They were made to lie there as if they were injured wild animals. We drove towards Cacuso in silence, and the only sound that one could hear was coming from the captured bandits. I did not want to look at them because for me listening to their cries was bad, but it was also very traumatic to see their agony. We arrived in Cacuso and disembarked at the guardhouse. When I saw the car that Caroline was travelling in, I rushed inside to see if they were okay. As I was about to enter, I saw Comrade Jerome coming from one of the rooms, and he passed me without saying anything, which was a very unusual thing for him to do. Normally he would shake my hand and ask me how I was doing, and we would share a joke or two, but that day he was different. I wondered what was wrong, but I did not ask him, I just went to the room he came from. There, I found Dimakatso and Joyce squatting in front of Caroline, who laid on the floor with a bandage over her head and a smile on her face. I knelt next to my friends without saying anything. I touched Caroline's soft hand and thought to myself that at least she was still alive. "Is Caroline going to sleep here?" I asked. Both Dimakatso and Joyce looked at me without saying anything. Their silence was killing me inside. "Don't you want to talk to me, comrades? Can we not at least wash the blood from her face?" I asked.

"Okay, if that is what you want, let's do it. I'm going to fetch some water, wait here," said Dimakatso with anger in her voice. She left and came back with a bucket of water and a facecloth. I just looked at them washing Caroline's body, with no idea in the world that my friend was dead. I looked at her beautiful, hairy body lying there with that lovely, naughty smile of hers and it reminded me about the comments made by our company commander, Comrade 26. He used to shout at Caroline for arriving late for roll call, "Do you want to neutralise me with that smile? Get to the formation, otherwise ... ozo kgakgaba nje ke nyoka." (Meaning she was going to crawl like a snake.) I remember Caroline would keep on smiling as if her life depended on it. She was a very beautiful and humorous person; she had a line of hair from her pubic hair to her breasts, which made her very sexy.

They finished washing her body and started to take off the bandage on her head. As they did that, I heard a funny sound like bones cracking, but I ignored it. The two comrades continued with the activity until they reached the last bandage, which was the one that exposed the severity of Caroline's wound.

"*Oh, God! Why her? She did not deserve to die!*" I thought. It was only then that I realised that Caroline was dead because I could see where the bullet had entered and exited. She was shot from the left, and the bullet protruded through to her right side. That was the worst day of my life; I never imagined that I was so naïve to fail to see a dead person. I mean, Caroline lay there for more than an hour, and I did not have a clue that she was dead!

Caroline was buried in Caculama, our training camp in Malanje. I happened to be a speaker at the funeral, but cannot remember what I said. The only thing I can still remember is that I was crying so much that no one was able to console me. I really felt empty without her, even now, while writing this book, I know deep down in my heart that she was the most amazing person. Her naughty smile, beautiful, big eyes and her sense of humour will remain with me for the rest of my days, and I cherish the time I spent with her. We drove back to Cacuso immediately after her burial.

Three days after Caroline's funeral, I was in my caravan with Thabang, one of my brothers from Bloemfontein, cleaning my gun. Thabang was standing next to me on my right-hand side when suddenly I heard the sound of a bullet. After the shock, I looked at Thabang, and I realised that he was also shocked and confused, but I was just happy to see him alive. As I was trying to think about what could have happened, Comrades Thabethe, Rex and AB were at the door. "Comrade Ruth, are you okay?" asked Comrade Thabethe. They entered and found Thabang still in shock.

"Chunku, what happened?" AB asked me.

"I was cleaning my weapon, and I think one bullet was left in the chamber by mistake because when I released the trigger that bullet went off," I said and Thabang confirmed this.

The three comrades told us that they came to investigate the situation after they heard a shot. They also said that Comrade Chris was actually worried about me after the death of Caroline. I told them that I was fine, and they did not need to worry about me. They left with Thabang, and I was left all by myself. I just stood there thinking about the events of the day, but mainly about Caroline. I could not comprehend as to why she had to die the way she did and felt that if she had to die, she was supposed to have died in a skirmish with the enemy at home, not in the bushes of Angola. My main concern was that MK did not have a lot of female comrades, and therefore, we could not afford to lose any more females. In about two months, we already lost two females, JJ and now Caroline, and it was a tragedy!

I tried to sleep but struggled because I just couldn't get Caroline out of my mind. I decided to walk to the guardhouse, where I met Comrades Diliza and Zanempi at the door. They look pleased to see me, especially Comrade Diliza, who always declared his love for me. Although I always laughed at him as I did with everybody else, I must say that I had strong feelings for him. I did not want to be in a relationship with him because of my respect for him, and I also thought that he deserved a lot better than what I could offer him, especially after what had happened to me in the past years. When I looked at Comrade Diliza, I thought he deserved to marry a virgin; someone who had never been touched before. He was such a wonderful and humble person. He was too good for me, and I did not deserve such a wonderful person. We discussed the matter numerous times and finally agree to remain friends. One thing I loved about him was his intellect and humbleness.

I shook Comrade Zanempi's hand, and as I was going to shake Comrade Diliza's, he ignored it and instead gave me a very tight hug and a kiss on the cheek. I felt so awkward because Comrade Zanempi was standing there looking at us. I tried to free myself from Comrade Diliza, but he held me as if he did not want to let me go. I must say it felt good, but it also felt so bad because I had made a decision a long time ago that I would never fall in love with him because he was such a wonderful person who deserved better. At the same time, I was wondering as to why something so good could feel so bad.

He looked at me and said, "Ruth, you know what? I love you so much and to show you that I love you, I am going to let you go, and I pray that someday, you will realise that I loved you with all my heart and soul. Maybe someday when you realise that I loved you truly, I shall not be on this earth any longer, but you should always know that Diliza loved you."

As I heard those words, my knees felt weak, and I did not know what to say. He was taller than me, and when I looked up, I saw tears running from his beautiful, brown eyes. I wanted to kiss those tears away, but I just looked at him and said, "One day, you'll find someone who deserves you," and with that, I let myself loose and walked away from him.

I decided that I would not be good company for anyone at the guardhouse after my encounter with Diliza and, therefore, decided to go back to the caravan. There I found Dimakatso and Joyce smoking outside. I greeted them and told them that I was going to bed because I felt tired. They both laughed at the same time, saying, "We understand, it's not easy to carry baggage everywhere you go. Go and sleep because both of you need the energy to survive the rough circumstances of Cacuso." I just looked at them and said nothing.

***

"Ruth, wake up, it's 18:00 pm and almost time to eat. Oh, and Comrade Diliza is here to see you," I heard Dimakatso's voice. I looked up and saw Comrade Diliza standing next to Dimakatso. *Damn you, Dimakatso, why did you let him in?* I said to myself.

"Comrade Ruth, I'm sorry to have come to you unannounced, but I felt I couldn't sleep without talking to you. I know we have agreed to remain friends, but I feel so jealous when I see you with AB. I feel that I am the one who is supposed to be with you, not him. Comrade Ruth, you know that we have a lot in common, amongst other things it is our political understanding. You know that we can have political discussions, talk about social life and everything under the sun. Hence, I believe we can make it as a couple. Ruth, I beg you, please understand the love I have for you! We can actually put this relationship on trial; let's say for two months. If it doesn't work, I will be satisfied that I cannot have you," he calmly said without sounding aggressive or agitated.

The way he said all those things made me think twice about my relationship with AB. Was our relationship a sustainable one? Did he intend to make me his wife, or was it ephemeral? Those were some of the questions running through my head.

"Comrade Diliza, it is a fact that I love you, but I cannot have a relationship with you. You deserve a better person than me, and I promise you that you will find someone who shall love you and be a better wife and mother to your children than I could ever be. I can't have a relationship with you, and that is it," I said, climbed out of bed and left him where he was standing to get some water for a bath before dinner.

Back at the caravan, to my relief, I saw that Comrade Diliza had left. I took a quick bath and left for the guardhouse, where I waited for the roll call before dinner. There, I met Dimakatso and Comrade Tebogo who were chatting and laughing. They looked like mischievous teenagers who ate the forbidden apple and were trying to revisit the scene. I greeted them and passed because I did not want to disturb them in their endeavour to enjoy each other's company.

At the guardhouse, I looked for other comrades to pass the time. I found Comrades Green, China and Shoabate drinking tea. I joined them, and we had some political discussion which led to the discussion about our mission in Cacuso. We felt that we were losing many Comrades on the Eastern Front, which was problematic. Although we understood the objectives of our engagement, it was still rather painful to see our comrades dying as they did. After dinner, I felt tired and went to bed.

The following day I woke up feeling a lot better and I had forgotten about Diliza and everything that we discussed. I went for breakfast and waited for the next order. While waiting, I met with Comrade Thabethe, who was happy to see me after the shooting incident in my room. He told me that he had spoken to AB, who confessed his love for me, but was worried that I was too young to be married to him, so he requested Thabethe to talk to me about his proposal. Although I felt a bit fascinated by what he told me, I did not know what to say because I was not ready for marriage. I was too young, and my priority was to go and fight inside the country. "Ta-Vic, I love him, but I cannot marry him. I have my ambitions, and marriage is definitely not one of them. Please tell him that I love him." Thabethe told me that he understood what I was saying and that he would pass on the message. I thanked him and left.

We were involved in some operational activities between Cacuso, Kwanza-Sul, and Kanandala for about four weeks. It was a bit relaxed because the bandits were not as active as before during our first days on the Eastern Front. Our mission was to monitor and ensure that the communities were safe and free from any harassment by the bandits.

The comrades deployed in Kanandala were those who had stayed for long times in the camps, and they showed a high level of nostalgia which one could easily interpret as anarchy and lack of discipline. One could even say they were enemy agents. Whenever I was in Kanandala, I would sit with them and listen to their individual stories. The fact that some of them had never left Angola since their arrival in 1977 baffled me. They were moved from one camp to another, and I could just imagine their frustration because I knew the feeling. They were desperate to go back to South Africa to fight, but due to the situation, they were not sent to the front. This led to a lot of frustration, and it manifested itself in anarchic behaviour like drinking on duty, and random shooting, which was unacceptable behaviour.

It was during this period that I became aware of problems in our ranks. These problems included the fact that members wanted to go home to fight but were not given the opportunity. I really understood what they were saying, but I felt that the manner in which they addressed the issue was not right. My opinion was based on what I had experienced in Lesotho, and I did not want the same happening here, so I avoided discussing the issue.

One day on our way back from Kwanza-Sul, I met with AB after almost two months of not seeing each other. I was very happy to see him again, and the feeling was mutual because he actually cried when he gave me a very tight and warm hug. I did not understand why he was crying, and then he asked me if we could go back to his place to talk. We walked hand in hand while kissing like new lovers, and when we finally reached his place, we found Comrades

China, Green, Tshepo, Jerome, and Simpi drinking tea and discussing the political situation at home, especially in Natal. I greeted them and went straight to AB's room, leaving him with them. After about two hours alone, he finally joined me with a plate of food which consisted of rice, vegetables and corned meat. We ate in silence, and I was very anxious to hear what he wanted to tell me, but he said nothing, and I did not ask him because he was the one who brought up the matter. After eating, he took the plate to the kitchen and did not come back immediately; he stayed with his comrades, which made me mad because I felt that he was ignoring me. After thirty minutes, he returned and slept beside me with his hands on my stomach, which was unusual because he was actually brushing over it. "Why are you playing with my tummy?" I asked while thinking about what Dimakatso and Caroline thought about me being pregnant. Here he was with his hand on my stomach, and I felt very uncomfortable.

"Chunku, please look at me. Do you realise that I also came back today, and I have been away from you for more than two months? During this time, I have been so worried about your health and your safety. Chunku, before I left, Jerome confirmed to me that you were pregnant and I felt so bad because you are so young and I know your ambitions, and I feel so bad that I made you pregnant at this crucial time in your life. Tell me, are you prepared to be a mother?" he asked nervously.

"No, I can't have a child because I'm not going to be a good mother, and I don't want my child to suffer the way I suffered as a child. I don't want to bring a child that I'm not going to take care of into this world. Honey, my mother did not take care of me; she never loved me, and I wouldn't like my child to go through that."

I realised that AB was crying, and I could not understand why. He gave me a warm, tight hug and told me he was going to take care of the child and me. "Chunku, you know

I love you so much, and I swore I would never hurt you, ever. I loved you the first time I laid my eyes on you, and I have never looked back since that day. You know I have a son in Tanzania, but that will never stop me from loving you and our unborn child. I understand that Doctor Mantu will be visiting Cacuso tomorrow; I want us to see her so that she can advise us on how you can take care of yourself and the baby. Baby, I want the best for you and the baby, that I assure you, and maybe when the time is right, we will be a family. I don't want to talk about marriage now because I know exactly how you feel about it, but you must know that there is nothing that will make me happier than to have you as my wife. I'll give you time to think about it."

(Dr Mantu Tshabalala was one of the comrades who left South Africa in the sixties to join the ANC in exile. She was amongst the few female comrades who joined MK and later on went to the Soviet Union to study medicine. Comrade Mantu had a soft spot for soldiers, and she was particularly concerned about the female comrades in the camps. She would always encourage female comrades to go to school to further their studies. Comrade Mantu was a beautiful woman; I remember her being hairy like the late Caroline, a bit dark in complexion with beautiful legs. She was amazingly beautiful!)

I was very confused, and I could not comprehend what AB was saying. Since the first rape incident, I never thought about marriage or being a mother. *"Why does he think I will be a good wife or mother? Is he not aware that an apple does not fall too far from the tree?"* I thought and started crying. We cried together in each other's arms, and I think we dozed off because we were woken by a knock on the door. AB jumped up to open the door only to find Comrade Simpi there.

"Comrade, we are going to the guardhouse. Where is Comrade Ruth?" he said.

"She is here with me. Are there any problems?" AB asked.

"No, there is no problem, but we are wanted at the guardhouse, and Dimakatso told me to call both of you because it seems as if we are going to Kwanza-Sul," Comrade Simpi concluded.

"Comrade Ruth cannot go to operations because she is not feeling well and Comrade Jerome knows that," AB said. I jumped out of bed, slunk my AK over my shoulder, and went towards the door.

"Comrade Simpi, I'm not sick. Comrade Abel, since when are you my spokesperson? You'll find me at the guardhouse," I said with insolence. AB grabbed my hand and held it behind my back.

"You are not going anywhere; do you want to be killed? What about the baby you are carrying? Stop being so stubborn. Comrade, tell the officer on duty that I'm coming. I just need to talk sense to Comrade Ruth's head."

"Ok, I'll tell him," Comrade Simpi responded, leaving us behind.

"Ruth, I'm telling you, not asking you! You are not going anywhere. If needs be, I'll stay behind with you; there is no way I am going to let you go to that dangerous place in your condition. I have actually let you do whatever you want for a long time, but not anymore. You are carrying a precious baby, and I cannot let you endanger it, there is no way! I'm going to protect you and the baby with everything I have. I'm going to the guardhouse to tell everybody who cares to listen that you're pregnant with my baby and there is no way I'm going to allow you to be involved in operations," he said, still holding my arm at my back. This was the first time I saw AB so angry with me; he changed from a crying baby to this father figure I never had. "I joined the struggle alone; there is no one who'll tell me what to do at any given time. This is my life, and if I die, I know no one will cry for me, so please stop trying to be my father. I'm going with or without you," I said, almost in tears.

Ruth Mantile

I knew AB meant well, but I did not want people to know that I was pregnant. The other thing was that I hated to be treated differently. AB looked at me and let go of my hand with tears in his eyes.

"Chunku, do whatever you want, but you must know I'm going to Comrade Chris to tell him that you're pregnant with my child and I'm going to tell him to send you to Luanda because Cacuso is dangerous for you and the unborn child," he said while crying.

I left the room, and as I was closing the door behind me, he grabbed the handle to open the door. "Please wait, I'll go with you. I don't want to fight you anymore, let's be civil about this." He said this holding my hand with a gentleness I knew, and not with the roughness he grabbed me in the room. We walked in silence until we reached the guardhouse where Comrades were waiting for us. We marched and saluted the officer on duty, who was Comrade Mafela, a friend of AB.

"Comrades, let's go and get our logistics and assemble here again here at twenty-two hours sharp! Battalion dismissed, except for Comrades Abel and Ruth". The battalion dismissed, and we were left alone with the OD.

"What happened? Comrade Simpi told me something about you, which was worrisome," Comrade Mafela asked with concern on his face.

"Comrade Mafela, AB makes me feel as if I'm an invalid; he wants to control me like his child," I said.

"Buda (as they called each other), Comrade Ruth is pregnant, but she doesn't want to listen to the voice of reasoning. I told her that she needs to relax and that she should not take part in any of the operations, but she is so stubborn and doesn't want to listen to me. The thing is; I don't want to lose her like Jerome lost Caroline in this fucking war. I love her too much to lose her!" AB said while sounding as if he was about to cry.

Comrade Mafela looked very perplexed by what he heard, and he seemed to be out of words. He just looked at us and said nothing. After a while, he said, "Comrades, I'm really baffled by what I've just heard; needless to say, I'm so disappointed by both of you for not taking preventive measures. I cannot comprehend how you could be so careless; you should know that a child comes with many responsibilities, which I think Comrade Ruth is still very young to carry. It does not help at this stage to lecture you because this is after the fact, Comrade Ruth, in essence, I would like to agree with Abel about your safety. Indeed, we need to ensure that you do not get involved in operations; a pregnant woman needs to relax and eat properly so that the child can get good nutrition. I would excuse both of you from this operation because I would like you to see Dr Mantu tomorrow. Is that clear?"

"Yes, it is clear," we said simultaneously, and with that, we left Comrade Mafela standing there. We went to my caravan, where we met Comrade Dimakatso and Joyce on their way to the guardhouse. I wished them well and went into my room. We didn't have much to say to each other that night, and I guess there were lots of things that needed to be resolved between us.

I had two concerns, one being the attitude of comrades towards my pregnancy. Secondly, I did not want to be like my mother, but I did not know how to be a different mother. I guess AB had his own worries, but we did not discuss our fears with each other. I think I fell asleep because when I woke to go to the toilet, I saw him sleeping on Dimakatso's bed.

The next morning, we woke and went to the formation without saying much to each other. We had our breakfast together and then waited for Dr Mantu's visit. We didn't know when to expect her, but at least she was already in Malanje. I really wished that she would tell me that the first diagnosis was wrong and that I would not be pregnant.

"Comrade Ruth, Doctor Manto is ready to see you," called Comrade Mafela.

"Thank you, comrade. Where is AB?" I asked.

"He just went to the toilet; he'll be back to join you and the Honourable Doctor," Comrade Mafela said while holding my hand to escort me to Dr Manto who was in one of the rooms of the residence. After we greeted each other, Comrade Mafela excused himself so that I could talk to the doctor.

"What did you say your name was?" Dr Manto asked.

"My name is Comrade Ruth Mantile," I responded.

"Comrade Ruth, what is your problem? Actually, how do you feel? I was with Comrade Chris, and he seemed worried about you, but he did not tell me why he was worried. So please tell me what is bothering you?"

"Comrade Manto, I don't know what is wrong with me, but there are comrades who are saying I'm pregnant. What I don't understand is that I don't feel anything, and my tummy is still the same. I'm not sick or anything like that. I really don't know where they get those ideas from!" I told her.

"Please lie on the bed so that I can have a look," Dr Manto commanded. As I was busy undressing, I heard a knock at the door, and the person did not even wait for a response and just walked into the room. Dr Manto shouted at the person for coming in without permission and then I heard AB's voice. All of a sudden I heard Dr Manto laughing and I can't say that I blamed her. AB was one of those people who made a difficult situation bearable with his huge heart and sense of humour that left everyone in tears, and I think it did the trick because they talked for a few minutes and then turned to me.

"Chunku, please don't panic. Tell Comrade Manto everything. She is going to assist us, and I trust her a lot," AB said.

"Comrade Ruth, let's check what the problem is," she said.

She pushed my 'biports' and inserted her fingers inside while making movements as if she was feeling something inside, and I felt the same pain I felt when I visited the Cuban gynaecologist. She continued doing that for some time and later on instructed me to relax my muscles because otherwise, she could not feel what she wanted to feel.

"Comrade, she is definitely pregnant, and from my experience, she is almost six months, which is a very delicate time. Comrade Ruth, you have to leave this place as soon as possible because the conditions here are not conducive for yourself and the unborn child. I would, therefore, speak to Comrade Chris Hani about your situation," Dr Manto said.

"Comrade Manto, please don't tell them I'm pregnant because I think we still need a second opinion on this. I cannot believe that I am pregnant; it is impossible!" I said.

"Chunku, it is fine because I will be with you throughout the way. I know we can do this together because I really care about you and love you very much! I will never allow anything bad to happen to you. Let's agree that you're going to Luanda and I'll come and visit you there," AB tried to reassure me.

"Take these tablets; one three times a day. They are folic acid and good for the unborn child and the mother. Keep well and take care of yourself. I'm going to talk to Comrade Chris, and we'll take it from there." After having said that, Comrade Manto left us.

We went to AB's room and just hugged each other without saying anything. I really felt very safe around AB. I did not know why, but maybe it was because of his way of displaying his love and affection for me. He never held back his feelings; he cried when he felt like it and loved me unconditionally. We just slept in each other's arms until morning when I went to my place to take a bath.

"Good morning, Comrade Ruth, I have been instructed to tell you that you should pack your clothes because you'll be leaving for Luanda tomorrow morning." When I looked, I saw Comrade Simpi, who looked rather worried.

"Ok comrade, thanks," I said, not even looking at him. *"Oh God, how am I going to look at the people who believed in me? I know most of them are so disappointed in me. How are they going to look at me? Will they still love me, or will they reject me? What am I going to do when I arrive in Vienna? Surely everybody knows about my condition by now,"* I asked myself, but I did not have answers to all the questions that were running through my mind. I decided to go and look for AB so that I could tell him about my trip to Luanda.

"Chunku", I heard AB calling me from a distance. I turned around to see him running to me with a big smile on his face. When he was close enough, he picked me up and kissed me. That felt so wonderful after the bad news.

"AB, I was actually coming to see you. I need to talk to you about something serious, and I think we need to go to a quiet place so that we won't be disturbed. Do you know of any place we could go to?" I asked.

"Chunku, you sound so serious, what's wrong? Let us go to my room, there is no one there," he said, and we walked to his room. I was very anxious because I did not know how he was going to react when I tell him the news.

"Sweetheart, I think we need to talk about something which has been bothering me for some time now. You heard what Doctor Manto said about the duration of my pregnancy? Just to refresh your memory; she said 'almost six months' and we have only been together for five. If her calculations are correct, it means that this baby is not yours," I concluded with absolutely no idea how he was going to react. AB looked at me as if he did not understand what I was saying.

"Are you listening to me?" I asked with panic in my voice.

"Ruth, I don't care what you're saying. The fact is: I love you, and if those calculations are correct, I've been with that baby since the inception. Therefore, no one is going to deprive me of him. He is my child and no one else's!" he said with tears rolling down his cheeks. He held me very tight and said, "I love you so much, and I will always love you. Please don't deprive me of this baby." He then kissed me and put his hand over my stomach, which was not even showing.

After our discussion, I felt as if a heavy load was taken off my shoulders because I felt that it would not have been fair to AB if I had allowed him to believe that the baby I was carrying was his while I knew it was not. I must say that deep down in my heart, I wished he was the father of my son, but that was only a wish.

"AB, I got a message that I'll be going to Luanda tomorrow morning. I so wish that you could come with me, but unfortunately in MK we follow orders. Honey, please take care of yourself and do not place your life in danger unless it is absolutely necessary! I love you too much to lose you in the bushes of Angola. Promise me that you are going to be careful?" I said.

"Chunku, I promise I'm going to be careful; don't worry about me. You're the one who needs to take care because you're carrying my boy, who might be the next commander-in-chief of MK," he said, kissing me on the cheek.

"Let's go and get food, it's already time for lunch," AB said, holding my hand. We left his residence for the barracks to get food, and I remember that day we ate rice and corned meat, which I did not enjoy at all because it was too salty. Amazingly, the other comrades I was with, including AB, seemed to enjoy the food, and I did not hear them complain about the salt at all. After lunch, we left the barracks with AB for my room, where we just sat and talked about the future, which included the liberation of South Africa. The thing that amazed me most about our relationship was the fact that the struggle dominated our discussions. We could talk about the ANC, SACP, MK, and other international politics without getting bored with each other.

FOURTEEN

A presumed curse turned into a blessing

THE FOLLOWING DAY AFTER breakfast, Comrade Mohlakwana, fetched me. He told me that we were going to fetch Comrade Chris, who was going to leave with us for Luanda. I started to panic, and I really wished that Comrade Mohlakwana did not tell me.

"Good morning, Mpoetsi, how are you doing?" Comrade Chris asked with a smile on his face. I actually thought he was sarcastic because I believed he knew exactly how I was.

"I'm fine, thank you, and how are you, Comrade Chris?' I responded with a trembling voice.

"I couldn't be better. Tell me, where is Noxolo? Are you guys still going to Lesotho?" he asked.

"I'm not sure where she is because I got a letter from her informing me that she had already left for Lusaka, but I don't know what is happening there," I responded.

"That's fine then. Let's see what the future holds for us," he said. I thanked God that he ended our discussion because I thought if he continued, we would end up having to talk about my pregnancy, and I was not prepared to discuss it with Comrade Chris in particular. I decided to sleep all the way to Luanda.

"Comrade Ruth, wake up, we have arrived in Luanda," said Comrade Mohlakwana. When I opened my eyes, I realised that we were actually at Res One where Comrade Chris would be staying for the duration of his stay in Luanda.

"Mpoetsi, don't worry about anything; I'll arrange for you to join Noxolo. Please take care of yourself, bye," he said to me.

"Thank you, Comrade Chris, I'll do that," I said, thanking God that Comrade Chris, throughout the trip did not mention anything about my pregnancy. He got out of the car with his bodyguard and went inside.

We left Res One for Vienna transit camp with Comrade Mohlakwana. I was very nervous and thought that the comrades would be waiting for me so that they could ask funny questions about my pregnancy and who the father of my baby was. I knew that some comrades would be sincere, but I also knew that the others would be sarcastic, and I decided that if anyone showed any nastiness, I would respond in the same way.

When we arrived in Vienna, the place was quiet, and it felt like there were no people in the camp. Comrade Mohlakwana dropped me at the administration block, where Comrade Motlatsi, my homeboy, welcomed me. He took me to the tent that I previously shared with Mpumi, who had left Vienna already. I took my luggage in and went to sit at the empty swimming pool. As I was sitting there, Comrade Grace, whom I left in Vienna on my way to the Eastern Front, joined me.

"Good day, Comrade Ruth. How are you and how was the situation in the front?" she asked.

"I'm fine, thank you, Comrade Grace. The situation in the front was terrifying, but tolerable because I believe that is what has brought us here. The freedom of the Angolan people will influence our own liberation in our country; therefore, the Eastern Front has given me an experience that I'll cherish for the rest of my days," I responded. She was quiet for some time, and I knew exactly what her next question was going to be because she was one of the biggest gossipers in the camp.

"Comrade Ruth, I understand that one of you are pregnant? Who could it be? I thought all of us got loops; I wonder what happened to the poor comrade?" she asked and if I did not know her, I would have believed that she was empathising with the poor, pregnant comrade. But I did and was not impressed by her question because I knew she just wanted a juicy piece of gossip to spread around.

"Mme Grace, why don't you come out with it? Don't pretend as if you don't know what is happening. Don't beat about the bush. Ask me what you want to ask me," I said.

"You know how people talk, and sometimes I don't take them seriously, but I heard from someone that Dimakatso is pregnant and that she is very frustrated because it means she can't go to the front. I hear she will have to go to Tanzania instead. Frankly speaking, I never believed what I heard, and as a result, I don't know how to confirm the information," Mme Grace concluded.

"Mme Grace, let me make it easier for you; you know exactly who is pregnant, so stop fooling around. It is me; I'm pregnant. I am not happy, but it's not the end of the world. Another thing – I know I'm not indispensable, and therefore someone else can take my place at the front." I was really annoyed by her insinuations, but I kept my cool. She looked at me without saying anything, and we just sat there looking at the geese walking around the camp. By the way, we had a lot of geese in Vienna, and apart from the mango tree leaves, they made the camp very dirty. You would find their waste all over the camp and because of this, we had to clean the camp almost uninterruptedly, as I mentioned earlier. I left Mme Grace at the swimming pool and went to sleep.

I overslept, and when the bell rang for supper, I quickly went to the formation. I felt as if I wasn't supposed to be there and told the officer on duty that I was going straight to the kitchen to get my food. "From now on, I'm not going to wait in the formation anymore. I will just register my presence and go straight to the kitchen to get my food because I'm a patient," I said and left for the kitchen without waiting for a comment. "You're still a spoilt child, do you know that?" said the OD, Comrade Bheki, whom I met in Caculama. I just smiled at him and proceeded to the kitchen.

After supper, I went and sat at the swimming pool, waiting for the other comrades to finish eating. There was going to be a jazz hour where comrades would be singing revolutionary songs until around 21:00 pm. To me, jazz hour was very emotional because that was when one realised the seriousness of the armed struggle. That evening, I sat there, admiring the morale and enthusiasm of the comrades, which reflected their determination to fight and overthrow the apartheid regime. I wondered why the leadership couldn't send us to the front because I knew that staying in Angola frustrated the comrades. The other thing that crossed my mind was the fact that a lot of comrades who had to stay in Angola so long, decided to get married either to Angolans or to their own comrades because they were getting older and time was not standing still. There was nothing wrong with getting married, but the problem with that was the fact that very few people would agree to leave their families to go and fight, especially those who had children. After jazz hour, I went straight to bed.

The following morning, I woke up, got water from the kitchen and took a long bath because, in my condition, I was free to stay in my tent and not go to the formation. I did everything on my own terms; no more commands. Comrades treated me with respect and dignity; from the comrades working in the kitchen to the camp's commander, Comrade Pro, and this humbled me a lot.

The kitchen staff would prepare special food for me, and Comrade Pro would instruct Comrade Mhlakwana to take me to the beach every second day. Throughout my stay in Vienna, everybody really made an effort to take care of me, which I appreciated a great deal because that was not what I had expected.

During lunchtime, the officer on duty called me and told me that I needed to see Comrade Vooki. Comrade Vooki was one of the comrades I respected a lot, and he was part of the ANC Intelligence. I first met Comrade Vooki in Kamalundi, where he was part of the camp administration responsible for intelligence and security in the camp. Comrade Vooki was a very humble person, always smiling. I actually thought he was from Bloemfontein because of his knowledge of the Setswana language and the fact that he would always be around comrades from Bloemfontein. I must say, throughout my stay in Angola, I was convinced that Comrades Goodman, Vooki, Kitso and Commander 26 were also from Bloemfontein.

I went to the administration block where Comrade Vooki was. I knocked at the door, and a man's voice ordered me to come in. As I entered, I saw Comrade Vooki as clean as ever with a big smile. "Come in Comrade Ruth, how are you doing? I heard what happened, but do not worry, everything will be fine. We have informed Comrade Mzwai about your situation, and he advised us to send you to Lusaka immediately so that he could see what he could do because SACTU wants you in Lesotho, as you know. What are you saying about that?" he asked.

"I do not have a problem with that; actually, I think that would be better for me because I do not feel comfortable staying here. I get panic attacks every now and then; I am always anxious as if something is going to happen to me, and I am so afraid of Comrade Mzwai," I responded. Comrade Vooki laughed before he told me not to worry about uTata, "You know Comrade Ruth, Tata is a very understanding person. After Comrade Morris told him about what happened to you, he was so furious with the perpetrator, and he immediately ordered his arrest. Therefore, you do not need to worry about him. He is aware of your situation."

"Thank you, Comrade Vooki. I will hear from you about the arrangements," I said while standing up and shaking his hand.

Three days after the meeting with Comrade Vooki, information came that all my documentation were ready, and I was to leave for Lusaka in two days. Two days seemed to be far away, but I was happy to hear that I was finally leaving. I was so bored in Vienna, and although from time to time somebody would take me to the beach or the market, it was not enough because most of the time I was alone as people went to their different businesses of the day. Honestly, my problem was that everyone who saw me knew with no shadow of a doubt that I was sexually active, which I hated because, for me, sex was a private matter.

The day before I left Vienna, I got a letter, which I thought was from Noxolo as she was the only person who used to write to me. To my surprise, it was from AB. It read as follows:

> Dear Chunku, I'm writing this letter with tears in my eyes, and I wish you were here to wipe them with your soft hands. I miss you so badly that I do not know what to do, but the only hope that I have is that we are going to meet on the freedom day when our country is free. I want you to take care of our baby, and if I die, please tell him that I loved him with all my heart and soul.
>
> Chunku, the other thing is that the National Commissar came to see me and told me that they decided to send me to Tanzania as a form of punishment for impregnating you. I told him it was ok with me because anyway I was going to be with you and I will see my other son, but he did not tell me when that would happen. Enough about that. Chunku, I wish I were an orator so that I could write

you a million letters, but I think this will suffice for now. Until we meet again. Love you always. Abel.

"Wow, I love you too," I said to no one in particular. The letter made me so happy, and it made me love and respect AB more. In my life, I had never met anyone who would sacrifice his life and happiness for me. AB knew that the child was not his, but he never denied the child I was carrying nor me. He was one of a kind; there was no one like him. I replied to his letter promising to love him 'till eternity'.

I woke up in the morning and after washing and eating my transport to the airport was already waiting for me. After saying my goodbyes, we left for the airport with Comrade Peggy, whom I first met at the store in Luanda. When we first met, we did not say much to each other, and I did not even know that she was also pregnant. Peggy was a tall, dark in complexion lady with a beautiful smile, and she spoke Zulu, and I guessed that she was from Natal. We arrived at the airport, and the comrade who took us there gave us our papers and left us. Not long after we boarded our flight, we took off and arrived in Lusaka without hassle. Comrade Javel took us from the airport to the Charleston residence, where we found several people from different parts of the world. I remember the person responsible was Comrade Lerumo, who was probably in his thirties. We found three students from Cuba, about five girls on their way to SOMAFCO and Comrade France, a resident at Charleston. After the introductions, we were given the layout of the residence and its programmes. We went to our room and for some reason ended of dozing off because one of the girls had to wake us up for supper. The food consisted of rice, chicken and some vegetables. I only managed to eat chicken because I could not stand the smell and taste of rice, which started in Vienna before I even went to Cacuso. Every time I smelled rice, I used to feel nauseous and did not know what was wrong with me. Obviously, I only found out later that I was pregnant and that this was the cause of the queasy feeling. That is how naïve I was back then ...

After dinner, Comrade Lerumo told Peggy and me that nobody would be sleeping in the house and that we had to put on our tracksuits and training shoes so that we could go somewhere else. I did not even ask because I knew the security situation in Zambia and the other Frontline States. After the briefing, we went to our room and found that everybody was already in tracksuits waiting for us. We changed and joined the other comrades, of which Comrade Lerumo was our guide.

It was now dark, and I could not see the route we were talking, but I trusted Comrade Lerumo's leadership. We passed dark houses that looked dilapidated and inhabitable, which made me feel worried. After about fifteen minutes, Comrade Lerumo stopped in front of a house that looked like a shack without lights. He put his AK-47 on the ground and fumbled in his pockets for the keys. Everybody but me went inside, and Comrade Lerumo said to me in a gentle voice, "Comrade Ruth, get inside. This is where you will be sleeping every night as long as you are here. This is for your own safety, and you should be able to understand better than these kids." He turned around and opened the way for me to enter the dark room.

I cannot tell you how and when I finally slept, but one of the comrades woke me up and said it was time to leave. When I looked outside, it was still dark and was told that it was 5:00 am. For security reasons, we had to leave before the community woke up and just like we came, we left – in silence.

We arrived at the residence, and I took a bath and went for breakfast. After that, Peggy and I washed the dishes while others cleaned the house. One thing I admired about Charleston was the spirit of working together, and it reminded me of Angola. If there was something that the ANC and Umkhonto weSizwe instilled in us, it was teamwork, and as a result, even the toughest task always seemed easy because we did it as a team. My stay in Lusaka was easy because I would get visitors who would take me out for lunch, and others would take me for walks in the vicinity. Comrade Mmuso, in particular, would fetch me and take me to town just to walk and he would say it was a good exercise for the baby. Although the comrades tried to make me feel comfortable, I still felt embarrassed for them to see me pregnant. To me, it felt as if I had betrayed the struggle because the ANC and MK had invested so much in me, and there I was: pregnant! Yes, I knew that I did not do anything wrong, but when I had to see Comrade Mzwai Piliso, I felt really bad. A comrade I did not know came to fetch me, and we drove in silence to the ANC's HQ where I was to meet the most feared comrade in the ANC. The driver took me to his office, and the secretary told me to wait. I had barely sat down when Comrade Mzwai entered his office. I stood at attention, not knowing what else to do. He greeted me and continued walking into his office. "Ngena comrade," the secretary said.

"Good morning, Tata," I said, wishing I was invisible so that he couldn't see the embarrassment on my face. "Good morning, comrade, how are you doing, and when did you arrive in Lusaka?" he asked politely, which really surprised me.

"I arrived three days ago, and I am good, Tata," I said without looking at him.

"Ruth, I have heard about your plight, and we made a decision that the perpetrator will be punished. We are very sorry about what happened to you. I was talking to Comrade Chris, and he told me that you were supposed to go to Lesotho to do political work and establish cells inside the country for SACTU. With your circumstances now, he was not sure what to do. I told him that he should have requested me to release you because you fall under my structure," he said while laughing. He continued by saying that it was a bit risky to go to Lesotho while pregnant because the medical facilities were not good, but he still gave me a choice to stay in Lusaka. I told Comrade Mzwai that I'd rather go to Tanzania to deliver my baby and after that resume my duties.

"That is fine; I will arrange that you get your documentation on time because there is a rule that prohibits pregnant women from flying when they reach a certain term of their pregnancy. I wish you well and please take care of yourself," he said while shaking my hand. I left Comrade Mzwai's office feeling very relieved. What I saw of him was contrary to what I heard. He was a leader, and I was happy that as the leadership, they took collective responsibility for my issue. I was so happy to belong to this organisation, which had a strong, accountable, and collective leadership.

After my meeting with Comrade Mzwai, I went back to Charleston, where I found the comrades playing chess, which was not my strong point, but I was prepared to learn. I joined them, and they gave me some lessons, and because I was a good student, I developed a serious interest in chess. I played it every day after doing my chores, and I must say it was very interesting. After staying in Lusaka for two months, we flew to Dar es Salaam in Tanzania.

We arrived at Mwalimu Julius K Nyerere International Airport in Dar es Salaam in the evening, but as we embarked from the flight, I felt a very hot breeze on my face. The weather was very humid and hot. We went inside and straight to immigration, where many security-related questions were asked. The way they performed their work impressed me. They displayed concern about knowing all the people who were entering their country and did this with diligence. We had not been waiting long when I heard a short man standing between Peggy and I, saying, "Dumelang comrades, is this your luggage?" We greeted him and showed him our luggage. The comrade led us to a Land Rover 110, which was parked just outside the airport. After loading our luggage with the assistance of a Tanzanian fellow, we drove off, and that is when he introduced himself. He told us his name (which I forgot, and I do not think Peggy remember as well), we told him ours, and we continued driving. The traffic was a nightmare; we moved very slowly, and I thought there was an accident somewhere ahead.

"Comrades, this is how slow the traffic in Dar es Salaam is, especially in the evening, and it is going to take us about two hours to arrive at our destination. I know you are tired, but there is nothing I can do," he said with a smile on his face.

"No problem, we understand," said Peggy in deep Zulu. While driving from the airport, I realised that Tanzanians were fast and reckless drivers that overtook anywhere and in any way, even when there was oncoming traffic. It was really terrifying to see how they drove! We were on the road for almost an hour when the comrade said, "At least we have finally arrived." I looked around and saw houses that almost looked alike with a bit of influence from European and Arabic architectural styles. "This is one of our residences in Dar es Salaam; it is in Temeke area, and as a result, comrades refer to the residence as 'Temeke'. Several comrades are staying here permanently, and others are in transit, either to Mazimbu or to school in Europe. I have already informed Comrade Zodwa about your arrival, and she is expecting you," he said while unloading our luggage. He then led us to the house, and without knocking, he pushed open the door and called out for Sis Zodwa. To my surprise, I saw a beautiful woman with a body to kill for coming out of one of the rooms. She had the most beautiful and genuine smile.

"Wow, you are so beautiful!" I said, extending my hand in greeting. I realised that she felt awkward because she started blushing before she gave me her hand.

"Thank you, comrade. You made me shy," she said while giggling like a teenager. "My name is Zodwa, and I am responsible for this residence. I live here with my husband and two sons. There are other people also staying here, but they are out now. I hope you will enjoy your stay with us," she said, shaking our hands.

"Comrades, you will be staying in this room," she said, pointing to a door that faced the main door. "The room is nice because of its ventilation, and you will not have problems with mosquitoes because it is far from the door, which stays open throughout the day. I think you will enjoy staying here," she said, opening the door.

The room was clean and looked comfortable for two pregnant girls. We thanked her for her generosity and sat down on our beds while Comrade Zodwa called out to the comrade to bring our luggage. After he brought our luggage, he told us that he was leaving, and he would see us around. We thanked him for everything, and he left. Not long after they had left, we heard voices outside, but we were too tired to investigate. Suddenly there was a knock on the door, and the person walked in uninvited. "Sani bonani, mina ngi gu Dudu, ngi hlala lana," (Good day, I am Dudu, and I am staying here), she said, shaking our hands.

"My name is Ruth Mantile; I am from Angola," I said. Peggy also introduced herself. Dudu told us that she had a baby girl, and the father of the child was in Germany for studies. We listened to her stories about Tanzania, and the Charlottes in Mazimbu, where young mothers were staying. She also explained the birth procedure which, in my mind, was very scary.

As I was listening to Dudu, I realised that she was a very intelligent young girl. I just wished that she could shift her focus from the father of the child and concentrate on bringing up her child and go to school. It was now past midnight, and I excused myself because I was tired and wanted to sleep. I do not know when Dudu left the room, but when

I woke up in the morning, Peggy was still sleeping. It was too hot to sleep; I had never experienced such heat in my life, and although Angola was hot, Tanzania was ten times worse. After taking a bath, I sat outside, just looking at the people in the dusty streets.

As I was sitting there, I saw a man pushing a wheelbarrow wearing a long, white cloth that looked like a dress. He walked in a very peculiar way as if he had pain somewhere in his body, and for some reason, his dress was actually in the wheelbarrow. I never asked anyone about it then, but I learned later on that those people were actually hanging their testicles in the wheelbarrows. Otherwise, they could not move around because the swollen scrotum made it impossible for them to walk, and the testicles would touch the ground. Those men had enlarged scrotums due to a hernia in the groin, which was not painful. I was also told that they were not bothered by it, and instead, when told to go to a hospital, said it was a sign of wealth. This must be one of the most absurd reasons I have heard in my life!

We stayed at the residence without any events, except for occasions where Comrade Thandi, who had a child with Comrade Sebata, my homeboy, would fetch us to visit her where she was staying with Comrades Seanokeng, Nono, and the late Mamsy. Being there was a pleasant change of scenery because those comrades were nice and accommodating.

After staying in the city for about four weeks, we received information that we would leave Dar es Salaam the following day. I was excited because I was tired of living out of a suitcase and I really longed for stability and security. I liked Dar, but I knew in my mind that I was in transit and was always anxious about when we would finally leave for Morogoro. The following day after breakfast, the bus came to fetch us, and we said our farewells. Comrade David, who was one of our Luthuli Detachment members, drove the bus. He was a big man with a loud voice, and he came across as a talkative man.

The traffic into the city centre was terrible, and it reminded me of our first day in Tanzania. As Comrade David was negotiating his way around, I realised why there was so much traffic congestion in Dar es Salaam. Drivers showed very poor driving skills, big potholes were visible on the streets, and one could see very few traffic lights. Driving in Tanzania was a nightmare, but it looked as if Comrade David knew his way around.

I started to relax when we drove out of the city centre, and that was when Comrade David started talking. He spoke about Kongwa in the Dodoma region where the Luthuli Detachment's comrades trained. He told us that, at a certain stage, they were in Kongwa for over five years. They were getting frustrated and tired of staying in the camp, and some comrades, including Comrade Chris Hani, wrote to President Comrade OR Tambo for intervention so that they could go to the country to fight. He recalled that some of them even mentioned the fact that they were not even getting decent women. If a person met a woman, he had to pay for her services, which was not easy to do because comrades did not have money. This resulted in the comrades stealing things from the camp to sell elsewhere so that they could have money to pay for these services. Comrade David told us so many stories that reminded me of the camp life.

One thing I learned from his stories was that the ANC/MK was consistent in certain decisions they made. When the Luthuli Detachment arrived in the ANC, they were the cream of our struggle, but things changed with the arrival of the June 16 detachment. This was also the case with the arrival of the Moncada Detachment; June 16 became the old furniture. Every new detachment negated the previous one. The other issue, which I picked up in the conversation with Comrade David, was the failure of MK commanders to infiltrate soldiers inside the country.

The phenomenon of stifling the movement of guerrillas to infiltrate South Africa started with the Luthuli Detachment, and it continued throughout the armed struggle. I tried to understand why it was so difficult to infiltrate the comrades at the front, but couldn't and I still struggle to get a meaningful answer about the situation. We might say that during the sixties it was difficult to infiltrate the country because of the hostility displayed by the South African neighbours like Rhodesia, Lorenzo Marques (now called Maputo) and South-West Africa (now called Namibia), but then those countries became free, and still, only a few people infiltrated South Africa. One could even think that there was a concerted effort to sabotage our armed struggle and render our comrades in the camps useless. I think their prolonged stay, while our people were dying on the streets of Soweto, Gugulethu, and Langa, brought discontentment, which led to mutiny at a certain stage. They did not understand why we were fighting and dying in other countries, while the people of South Africa were waiting for us to liberate them. Yes, we understood the question of internationalism, but our priority was to first liberate our own country and then assist our allies.

Comrade David spoke for over two hours, and I laughed when he realised that he spoke for more than two hundred and thirty kilometres. He said, "Comrades, I am so embarrassed to realise that I have spoken so much! I was not even aware that we have reached Mazimbu." As he spoke, I looked around and saw a big portrait of Comrade Solomon Mahlangu with his celebrated words: *'My blood will nourish the tree that will bear the fruits of freedom. Tell my people that I love them, and they must continue with the struggle.'*

In Mazimbu, the bus stopped at a boom gate guarded by a uniformed man. Comrade David spoke to him in his language, and I could not understand a word they were saying. They were laughing, and the man opened the gate for us.

"Welcome to Mazimbu, comrades! You have to make sure that you enjoy your stay; I am taking you to 'the Charlottes' where you will be staying. The Charlottes was built to accommodate young mothers, and it is a good place to bring up children," Comrade David said. We drove passed houses with beautiful gardens until we reached a place that looked like a boarding facility. "Here we are, comrades. Welcome to the Charlottes," he said. He stopped the bus and rushed to one of the dormitories. A few minutes later, he came out with a beautiful woman who seemed as if she wasn't surprised to see him. They were laughing as they approached the bus hand in hand. "Dumelang ma-comrade," the woman greeted us with a beautiful smile.

"Dumela Mme," I said, extending my hand. Peggy did the same.

"Comrades, please come with me. Comrade David will assist us with the luggage. My name is Comrade Christina, and I am the matron at this facility. Inside you will find other comrades who are single mothers because this facility is meant for young and single mothers," she said. We introduced ourselves to her, and she led us to a very quiet and deserted dormitory.

"Comrade Ruth, you will stay in this part of the facility. The comrades who are staying are working mothers because their children are over two years old. You will meet them in the evening," she said while assisting Comrade David with my luggage. They then left to show Peggy her room.

My room had six beds, which meant that six people were staying there. The room also had closets for everyone. The architecture was beautiful and modern. I was tired, and I think my baby was growing fast because I had swollen feet and it was difficult for me to walk fast. Therefore, I decided to sleep until Peggy woke me up for dinner. She led me to the adult kitchen to fetch food, and also showed me the children's kitchen. She told me that she already met some of the other comrades while I was sleeping, and I told myself that I would meet them eventually.

I really enjoyed our stay in Mazimbu, and the people who lived with us were also very nice. Naledi was one of those comrades who were selfless. She used to share things with us as if we were her sisters or friends. She was as beautiful as her heart and very tall. She had a daughter who was also very beautiful but had terrible eczema. I felt so sorry for her because she would keep on scratching herself. I really wished that she could leave Tanzania for a place that was not so hot and humid because the weather certainly worsened her condition.

Peggy, who came from Kwa-Mashu in Natal, and I became very close in Mazimbu. We went everywhere together, and the comrades at the Charlottes ended up calling us 'two tons of fun' because we were both tall and huge; Peggy's complexion was dark, and mine was lighter, and we really looked like them. She was a very funny person to be with and the only girl in her family. She had two brothers of which one was also a member of MK.

Peggy left the country through Botswana with her boyfriend Zweli, who was the father of her unborn child. She only said good things about Zweli and their intention to get married, and I admired her and the fact that she was enthusiastic about marriage, which was something farfetched for me.

There was not a lot of things to do in Mazimbu, especially for us who were pregnant. We would go to town or to the clinic at Morogoro Hospital and have lunch at a shop called Soda Baridi (cold drink) where we would have something very cold to drink. Peggy taught me that Zulu women did not do 'Indlamu', but 'ba ya Sina', and she would then start performing for me not caring who was watching or that she was pregnant. I remember she would praise me and say, "Umuhle nje nge ndoni ya manzi." At first, I did not understand what she was talking about until one day during

— Ruth Mantile —

one of our trips to Morogoro Hospital, she showed me the fruit she was talking about. She explained to me that the fruit grows along the riverbanks and its skin is as smooth as mine, and that is why she said I was as beautiful as that fruit. Peggy and Noxolo were the sisters I never had ...

***

"Ruth, please wake up! I have terrible pains." I thought I was dreaming, and I turned and tried to change my position. I heard the voice again, "Ruth, please wake up!" I opened my eyes and saw Peggy almost in tears.

"What is wrong? What time is it?" I asked her.

"I do not know; please let us go to the clinic because I have serious abdominal pain and my water broke," she said, sounding very desperate. I climbed out of bed, brushed my teeth, and we walked to the clinic.

My watch said it was 4:50 am, March 4, 1984, and it was still dark outside. We walked, and fortunately, Peggy was a strong woman because she remained calm and in control. We finally arrived at the clinic where we found Comrade Ivy, who immediately took us to Morogoro Hospital because she said it was dangerous for Peggy and her unborn child. She did not explain further, and we got into the ambulance and drove to the hospital.

On our arrival, Comrade Ivy rushed inside and came out with two male nurses and one female nurse. All four of them helped Peggy out of the ambulance to what looked like a maternity ward, and I followed them carrying Peggy's bag.

They took her to a ward with 'WAITING ROOM' written on a sign, and a lot of women were sitting there. The room was crowded and smelled terrible, and I felt nauseated but kept my pose for Peggy's sake. They placed her on a bed for a checkup, but soon after nurses took her to another room adjacent to the waiting room.

I followed them into the other room with a 'MATERNITY WARD' sign over the door. It was crowded with women sharing beds, and it felt as if there was no oxygen in the ward because of the terrible smell. I was really getting scared when I saw old women crying and behaving like lunatics. They would scream and shout on top of their voices, and although I could not understand what they were saying, I could see the anguish on their faces. Some would violently grip their beds or anyone who was near, and even though I could see that Peggy was in pain and holding her stomach, she remained calm.

"Comrade Ruth, let us go because Comrade Peggy will be admitted. We will come for a visit in the afternoon," Comrade Ivy said. I said goodbye to Peggy, with the promise to come back later that day and we left for Mazimbu. In the afternoon, when we returned to the hospital, Peggy had delivered a baby girl she called Busisiwe (Blessing). She was tiny but cute.

"Congratulations! I am happy for you! How were the pains?' I asked Peggy, who looked tired. She did not answer but smiled at me.

"Comrade Peggy, will you be able to walk to the ambulance? You have been discharged, the nurse just told me," Comrade Ivy informed Peggy, who looked very happy to hear the news.

"Yes, I can walk," she said, trying to get out of bed. We assisted her and managed to walk her out of the hospital. I held Busisiwe, and her bag and Comrade Ivy held Peggy. We drove to Mazimbu in silence.

Busisiwe was a very sweet little girl; she only cried when she was hungry. I spend most of my time with Peggy assisting her with Ma-Busi, as we called her. I only went to my room at night to sleep. On March 7, the Charlottes was blessed with a baby boy. The mother was Nombulelo from SOMAFCO, a very intelligent woman indeed. I admired her for her political understanding and her activeness at school.

Ruth Mantile

On March 8, I started to have terrible stomach pains, and I even experienced some diarrhoea. After some time, the diarrhoea stopped, but the cramps continued, and that was when other the comrades encouraged me to go to the clinic, which I hated. On arrival at the clinic, a doctor checked me and referred me to Morogoro Hospital. I was very angry because I did not want to go to Morogoro Hospital, especially when I thought about the conditions. On my arrival at the hospital, after all the administration issues were resolved, they admitted me for observation to the same waiting room where Peggy was a few days earlier. I was allocated a bed, and luckily, I slept alone. The pain continued, but I was given nothing for pain relief because they were afraid that it would harm my unborn baby, and I stayed like that for three days. On the third day, it became worse, and I did not know where the pain came from. Later that day (I remember it was a Saturday afternoon), the nurse told me not to move around, and that if I wanted to go to the toilet, I must call her. I wanted to ask her a lot of questions, but because of the language barrier, I could not explain how I felt.

The pains were getting worse, and I was not sure if they were labour pains or just stomach cramps. Although they came in intervals, they were terrible. At around 20:00 pm, the pain was nonstop, and I just started screaming. Two nurses came running, and they looked at me, said something to each other, and I saw one nurse leaving my bed. The nurse who stayed next to my bed looked younger than the other one, and I told her that I had to go to the toilet. She looked at me as if she did not understand what I was saying, and instead of answering me, she looked at the patient next to me and spoke to her in their language.

The patient looked at me and said, "You are not allowed to go to the toilet now, because you are about to deliver your baby. That is why you are in so much pain. The other nurse is going to call the sister in charge to come and check on you." I thanked her and continued nursing my pains, happy to know that my condition would soon be getting better.

As I was lying there, I felt the urge to push, and I think the nurse realised this because I heard her saying something to the patient next to me. "Do not push, please wait for the sister in charge," and as she was saying this, I saw the older nurse running through the door with two other nurses. "We are going to move you to the maternity ward," the nurse told me.

They helped me out of bed to the maternity ward, but before we could reach the ward, the excruciating pain came back, and it was worse than before. They rushed me to an empty bed and told me to open my thighs. I do not know what she was looking for, but I remember that I pushed because I had a sudden urge to do so. "Do not push!" I heard the sister in command say, but it was too late. I pushed and pushed until it felt as if something heavy was out of me, and I fell into a deep sleep.

"It's a baby boy," I heard the nurse say to no one in particular. I looked up and saw a baby with a very pale face. He was crying so hard, and at a certain stage, I thought I heard him losing his breath, but he was not; he was just crying with breaks in between. I was so desperate to hold him, but the nurse was busy doing something to my baby. I was still wondering about what she was doing when she said, "Here, take your baby." I did not care about the unfriendly nurse because I just wanted to see and hold my beautiful, handsome prince. She placed my son on my chest and said, "Congratulations!" I thanked her and concentrated on the little man in my arms.

I looked at his little fingers and toes, which looked very tiny. I remember he had two funny toes; his second toes were longer than the rest, but I was happy that he was alive and healthy. I remember smiling for the first time in months, and I heard myself saying, "I'm going to love this boy."

I never thought I would survive the pain of childbirth and all the circumstances surrounding my pregnancy, but I survived, and evolved into a strong woman, against all the odds.

-The End-

www.ingramcontent.com/pod-product-compliance
Lightning Source LLC
Chambersburg PA
CBHW022110040426
42450CB00006B/652